Solidarity: Nature, grounds, and value

Manchester University Press

CRITICAL POWERS

Series Editors:
Antony Simon Laden (University of Illinois, Chicago),
Peter Niesen (University of Hamburg) and
David Owen (University of Southampton).

Critical Powers is dedicated to constructing dialogues around innovative and original work in social and political theory. The ambition of the series is to be pluralist in welcoming work from different philosophical traditions and theoretical orientations, ranging from abstract conceptual argument to concrete policy-relevant engagements, and encouraging dialogue across the diverse approaches that populate the field of social and political theory. All the volumes in the series are structured as dialogues in which a lead essay is greeted with a series of responses before a reply by the lead essayist. Such dialogues spark debate, foster understanding, encourage innovation and perform the drama of thought in a way that engages a wide audience of scholars and students.

Published by Bloomsbury

On Global Citizenship: James Tully in Dialogue
Justice, Democracy and the Right to Justification: Rainer Forst in Dialogue

Published by Manchester University Press

Cinema, democracy and perfectionism: Joshua Foa Dienstag in dialogue
Democratic inclusion: Rainer Baubock in dialogue
Law and violence: Christoph Menke in dialogue
The shifting border: Ayelet Shachar in dialogue
Toleration, power and the right to justification: Rainer Forst in dialogue

Forthcoming from Manchester University Press

Rogue theodicy: Glen Newey in dialogue
Autonomy gaps: Joel Anderson in dialogue

Solidarity

Nature, grounds, and value
Andrea Sangiovanni in dialogue

Andrea Sangiovanni

with responses from:
Rainer Forst
Jared Holley
Avery Kolers
Catherine Lu
Sally Scholz

MANCHESTER UNIVERSITY PRESS

Copyright © Manchester University Press 2023

While copyright in the volume as a whole is vested in Manchester University Press, copyright in individual chapters belongs to their respective authors.

An electronic version of this book is also available under a Creative Commons (CC BY-NC-ND) licence, thanks to the support of Horizon 2020, under ERC Consolidator Grant 771635, which permits non-commercial use, distribution and reproduction provided the editor(s), chapter author(s) and Manchester University Press are fully cited and no modifications or adaptations are made. Details of the licence can be viewed at https://creativecommons.org/licenses/by-nc-nd/4.0/

Published by Manchester University Press
Oxford Road, Manchester M13 9PL

www.manchesteruniversitypress.co.uk

British Library Cataloguing-in-Publication Data
A catalogue record for this book is available from the British Library

ISBN 978 1 5261 7267 9 hardback

ISBN 978 1 5261 7268 6 open access

First published 2023

The publisher has no responsibility for the persistence or accuracy of URLs for any external or third-party internet websites referred to in this book, and does not guarantee that any content on such websites is, or will remain, accurate or appropriate.

Typeset by
New Best-set Typesetters Ltd

I rebel, therefore we are.
Albert Camus, The Rebel

Contents

Notes on contributors   *page* viii
Series editor's foreword   x
David Owen

Part I   Lead essay

1 Solidarity: nature, grounds, and value   3
    Andrea Sangiovanni

Part II   Responses

2 Solidarity is not joint action   137
    Avery Kolers
3 The (anti)colonial limits of solidarity: history, theory, practice   154
    Jared Holley
4 Collective transformative hope: on *living* in solidarity   182
    Sally Scholz
5 The meaning(s) of solidarity   205
    Rainer Forst
6 Solidarity and structural injustice   222
    Catherine Lu

Part III   Reply

7 Response to critics   241
    Andrea Sangiovanni

Index   271

Contributors

Rainer Forst is Professor of Political Theory and Philosophy and Director of the Research Center 'Normative Orders' at Goethe University Frankfurt. In 2012 he was awarded the Gottfried Wilhelm Leibniz Prize of the German Research Foundation. Important publications are: *Contexts of Justice* (1994, published in English 2002), *Toleration in Conflict* (2003, Engl. 2013), *The Right to Justification* (2007, Engl. 2012), *Normativity and Power* (2015, Engl. 2017), *Die noumenale Republik* (2021, Engl. forthcoming). He is the author and subject of two volumes in the Critical Powers Series: *Justice, Democracy and the Right to Justification* (2014) and *Toleration, Power and the Right to Justification* (2020).

Jared Holley is Lecturer in Political Theory at the University of Edinburgh, having previously held a Marie Skłodowska-Curie Fellowship for the project 'Anticolonial Solidarity: analytical clarification through historical reconstruction'. He is the author of *Rousseau's Politics of Taste* (forthcoming, Edinburgh University Press) and several articles, the most recent of which is 'Racial Equality and Anticolonial Solidarity: Anténor Firmin's Global Haitian Liberalism', *American Political Science Review* (2023).

Avery Kolers is Professor and Chair of Philosophy at the University of Louisville. He is the author of *Land, Conflict, and Justice: A Political Theory of Territory* (2009) and *A Moral Theory of Solidarity* (2016), as well as numerous papers in applied ethics and social and political philosophy. He is working on a book about what political theory can learn from the individual and collective goods we realize in athletic activity and games. A recent paper in this vein is 'Groundwork for the Mechanics of Morals', *Canadian Journal of Philosophy* (2021).

Catherine Lu is Professor of Political Science at McGill University in Montreal, Canada. Her research interests intersect political theory and international relations, focusing on critical and normative theoretical studies of colonial international order, structural injustice, and global justice; alienation and reconciliation; and cosmopolitanism and the world state. In addition to writing articles on these themes, she is the author of *Justice and Reconciliation in World Politics* (Cambridge University Press, 2017) and *Just and Unjust Interventions in World Politics: Public and Private* (Palgrave Macmillan, 2006).

Sally J. Scholz is Professor of Philosophy at Villanova University. An award-winning teacher and researcher, Scholz works in social philosophy on solidarity, oppression, violence, and just war theory. Publications include the books *Political Solidarity*, *On de Beauvoir*, and *On Rousseau*, and *Feminism: A Beginner's Guide*. Scholz has co-edited numerous books and special issues, and served as editor for *Hypatia*, *Journal of Peace and Justice Studies* and the *APA Newsletter on Philosophy and Feminism*. In addition, Scholz is a leader in the profession, serving on the board of the American Philosophical Association and president of the North American Society for Social Philosophy.

Series editor's foreword

Andrea Sangiovanni has established himself as one of the most innovative and important political philosophers of his generation through a series of conceptual and theoretical works that range from his path-breaking articles on practice-dependence[1] and the sites of justice[2] in political philosophy to his continuing normative engagement with the institutional structure of the European Union.[3] In his powerfully argued book *Humanity without Dignity* he grounds human rights not on an appeal to the concept of dignity but in the moral right of each person not to be treated as inferior to other persons. He defends this argument through a substantive account of being treated as an inferior manifest in dehumanization, instrumentalization, infantilization, objectification, and stigmatization.

1 See, for example, 'Normative Political Theory: A Flight from Reality?' in *Political Thought and International Relations*, ed. D. Bell (Oxford: Oxford University Press, 2008), pp. 219–40; 'Justice and the Priority of Politics to Morality', *Journal of Political Philosophy* 36(2) (2008): 137–64; 'How Practices Matter', *Journal of Political Philosophy* 24 (2016): 3–23.
2 See, for example, 'Global Justice, Reciprocity, and the State', *Philosophy & Public Affairs* 35(1) (2007): 2–39; 'The Irrelevance of Coercion, Imposition, and Framing to Distributive Justice', *Philosophy & Public Affairs* 40(2) (2012): 79–110.
3 See, for example, 'Solidarity in the European Union: Problems and Prospects', in *The Philosophical Foundations of European Union Law*, eds. Julie Dickson and Pavlos Eleftheriadis (Oxford: Oxford University Press, 2012), pp. 384–412; 'Solidarity in the European Union', *Oxford Journal of Legal Studies* 33 (2013): 213–41; 'Non-Discrimination, Free Movement, and In-Work Benefits in the European Union', *European Journal of Political Theory* 16 (2017): 143–63; 'Debating the EU's raison d'être: On the Relation between Justice and Legitimacy', *Journal of Common Market Studies* 57 (2019): 13–27.

Sangiovanni's concern with moral equality construed in these terms offers one route through which an interest in solidarity naturally arises, since an important site of solidarity is that of groups who are treated as inferior and engage in political struggle against their being so treated. But a second route arises directly from his work on the European Union and its commitment (at least in principle) to solidarity between member states. The fact that his work raises the issue of solidarity from these two different directions is a reason why Sangiovanni finds himself confronting the general question of whether the use of the word 'solidarity' in both contexts can be seen as particular specifications of the same concept or not, and hence the question with which he begins the lead essay of this volume concerning the nature of solidarity, its grounds, and its value. The ambitious aim of this essay is to offer a general account of solidarity that has sufficient structure to be empirically and normatively valuable, to distinguish solidarity from other normative concepts, and to encompass an important range of standard uses.

At the heart of Sangiovanni's account is an understanding of solidarity as 'a particular form of *joint action* characterized by a typical profile of commitments, intentions, and attitudes, and triggered by, *inter alia*, an identification with others on the basis of a shared cause, role, way of life, condition, or set of experiences'. There are reasons to favor such a general concept of solidarity if it helps us make sense of the history of solidarity and the diversity encompassed by that history, as well as the normative attractiveness of practices of solidarity as egalitarian and mutualistic forms of cooperation among strangers directed to overcoming significant adversity. Sangiovanni's engagement with the history of solidarity is a way both of supporting his conceptual account and of fleshing out the kind of practices which that account would encompass. The third part of Sangiovanni's account turns from the history of the concept of solidarity to the normative grounds of the practice of solidarity and to making the claim that identification is paradigmatic of solidarity. Finally, Sangiovanni addresses the value of the practice of solidarity. Here he is concerned to argue that solidarity has non-instrumental value and to differentiate solidarity from a value that it is often identified with, or reduced to, namely, justice.

That Sangiovanni has produced an original, substantive account of solidarity is amply demonstrated by the range of arguments and objections which his interlocutors raise in their critical essays. His response to these essays should be seen as just the start of the dialogue that this innovative contribution to the debate on solidarity will provoke.

David Owen

Part I

Lead essay

1

Solidarity: nature, grounds, and value

Andrea Sangiovanni

Introduction

Many today have the sense that collective action is futile in the presence of large transnational social and economic forces. They worry about our increasingly fragmented, unequal, and divided politics. They worry, too, about the decline and stagnation of their societies and institutions. People sense the need for some form of collective resistance and mobilization that looks beyond normal electoral politics, and are hungry for forms of meaningful and transformative joint action. It is no surprise that calls for solidarity are heard everywhere. This book puts forward a critical proposal to guide our reflection on what solidarity is, and why it should move us.

How is solidarity distinct from other, related ideas, such as altruism, justice, and fellow-feeling? What value does acting in solidarity with others have? What reasons do we have to act in solidarity with others? Answering these questions is important for at least three reasons. First, less attention has been given to solidarity than to other more established values such as justice, liberty, legitimacy, equality, patriotism, dignity, and so on. Second, solidarity has had a long history of inclusion in Christian, socialist, and nationalist arguments, as well as in those social movements inspired by them (e.g., feminism, civil rights). Solidarity is, furthermore, now gaining ground again as a rallying cry in debates, for example, within bioethics,[1] human rights,[2] contemporary social movements[3] (Black Lives

---

1 Prainsack and Buyx 2012.
2 Vasak 1979; Wellman 2000.
3 See, e.g., Shelby 2009; hooks 2015a; Scholz 2010.

Matter [BLM], Occupy, MeToo), the COVID-19 pandemic, and constitutionalism[4] (consider that eighty-five polities across the world refer to solidarity in key areas of their constitution, including Albania, Algeria, Angola, Bangladesh, Bhutan, Cameroon, Chile, Colombia, Israel, Morocco, Romania, Spain, and the European Union [EU]). Third, the study of solidarity lies within the broader class of what we might call *associational* ethics – the ethics of life in associations and within social relationships that extend beyond relations among intimates. Other members of the class of associational ethics include the ethics of larger social and economic collectivities, such as corporations and social movements. This area has been much less studied than the ethics of family and friendship, on one hand, and the classical concerns of political justice such as the state, human rights, and international relations, on the other.

And yet the uses to which solidarity is put and the contexts in which it arises are so many and so various that many feel the concept to be hopelessly vague and amorphous. So vague is it, it is often said, that it ends up bleeding into other related notions – such as altruism, community, mutual concern, fellow-feeling, justice – and therefore quickly becoming indistinguishable from them. The temptation is to eliminate the term and use its clearer relatives instead. Another temptation is to proliferate the possible kinds of solidarity, each of which identifies a distinct concept of solidarity.[5] The existing literature often distinguishes, for example, between *political, social,*

---

4 See www.constituteproject.org (accessed May 15, 2023) for a searchable list of over 200 constitutions across the world. See also the instructive discussion in Brandes 2021. Constitutions refer to solidarity in a wide variety of contexts. I list several of them: background inequality among regions within the country (e.g., Argentina, Chile, Spain, Germany); ethnic, linguistic, and religious conflict (e.g. Bangladesh, Spain, Nepal); social rights provisions (e.g., Poland, EU); intergenerational justice (e.g., Belgium, Portugal); terrorist attacks and natural disasters (e.g., Bolivia, EU); national unity (e.g. Thailand, Vietnam, Portugal); expressions of support for other socialist and/or postcolonial countries or for pan-Africanism (e.g., Cuba, Cameroon, Mozambique, Nicaragua). For the EU, see, e.g., Ross and Borgmann-Prebil 2010; Sangiovanni 2013; Somek forthcoming.

5 See, e.g., Derpmann 2015, p. 85: 'There is plainly no distinct philosophical concept of solidarity that equally supports the notions of solidarity with humankind, towards the unfortunate and the oppressed, and among a revolutionary army or a football club.'

civic, and *human* uses of the term 'solidarity'. *Political* solidarity – described as central to social movements such as socialism, feminism, and civil rights – is often referred to as oppositional and goal-directed in ways that social, civic, and human solidarity are not;[6] the *social* solidarity deployed in the solidarist writings of, for example, Auguste Comte and Émile Durkheim, is taken to be primarily descriptive and sociological in contrast to the other, more normatively oriented concepts;[7] *civic* solidarity is depicted as primarily institutional and narrowly defined in terms of the welfare state;[8] and *human* solidarity – as, for example, deployed in the social teachings of the Catholic Church – covers the whole human race in ways that other usages do not.[9]

This way of characterizing the field of meanings can be useful, depending on one's theoretical aims, but it obscures whether there is anything but a very loose and abstract concept that might unite them. What makes each of these an instance of *solidarity*? Is there a characterization of solidarity that can show each of these different usages to be a particular specification of an overarching concept that has enough content to be meaningful? Or are they merely tied together by very loose family resemblances?[10] Or, even more starkly, do they describe entirely different concepts that share only a string of letters (in the same way as [institutional] banks share the same string of letters as [river] banks, or [sporting] bats the same letters as [flying] bats)?

The aim of this essay is to elaborate a unified concept of solidarity that can comprehend each of these usages while having enough structure to make it normatively and empirically fruitful in a range of other contexts, too. I will argue that solidarity is best understood, not as an emotion or kind of fellow-feeling, but as a particular form of *joint action* characterized by a typical profile of commitments, intentions, and attitudes, and triggered by, *inter alia*, an identification with others on the basis of a shared cause, role, way of life, condition, or set of experiences. Much of the account will be dedicated to

---

6 See, e.g., Scholz 2010.
7 See, e.g., Bayertz 1999b; Stjernø 2005.
8 See, e.g., Banting and Kymlicka 2017, Introduction.
9 See, e.g., Bayertz 1999b; Brunkhorst 2005.
10 Cf. Scholz 2010, pp. 18–21.

unpacking each of these aspects. Throughout I will be building on, re-elaborating, extending, and revising some of the key insights that have emerged in the recent literature. So as not to distract from the main line of argument, I will compare, where relevant, recent treatments in the footnotes.

There are five reasons why setting out a general account of the nature, grounds, and value of solidarity is a worthwhile endeavor.

First, there is unclarity in the literature regarding whether and to what extent solidarity is a normative and to what extent an empirical phenomenon. Is it more like justice (i.e., a normative concept) or more like the welfare state (i.e., a descriptive concept), or is it some hybrid of the two? (If the latter, what kind of 'hybrid'?) Closely related, what might it mean to *defend* a particular (normative or descriptive) conception of solidarity against other possible conceptions? What is the appropriate scope of solidarity? And what are its grounds? Identifying the relation between a higher-level, more abstract concept of solidarity and more specific concepts and conceptions *of* solidarity will allow us to answer these questions, and, in the process, to make conceptual room for *both* empirical *and* normative study of solidarity while clearly distinguishing them.

Second, in section 3 ('Grounds'), distinguishing between normative and descriptive uses of the term will also allow us to discuss the *value* of acting in solidarity *simpliciter* – a topic which has been addressed only sporadically in the literature on solidarity.

Third, delineating a general concept of solidarity will give us a formula for generating more specific concepts and conceptions of solidarity without worrying about whether they fit into one of the already enumerated categories (e.g., social, civil, political, human). Indeed, it will give us a framework for developing specific empirical and normative conceptions of solidarity for *any* context in which people act together to accomplish significant ends.

Fourth, one might wonder whether the exercise I will be engaged in throughout this essay will be merely 'linguistic'. What's in a name? Is the aim to trace the definition of a word in the English language?[11] Or to provide an account of ordinary usage? And, if

11 Cf. Van Parijs forthcoming, who writes: 'In this enterprise, I shall be guided by my own linguistic intuitions, and hence probably by the way the relevant words are used in French more than in other languages. This may account for differences with what readers more familiar with other languages may regard as the best explication of the concept.'

so, what's the point? The aim of this essay is not to capture the English definition of a word; I am not a lexicographer. Rather, my interest will be in the practice that gave birth to the term (especially in section 2, 'History') and that sustains it as a richly normative and evaluative social phenomenon. My aim, then, is to identify the concept that best captures what is fundamental, and valuable, about the practice. This marks a key difference. It is possible, for example, for the everyday English word as it is used today (and its associated concept or concepts) to *fail* in tracking the practice; it is also possible that the concept picked out by any one pattern of usage prevents us from seeing clearly what is valuable, distinctive, or normatively compelling about the practice. A useful analogy is to studies on the nature of law.[12] The point of such studies is not to uncover the meaning of the word 'law' in, say, the English language, but to

---

[12] See, e.g., Dworkin 1986. On some problems with Dworkin's attempt to make LAW into what he calls an 'interpretive' concept, see Plunkett and Sundell 2013b. My essay is, more broadly, an attempt at 'conceptual engineering'. See, e.g., Cappelen and Plunkett 2020. The particular form of engineering I am deploying assumes that we should take solidarity to be a *social kind* determined by historically evolving social conventions, norms, behaviors, expectations, and background circumstances. My account is intended to track this kind, not to reproduce the semantic values paired with current word usage. The idea, then, is that we need to reorganize and sharpen our basic concept of solidarity to better track the social phenomenon; as I point out in the text, current usage has, in many cases, led us astray. On social kinds, see Mallon 2016; Millikan 2000, pp. 18–20; Boyd 1991; Godman 2020. In section 2, I will argue that the concept becomes salient as a response to the breakdown of traditional ties of kinship, guild, and church, and responds to a need to find a large-scale form of social unity among strangers capacious enough to sustain a willingness to sacrifice for others. A parallel here is to the concept of sexual harassment. While the behaviors and practices tracked by the concept have been around for centuries, the concept only emerges in the late 1970s (for this history, see Brownmiller 1999; Fricker 2007, pp. 149ff). Once the concept comes into usage, in turn, it transforms the very category itself, including the meanings and possibilities of action and reaction associated with it (for other analogues, see Hacking 1999; Mallon 2016, chs 2 and 8). I think a similar pattern characterizes solidarity: the underlying pattern of dispositions, norms, behaviors, and attitudes has been around for centuries, but it only becomes theorized as a distinctive phenomenon, and enters public and social discourse, in the nineteenth century. Once it does, solidarity as a category of action becomes transformed as people begin to think of themselves as acting in, and out of, solidarity with others. (See below, second section and Sangiovanni ms.b)

provide an interpretive account of law as a practice. Doing so successfully requires attention to why the law is valuable, and why, and under what circumstances, something's being the law gives us reasons (and in some cases obligations) to follow it. The same thing goes, I argue, for solidarity.

I will delineate, in brief, a concept that can be fruitful in thinking more carefully about the social phenomenon and that can enter into both descriptive and normative inquiries. I will lay out, that is, an account that can be used both in describing and explaining the social world in which solidarity has figured (hence 'nature') and in evaluating and reforming it (hence 'grounds' and 'value'). This is why tracing the history of solidarity (as we do in section 2) is so important. The history both provides a testing ground for the usefulness of the concept introduced and is important for understanding the political uses and possibilities of solidarity, including what makes it relevant to social and political life today. Understanding how and when the concept of solidarity emerged – including especially what solidarity emerged as a response *to* – will help us appreciate the centrality and distinctiveness of certain aspects of solidarity that we might not have appreciated before.[13]

The account should therefore be assessed *not* according to whether it tracks our linguistic intuitions but according to whether it provides a useful tool for illuminating solidarity's history and the various contexts in which it has been used, for distinguishing it from related phenomena, and for making sense of what we find valuable and normatively compelling in solidarity.[14] In some cases (as I will indicate throughout), the account I defend is *revisionary* of current usage; in others, it tracks such usage more closely. I will also suggest not only a framework or set of tools for further discussion but when and why we should take ourselves to have good or genuine reasons to act in solidarity, and reason to believe that acting in solidarity is good in itself.

Fifth, and relatedly, if I am successful in showing that the overarching concept I propose is an accurate representation of the practice,

---

13 See the useful discussion of the importance of conceptual history to understanding which concepts we should use (and which we shouldn't) in Plunkett 2016.
14 See also Derpmann 2015, p. 84.

and that it is distinct from related notions, then it lends plausibility to the idea that solidarity, or being in solidarity with others, is an important social form in its own right, sufficiently rich to add to our social ontology, alongside other, more basic social forms, such as institutions, social groups, and social structures.

1 Nature

The first step in our account is to identify what kind of thing solidarity is. Is solidarity an emotion (like joy or anger)? A propositional attitude (like a desire or belief)? Does it name some kind of action or activity (like, say, dancing the tango) or institution (like the welfare state)? Let us begin with propositional attitudes. Propositional attitudes are mental states whose content is some proposition. This is why they are often (though not always) expressible by using a *that*-clause to indicate the proposition being related to (I desire *that* [we go to dinner together]; I believe *that* [the sun will rise].) But solidarity is not a mental state with some object expressed by a proposition. Solidarity is, as we will see, a type of action constituted by a relation among persons. The relations, furthermore, are identified *non-comparatively*. If I am taller than you, I possess a non-relational property, vertical extension, to a greater extent than you do. 'Taller than' is therefore only *comparatively* relational. If I am to the left of you, by contrast, then I do not share some non-relational property to a greater extent than you. While being to the left of depends on non-relational spatiotemporal properties, it is not defined in terms of the possession of those properties to a greater extent than someone else. 'Being to the left of', like 'being your uncle', is therefore a *non-comparative* relation. 'Being in solidarity with' is relational in this non-comparative sense: it is not defined in terms of the equal or greater (lesser) possession of a further, underlying non-relational property. It is also an essentially *social, interpersonal* relation, constituted, as we will see, by a characteristic set of other-regarding attitudes, behaviors, norms, and dispositions.

It is also not an institution. Rather, institutions might be the *product* of solidarity or *expressions* of it; however, it would be a mistake to say that solidarity simply *is* an institution. There are no conventional rules or norms establishing roles and positions in an institution called 'solidarity' (except in derivative senses, such as the French Second Republic parliamentary grouping named 'Solidarité Républicaine').

It bears perhaps the most similarity to a sentiment or emotion, but unlike emotions (such as anger) it is not marked by a corresponding, typical, and often automatic somatic response, and it does not function as a direct reflection or response to an object (e.g., fear as a direct response to the wolf's ferocity; grief as a direct response to the loss of one's friend). While of course a shared identity, or experience of injustice, might be, for example, a *reason* to act in solidarity, solidarity is not best characterized as itself a somatically marked, typical, and automatic response to sharing an identity, or an experience. Of course, this is not to deny that acting in solidarity with others is often accompanied and underpinned by typical emotions or sentiments of fellow-feeling or community. But it is hasty to conclude that solidarity is best understood as simply naming the feeling itself. One could act in solidarity with others and feel a wide array of emotions; the fact of solidarity would not come and go as the emotions change.[15]

Solidarity is, rather, best understood as a special kind of *joint action* constituted by a characteristic profile of interpersonal attitudes, norms, dispositions, and behaviors triggered by one's *identification* with another on the basis of a role, cause, way of life, condition, or set of experiences.[16] In elaborating this proposal, I will discuss the two components of this account in the following order: identification first, and then joint action. These components together define the core or paradigm concept of solidarity; there are also, as we

15 Rorty 1989, p. 190, for example, refers to solidarity as a feeling.
16 There are several differences between the account here and Sangiovanni 2015. This essay identifies a single concept of solidarity that can unite different traditions (rather than defending one tradition against others), explains how to use the concept to generate particular empirical and normative conceptions (and to distinguish more clearly between them), clarifies the symmetrical rather than unilateral nature of solidarity, provides an account of the value of solidarity, compares solidarity to other related or structurally similar concepts, including justice, love, and charity, amends the specific conditions required of joint solidaristic action (most importantly, this essay includes a discussion of the significance of identification – for more detail on the differences in condition, see below, note 26).

will see, instances of solidarity that share most but not all of the features of the core. The account I will provide will help us to identify why they are borderline or penumbral cases rather than paradigmatic ones.

1.1 Identification

It is often said that my identification with you *as a woman* or *as a worker* or *as an African-American* or *as a French citizen* or *as an antifascist* can provide me a reason, or even an obligation, to act in solidarity with you.[17] There are two questions to be answered. The first asks: What does it mean to identify with another in each of those ways? What are the relevant forms that identification takes? The second asks: *Why* and *under what circumstances* does identification give rise to genuine reasons to act in solidarity with others? Why does that appeal to what we share have normative force? In this section, I answer the former. I answer the latter in section 3.

One can identify *as* and one can identify *with*.[18] I might identify, for example, as a Norwegian. This means that I take myself to belong to a socially salient group; I will recognize that this will often affect my social interactions with others, both in the way that I present myself and in the way others perceive me. I might not, however, feel any particular attachment to that identity, or take it as in any way important to my self-conception. If I identify *with* my Norwegian nationality, then I do take it as important to my self-conception; I take membership to be meaningful; I feel attachment to my identity as Norwegian; I feel normative pressure to conform to the norms, attitudes, behaviors that typically define *being Norwegian*.

Identifying with *another person* takes a similar but importantly different form. One can identify with another person *as such* or on the basis of a *role*, *a cause*, *a condition*, *a way of life*, or *a set of experiences*. When I identify with someone (or, indeed, with a character in a novel), I identify with his life as he lives it. I enter his perspective; I imagine the world through his eyes.[19] Identification

---

17 For the importance of identification, see also Shelby 2009, p. 68.
18 Cf. the way identification as and with is presented in social identity theory in, for example, Hogg and Hains 1996, pp. 295–7.
19 On the role of imagination in identification, see Wollheim 1974.

with a person (like identification with a social identity) also has affective and normative dimensions. Affectively, I am drawn into his world; I am attracted by it. While I may be ashamed or disapproving of my attraction, I am attracted nonetheless; identification is never repulsive *tout court*. At the same time, I resonate with his attitudes and emotions. When he is consumed with contempt, I become hateful and want to take revenge on his oppressor; when he rejoices in his freedom, I am unbound. Normatively, I take his perspective as describing an ideal to which I want to conform. I align myself with his standards and expectations, his goals and projects; I make them mine; I see things the same way he does; I am changed by the way I see him in me, and judge my own actions from his perspective.[20] As Richard Wollheim puts it:

> In effect what we do when we identify with another is that we write a part for ourselves, based upon the other, in the hope that, when we act it to ourselves, we shall be carried away by the performance.[21]

When I identify with another, my imagining and sympathizing with their life is not just a way of learning about them but a way of modifying or transforming myself in the process.

Identification with a person as such is identification with a particular: it is an attitude *de re*. But I can also identify with someone on the basis of something else. I might identify with you *as a teacher* (role) or with you as a *climate change activist* (cause) or with you as a *mortal* (condition) or with you as a *Christian* (way of life), or with you as a *cancer survivor* (set of experiences). This kind of identification is not identification with a particular: I might not even know you personally. The attitude is *de dicto*: I identify with you on the basis of an indefinite description that we both satisfy, that defines a socially salient group, and that significantly structures our self-conception. Identifying with a person in this way also involves

---

20 Laplanche and Pontalis define the psychoanalytic (Freudian) conception of identification in the following way: identification is a 'psychological process whereby the subject assimilates an aspect, property or attribute of the other and is transformed, wholly or partially, after the model the other provides' (Laplanche and Pontalis 2018 [1973], p. 205). See also Scheler 2017 [1923] on sympathy, and the necessity of keeping the 'I' and 'thou' separate when feeling-with another and Lugones 1987 on 'world-travelling'.
21 Wollheim 1974, p. 191.

epistemic, affective, and normative elements. Epistemically, when I identify as a member of the relevant group, I seek understanding of the norms, attitudes, and behaviors that define the group. This understanding becomes interpersonal – a way of knowing how others see themselves and present themselves to others – when I come to know that you are also a member of the group. As a teacher, I know what it is like to be a teacher; I understand the challenges you face and the joys you experience. Affectively, when I identify with you, I feel both empathy and sympathy with your situation as a teacher, Christian, and so on; I am moved by and concerned with the challenges you face as a teacher, Christian, and so on. My understanding is acquired not just through knowledge of a series of true propositions about you, but via the ability to see the world through your eyes and be drawn, emotionally, into your perspective.[22]

Normatively, identifying with you in virtue of some cause, role, and so on has two components. First, I take your situation as giving rise to a set of normative expectations. When I identify with you as a Christian, for example, I have a structured set of beliefs about how Christians ought to behave, as Christians, in different kinds of situations. My identification is, in part, grounded in the sense that we share a normative perspective on the world governed by our special situation. There is a pressure, then, to seek a common view of the standards, norms, and expectations that govern our particular situation, or, alternatively, to bring our disagreements into the foreground, and make their characteristic shape and form definitive of who we are. Second, the flourishing of the group that forms the basis of our identification now forms a part of my individual flourishing. When the group succeeds or does well, I feel proud; when it fails, I feel shame or disappointment.[23]

---

22 On the importance of the affective dimension in understanding the identification that underlies solidarity, Carol Gould writes that empathy is required to 'understand the specifics of others' concrete situation, and to imaginatively construct for oneself their feelings and needs' (Gould 2007, p. 156). See also Bartky 2002, ch. 4, and Lu 2000, p. 256.
23 On vicarious pride and shame, see also Feinberg 1974, p. 237; A. E. Taylor 2015, p. 133; Mason 2000, p. 23. On the idea that identification with a social group can transform reasoning from an 'I' to a 'we' perspective, see also Sugden 2000, 2003. From a social identity perspective, see also Kramer and Brewer 1984, p. 1045.

The normative element of identification may not be readily apparent. We can clarify it by comparing it to identification with a cause, condition, way of life, or experience *directly* (rather than with a person on the basis of sharing one or more items on the list). When I identify with a cause, for example, I make the cause mine. I am committed to it and conceive of it as an important element of my practical identity, and hence an important element of my life (and hence my flourishing). Pursuit of the cause organizes my reflection and deliberation, and shapes the decisions I make. It gives my life direction.[24] I align my will with it on the basis of the values and aims it seeks to realize. The same thing is true of identifying with a role. The role is structured by a set of expectations, standards, and norms that are essential to it. When I identify with the role, I take those expectations, standards, and norms as important guiding commitments in my own life – commitments that I do not merely comply with but endorse and affirm. Similar things can be said with respect to a way of life, but also with respect to identifying with a condition or experience. When I identify as a cancer survivor, I take 'being a cancer survivor' as bringing with it a series of expectations, standards, and norms that partially define who I am. When I identify with my mortality, or with, say, my disability, I embrace it. That does not mean I welcome it or seek it out, but it does mean that I am not ashamed by it, or denying it, or seeking to resign myself to it. I take it as part of who I am, as something which ought to structure my life and give it direction. I can even, as we will see later, identify with my condition as *oppressed*, even as I fight to end it.

Note that identification with a cause, way of life, and so on is therefore not the same as desiring something for its own sake. I might desire, for example, the joy of basking in the sun for its own sake, but this does not make that activity something I identify with. It does not, after all, guide my life as an enduring project or

---

24 *Nota bene:* The structuring role of identification need not extend over an *entire* life. The structuring and commitment may hold even over a brief period. As long as, during that period, the object of one's identification structures one's life in all the ways listed, that is enough. Thanks to Zofia Stemplowska for discussion on this point.

commitment. I have no ongoing emotional investment in it. And it does not structure my perspective on the world. It is also not the same as believing a cause, way of life, and so on, to be worthwhile. I might, for example, believe medicine to be a valuable pursuit, and hence worthy of identification, but not myself be invested in it in that way.[25] Indeed, identification, as we have seen, need not (although it usually does) come with the judgment that the cause, way of life, and so on, is worthy of pursuit in its own right. I can identify with my condition as oppressed, but not believe that oppression is something anyone has reason to pursue in its own right and for its own sake. While identification does require that I embrace, rather than deny, my condition as oppressed – to see it as having significant affective, normative, and epistemic bearing on my life – it does not require that I promote it.

The normative structure of identifying directly with a cause, way of life, condition, or set of experiences helps us to make sense of the normative element of identification *with another person* on the basis of one or more of those items. When I identify with you as a cancer survivor (experiences), or as a Christian (way of life), or as a mortal (condition) or as a teacher (role), or as an activist (cause), I take us as both identifying with each of these phenomena directly, and thus as seeking to structure our lives in important ways in relation to them. Furthermore, I desire that the group defined by our shared way of life, condition, and so on, does well, since my own interests are bound up with it. I also aim to come to a more unified and comprehensive view about what our (direct) identification with the cause, role, experience, condition, or way of life requires of us and what its meaning should be in our lives. Even if we come to accept that it has a different meaning to each one of us, we take the differences themselves to define the larger and more comprehensive perspective that the cause, role, experience, condition, or way of life gives us; the differences and disagreements, in part, define what it means to be, say, a teacher or environmental activist. Note that, unlike identification *de re*, this mutual role-taking and role-adjustment can take place without knowing personally the others aligned with

---

25 Cf. Scheffler 2010.

the cause, role, experience, or condition; we can gain access to different perspectives in a much more mediated way, including through articles, literature, art, narratives, second-hand reports, and so on.

It may seem that identification and solidarity are one and the same. If I identify with you in any of the ways that I have just described, then isn't this just to say that I am in solidarity with you? No. This is clearest with respect to identification with a person as such. We can, after all, be in solidarity with strangers. We do not need the intimate knowledge of another's life that identification in the *de re* sense requires. But it is also true of identification with another person in the *de dicto* sense. As we will see, to say that I *identify with* you as a cancer survivor and that I am in *solidarity with* you as a cancer survivor are two different things. To *be* in solidarity is, as we will see below, to *act* in solidarity. But identification can provide a *reason* to act in solidarity with you. Indeed, I will argue below that one or more of the forms of identification I just outlined are paradigmatic *grounds* for acting in solidarity with others.

1.2 Joint action

So far I have elaborated an account of identification and suggested that identification is not the same as solidarity; rather, we should think of it as providing a paradigmatic ground of solidarity. Understood in this way, identification is a *core component* of solidarity without being identical with it. I have not yet provided an argument for any of these claims. At this stage, we are merely articulating the components of the theory. The support for these claims comes later, when we contrast the account of solidarity with other, related notions, show the work that it can do in distinguishing and clarifying normative and empirical uses (including a critical assessment of reasons for acting in solidarity), explore its value, and place it in a historical context. The argument for the account, that is, emerges by showing its theoretical and practical role in elucidating the range and scope of its characteristic features, as they emerge in social and political practices, both past and present. Here, we lay out the way in which solidarity is a form of *joint action*.

Acting in solidarity has the following features.[26] We act in solidarity when, as a result of mutually identifying with one another on the basis of a role, cause, condition, set of experiences, or way of life,

1. we each intend to do our part in overcoming some significant adversity, X, by pursuing, together, some more proximate shared goal, Y;
2. we are each individually committed (a) to X and Y and (b) to not bypassing each other's will in the achievement of X and Y;[27]
3. we are committed to sharing one another's fates in ways relevant to X and Y;
4. we trust each other to play their part in X and Y, trust each other's commitment, trust that we will not bypass each other's will, and trust each other to share one another's fate.

(1) is intended to be compatible with a variety of theories of shared intentional activity; the important idea is that our action must be a form of acting *together* in order for it to count as acting in solidarity.[28] John Gardner provides a useful example (drawn from a novel

---

26 I defend a similar account of the conditions for solidary collective action in Sangiovanni 2015. Here are the differences: (a) (1) is stated in a way that is ecumenical with respect to the dominant accounts of collective action and shared intentionality (see also note 28); Sangiovanni 2015, by contrast, was committed to the view that shared goals without shared intentions were sufficient (for the importance of shared intentions rather than merely shared goals see, for example, Searle 1990); (b) *trust* is included as a core component of solidarity (otherwise agents who merely happen to share a goal and who do not expect one another's reliance could count as acting in solidarity); (c) the account contains a discussion of the importance and role of 'sharing another's fate', which is left unspecified in Sangiovanni 2015; (d) the conditions require identification as a trigger, whereas Sangiovanni 2015 does not.
27 On the importance of the fact that participants must intend to advance a shared goal (in our case, overcoming significant adversity) in part *by way of* the intentions of each in favor of the shared goal, see Bratman 2014, pp. 50–6, esp. p. 55.
28 The idea of acting with the intention of 'doing one's part', that is, must be further analyzed to make it non-circular. The account of solidarity I offer is meant to be ecumenical with respect to how it should be analyzed, as long as the account is scalable to larger groups. There is some doubt, for example, whether Bratman's account of shared action (Bratman 2014) – which depends on individuals' each intending that we *J* – is scalable (see,

by Ian McEwan) to make the distinction between mutually responsive, coordinated activity and truly *joint* activity.[29] Imagine that there are two people holding a balloon down by separate ropes in order to save an infant from flying up into a windy sky. Their each holding down the rope is required to save the baby. If only one were to hold it down, it would not be sufficient to keep the balloon down. In one description, let us imagine that each individual treats the other as if they were an aspect of the background circumstances to which they must adjust. While they have expectations regarding what the other will do, which will inform what they do in trying to save the baby, they do not, however, ever 'transform' the unit of agency in which their goal is encompassed.[30] Person A aims to save the baby, and so does Person B. But their goal is only held in *common*. It is not *shared*. There is no 'we'-perspective that rationalizes their individual actions; while they each act in ways responsive to the other, they do not act *together* as a 'we'. Accounts of collective agency aim to explain what is required in the attitudes and modes of reasoning of each to make their action truly joint, truly an instance of a 'we' that is more than a sum of 'I's'. My account of solidarity is meant to be ecumenical between them.[31]

Another example is useful in drawing the distinction between merely coordinated activity and truly joint activity. In the wake of a train crash, everyone's rushing to the exits while coordinating on the way – for example, by avoiding tripping on each other – is not a joint action and (therefore) not a form of solidarity. While they are aware of each other's intentions, are prepared to coordinate their actions, and are each aiming to avoid death by getting out of

e.g., Shapiro 2014). Bratman himself leaves it to others to figure out how (and whether) it might be adapted for larger groups (see Bratman 2014, p. 8). Gilbert 1996; Kutz 2000a; Tuomela 2013; Sugden 2000; Searle 1990, by contrast, are clearly intended to be scalable. The way I have stated condition (1) is most similar to Kutz's formulation precisely to avoid the reference to a set of individual intentions that we *J*. Given that, in forming an intention, we must take ourselves to settle the matter of our *J*'ing just by our intending it, Bratman's way of formulating the shared intention looks too demanding for very large groups (for this critique of Bratman, see, e.g., Velleman 1997).
29 Gardner 2002. I have taken the simplified version of the example.
30 For this way of putting it, see Sugden 2003.
31 See note 28.

the train, they do not *share* the goal that *everyone* (or some proper subset of individuals) get out of the train. There is no overlap in the satisfaction conditions – in the token activities or outcomes required to satisfy our goal – involved in any person's getting out: *my* getting out is not required to satisfy anyone else's plan to get out, and *everyone else's* getting out is not required for my plan to get out. If, on the other hand, those involved in the train wreck had each intended to do their part in the joint activity of *everyone's* getting out (or in some proper subset getting out), and if each of the other conditions (2)–(4) had been satisfied (along with an identification with others on the basis of our predicament), then it *would* have been an instance of acting in solidarity.

For us to share some more proximate goal, Y, required to overcome some significant adversity, X, how much agreement must there be in satisfaction conditions? There must be some overlap, but this overlap need not be extensive. This allows for solidary groups to be very loosely connected.[32] For example, if you and I both intend to do our part in overcoming current and past vestiges of racial oppression through public forms of resistance (and [2]–[4] are also satisfied), but your aim in publicly resisting government policy is to form a separate Black nation in Sub-Saharan Africa whereas my aim in publicly resisting is to pave the way to successful integration in broader American society, then there can be (let us assume) many token outcomes and/or activities that we agree would count as satisfying our more proximate goals (such as preventing the government from passing policies that undermine educational opportunity in the Black community, or that increase rates of incarceration). These more proximate goals, in turn, rationalize our cooperation in the here and now despite the fact that we have very different ideas about what the final ends of our action are.[33] If, on the other

---

32 Cf. Tuomela 2013, who argues that the we-mode characteristic of solidarity groups requires a single group reason on which the group acts and a goal that is set by the group for the group. See, e.g., Tuomela 2013, pp. 41–2 and ch. 9.
33 Cf. what Malcolm X told SNCC workers in Selma, Alabama, just before he was murdered in 1965. He worried that though they were struggling for a just cause, America would turn its back on them: 'I don't want to make you do anything you wouldn't do.... I disagree with nonviolence, but I respect the fact that you're on the frontlines and you're down here

hand, we have completely non-overlapping ideas about what would count as successful forms of public resistance, then we cannot act in solidarity because we cannot be said to share a goal in the relevant sense.

Similarly, if we realize that our preferred forms of public resistance sometimes work at cross-purposes, end up undermining the pursuit of our ultimate ends, and we do nothing to coordinate so as to stop this from happening, then we are not acting in solidarity. Solidarity requires joint action, and joint action requires, at the very least, coordination based on shared intentions. But we can still act in solidarity in the case in which we each pursue our preferred courses of action despite our knowledge that our public resistance would do even better if we united forces. This will be the case if some of us believe that there are other, overriding reasons (for example, of pride or community) to pursue, say, an emigration-based policy even if our public resistance would be more effective by uniting to further an integrationist legislative agenda. As long as we are not actively undermining our shared proximate goals or each other, there is no need to sacrifice our other, non-convergent goals for the maximal realization of the proximate goals. Consider, by contrast, forms of collective irrationality. Were we, as fishermen, each committed to preventing progressive poisoning of the lake that provides our catch, yet make no effort to coordinate our individual subplans (because we continue to garner temporary profit from individual exploitation of the lake's resources), then we cannot be said to be acting either together or, *a fortiori*, in solidarity.

To explore the amount of overlap required for solidarity, it is useful to pause and reflect on what have been called, in the social movement literature, the 'new social movements' (e.g., BLM, Occupy).[34] BLM is a grassroots movement with local chapters and

---

suffering for a version of freedom larger than America's prepared to accept' (from an interview with Taylor Branch; National Public Radio Transcript, Saturday, April 4, 1998), quoted in Dawson 2003, p. 240.

34 For the contrast with the organizations that were part of the civil rights movement, see, e.g., Harris 2015; Tillery 2019. On new social movements more broadly, see, e.g., Della Porta and Diani 2020.

no (officially recognized[35]) centralized leadership (although the founders play a prominent role in advocacy and coordination). It was formed, first as a hashtag, in response to the acquittal of George Zimmerman (who was charged with second degree murder and manslaughter for the killing of Trayvon Martin). It then coalesced in as a movement in the streets of Ferguson, Missouri, after the police killings of Michael Brown and Eric Garner. While its main aim, in this early period, was to rally against anti-Black police violence in the US, its agenda has expanded to include a wide range of issues in anti-racist politics. It is now, furthermore, global in reach, with local chapters in Australia, the UK, Denmark, and Japan, among others. Are the different chapters involved in the movement acting in solidarity with one another? Can they, for example, be understood to be acting *jointly* to overcome anti-Black racism? What would it take for us to say they are *not* acting in solidarity? The case of BLM Denmark seems straightforward. BLM Denmark is organized to fight for the rights of asylum-seekers and irregular migrants (the majority of whom are non-White) detained on Danish soil.[36] It is not, therefore, centered on fighting anti-Black police violence in the usual sense, let alone US police violence. And yet it seems clear that its intentions are sufficiently interlaced with US BLM movements to say that it is acting in solidarity. Both movements are, at their root, founded on a recognition of the global, interlocking, and interconnected nature of racist social structures, which have a long, interwoven history (think, for example, of the slave trade and European nineteenth-century colonialism, and its implications for more recent patterns of migration and immigration both into and from Africa, Asia, the Americas, and Europe).[37] Both movements

---

35 The umbrella organization the Black Lives Matter Global Network has an increasingly centralized structure, but it is not widely recognized as organizing and leading the movement on behalf of all its members. See, e.g., https://en.wikipedia.org/wiki/Black_Lives_Matter_Global_Network_Foundation (accessed April 9, 2022).
36 See, e.g., this interview with its leader, Bwalya Sørensen: www.youtube.com/watch?v=I8feE8cXf20 (accessed May 9, 2022).
37 See the comparison of US and Danish BLM movements in this study: https://rucforsk.ruc.dk/ws/portalfiles/portal/59105903/Group_21_Black_Lives_Matter_Semester_project.pdf (accessed May 15, 2023).

see themselves as involved, together, in a fight against such structures, and are prepared to support one another in doing so. When BLM Denmark takes its stand against refugee policy in Denmark, it understands itself as doing its part in a truly joint, transnational activity with BLM chapters in the US. It is evident that similar things are true with respect to all other international BLM chapters.

But are there harder cases where things aren't as clear? Consider the BLM10. In 2020, they severed ties with the Black Lives Matter Global Network (BLMGN), which is sometimes seen as the standard-bearer for the movement as a whole. They do not dissent from the broader goals of the *movement*. Rather, their grievance is with the transparency, accountability, and remoteness of the larger *organization*. In a public letter signed in December 2020, they expressed their concerns, among other things, over the lack of transparency regarding how much money the organization had raised, and the procedures for deciding to whom the funds should go.[38] They also believe that the increasingly centralized character of the umbrella organization has undermined the grassroots, decentralized nature of the movement. When the BLM10 organize local protests and activism against, say, police violence, are they acting in solidarity with BLMGN? It depends. As long as they are not actively and intentionally undermining BLMGN's activism, and as long as they would be prepared, when the chips were down, to support BLMGN (for example, were it to be attacked in the press by, say, an advocate of All Lives Matter), and as long as they each conceive of themselves as doing their part in the joint activity of overcoming racism, then, despite the disagreement, they can still be understood as acting together in solidarity in the pursuit of an anti-racist agenda. Solidarity, after all, does not preclude even profound disagreement (on which more below). But if their break from the larger movement also means that they are abandoning any attempt to coordinate their activity, or any sense in which they are working together in the name of a

---

38 For the most recent statement, dated June 10, 2021, see www.blmchapterstatement.com/no2/ (accessed May 15, 2023). See also the following press articles: www.politico.com/news/2020/12/10/black-lives-matter-organization-biden-444097 (accessed May 15, 2023) and www.nytimes.com/2021/06/04/us/black-lives-matter.html (accessed April 15, 2022).

common purpose, or any support for the work that BLMGN does as an organization, then they are no longer acting in solidarity.

Note further that an action being joint is, however, not *sufficient* for solidarity. Dancing the tango is a joint action but it is not (in usual cases) an instance of solidarity. Solidarity must involve *significant adversity*: acting in solidarity always involves overcoming weighty obstacles.[39] Moreover, in addition to not bypassing the will of other solidaries by, for example, coercing or deceiving them, (2) requires *commitment*, by which I mean that parties have a reflectively endorsed disposition to set aside self-interest (narrowly understood) in jointly overcoming significant adversity. This condition excludes cases where parties act together – say a group of thieves – but only out of self-interest narrowly understood, or only because they have been forced to do so via threats.[40] Acting in solidarity must therefore be a form of what Bratman calls shared *cooperative* activity.[41] Commitments,

---

39 Cf. Shelby, who argues that 'there are five core normative requirements that are jointly sufficient for a robust form of solidarity [identification with the group, special concern, shared values or goals, loyalty, and mutual trust]. By 'robust' I mean a solidarity that is strong enough to move people to collective action, not just mutual sympathy born of recognition of communality or a mere sense of group belonging' (Shelby 2009, p. 68; see also May 1996, p. 44; cf. Feinberg 1973, p. 677). But, on this view, a reading group might exhibit all five features, and move its participants to do things together, and yet it seems strained to say that a reading group's participants are in solidarity with one another. (Once again, it is strained not so much because it doesn't capture the ordinary English meaning, but because it seems to jar with the value and history of the practices in which the term has predominantly figured, and which make sense of the role we might want an account of solidarity to play.) It is also unclear, on this view, whether collective action is a necessary condition of solidarity, or whether two or more people can be in solidarity by holding the attitudes mentioned without ever acting together in some relevant sense. Might brothers be in solidarity by possessing all five of the listed attitudes, though they never act together in the pursuit of any goals, or come to each other's aid in any way? On whether shared values are necessary for solidarity, see section 3.
40 And so excludes cases of what Bratman calls 'opportunistic sociality' (see Bratman 2014, p. 72).
41 For the contrast between shared cooperative activity and shared intentional activity *simpliciter*, see Bratman 2014, pp. 86–7. Joint action in general, unlike solidarity, can tolerate severe coercion (as between a master and slave) as long as the coercion works to get the slaves to intend the joint activity *as such*, and the master intends to work by way of the slave's

furthermore, are robust: unlike intentions such as closing the door or waving to someone, they are not fleeting. They set our agency on course to achieve a goal; they are resistant to temptation.[42]

(3), furthermore, requires a commitment to 'share one another's fate'. Using the previous example, if the train crash survivors are not prepared to share each other's fate by exposing themselves to significant risks to help others, but are prepared to act together, then the action might still count as joint even if not solidaristic. To share another's fate is, that is, to be prepared either to tie one's fate to another's or to take on another's ill fortune as if it were one's own.[43] Examples of the former include the international chapters of the BLM movement. But they also include the Iranian woman who, in a protest, was the *second* (and third, and fourth …) to take off her hijab in a public square, stand up on a telecoms box, and wave it aloft on a stick.[44] Here it is as if she were saying: 'If you punish the first woman, you must punish me, too.' The fate of each woman now depends on the fate of the other. An example of the latter is the London marathoner who slowed down to help another struggling athlete across the finish line.[45] Here the first marathoner,

---

intention in favor of the activity. The only background coercion that would be compatible with solidarity, by contrast, is background coercion that is intended by all participants as a means of providing assurance (e.g., steeling one's will in cases of dangerous action or where the temptation to free-ride might be high); coercion designed to get another to intend the joint activity in the first place, as in the master/slave example, does not count as solidarity. For more on background coercion, see Sangiovanni 2015.

42 On commitments more generally, see Calhoun 2009.

43 If we take the idea of 'debt' metaphorically, then to be in solidarity one must be prepared – just as in the original Roman law formulation of a *jus in solidum* (from which our modern usage derives) – to take on another's debts as if they were one's own. For more on this history, see section 2.

44 www.theguardian.com/world/2018/feb/02/tehran-hijab-protest-iranian-police-arrest-29-women (accessed December 7, 2021).

45 www.theguardian.com/sport/video/2017/apr/23/london-marathon-runner-helps-exhausted-athlete-finish-race-video (accessed December 7, 2021). It is important that it is one *marathoner* sacrificing his own prospects of doing well sharing the fate of another *marathoner*. If it had been a general member of the public, and so no mutual identification with the cause of finishing the race together (and also a fortiori no mutual identification based on a shared condition or role), then it would have been an act of charity or aid, not solidarity. Thanks to Tom Parr for discussion.

in helping the second and hence giving up his own hopes of doing well, takes on the other's ill fortune as if it were his own.[46] In both cases, the participants thereby come to share an intention – to cross the line, to protest the injustice. If they are also committed to act via each other's will and trust one another to fulfill each of these conditions, then we can say they are acting in solidarity.

(4) requires participants merely to *trust*, without *knowing* or even *believing*, that others will do their part, will be committed in the various ways identified, and will share our fate.[47] Trust is reliance plus a distinctive practical stance toward others' actions and attitudes. Reliance only requires taking, in Strawson's terms, an objectivating stance toward an object. I can rely on the key to open the door just as I, the thief, can rely on the old man to leave his house every day at six. In both cases, if the key doesn't open the door, or the man doesn't leave his house, I can at most feel anger; resentment or a feeling of betrayal is entirely inappropriate.[48] Trust is different. When I trust that you will show up at ten tomorrow, I rely on you to do so, but I will also feel let down if you fail to turn up. Trust comes with a complex web of normatively grounded expectations and reactive attitudes. And so it is with solidarity. When I trust that you will do your part and are committed to sharing my fate, I do not merely rely on these things. I will also feel let down, betrayed, if you do not do your part (without good reason), if you are not committed to sharing my fate, if you are not committed to our cause, and so on. I am engaged with you and your actions as a participant in our joint struggle rather than merely as an observer trying to take into account what you will do. But notice also that trust, as a form of reliance, doesn't require belief, let alone knowledge,

---

46 The idea of 'sharing another's fate' therefore goes beyond the mere 'disposition to help' that Bratman identifies as key to shared intentional activity in general. See Bratman 2014, pp. 56–7. Solidarity is more demanding. However, it is important to note that participants in solidarity need not take each other to have *obligations* to share others' fates (again, dangerous actions provide a good example). Cf. Gilbert 2000. It is enough if they take themselves to have weighty reasons to do so.
47 For the notion of trust on which I am relying, see Holton 1994. See also Alonso 2009.
48 The trust condition also serves to deal with cases like Spy and Counter-Spy as elaborated in Kutz 2000a.

that you will do your part, be committed, or share my fate. I can decide to rely on the rope – given my lack of alternatives – even if I am not so sure it will hold me.[49] Similarly, I can trust my fellow solidaries to do their part, even if I am not so sure they will carry through – if, for example, our common action is very dangerous and there is a good chance that they will abandon both me and the cause when the going gets tough.

The commitment to share others' fates is also a feature of other complex attitudes and associated motivational states. But the way it functions in solidarity is distinct. To see how, it is worth comparing the way the commitment to share another's fate functions in love. There are two relevant differences. First, the lover has a broad and encompassing concern for the beloved's welfare. They take a full view of it and are therefore committed to sharing in the other's fate across the whole range of their life. The solidarist is permitted to take a narrower view of things: they can be committed to sharing the other's fate in what will often be deep and demanding ways, but that sacrifice can be focused on the other's fate only insofar as it bears on jointly overcoming significant adversity. I may, for example, risk life and limb for those participating in the protest as we challenge the oppressors, but I need not take, merely *qua* solidary, any particular view or make any particular sacrifice with respect to their attempts to reconcile with their distanced children.

The second difference with love is perhaps even more important. The lover, we say, doesn't just love the beloved as the bearer of some number of valued qualities, attributes, or even general properties. While of course we love our beloved in part because of their qualities, we do not love them only as the bearer of those qualities. Put another way, we love the person *themselves* rather than their qualities. If a twin showed up who bore the qualities to exactly the same extent and in exactly the same way as our beloved, we would not remain, like Buridan's ass, indifferent between them. Love is a *de re* attitude.[50] Therefore, when we share another's fate because we love them, we do so because of *them* rather than because they happen to be picked

---

49 Note that trust and reliance do require that one lack a belief that others will *not* do their part; the point is that it does not require a belief that they will. On this point, see Holton 1994, p. 8.
50 See, e.g., Velleman 1999.

out by a definite description ('the woman who is intelligent, impetuous, mischievous, ...').

When we act in solidarity with others and are committed to sharing their fate, this kind of *de re* attachment is not required. In most cases, we are committed to sharing another's fate not because of *her*, as it were, in particular, but because she is 'one of us', because she counts, that is, as someone who fits the indefinite description identifying the relevant social group. For example, we can be committed to sharing her fate because *she is a worker* (identification based on condition) or because *she is a fully participating member of the societal division of labor* (identification based on role) or because *she is a member of Extinction Rebellion* (identification based on cause) or because *she is a fellow national* (identification based on way of life) or because *she suffers because of and with me as a child of God* (identification based on set of experiences). This also explains why it is permissible to be committed to sharing her fate *only* in ways that are related to jointly overcoming significant adversity (by overthrowing capitalism, protecting the nation, alleviating suffering, and so on). Unlike in love, our commitment to sharing another's fate is therefore (most often) *de dicto* rather than *de re*. Our commitment need only be impersonal and general, rather than personal and particular.

This is not to say that there *cannot* be solidarity grounded on identification *de re*. Some of the most profound forms of solidarity are found between lovers, friends, and family, who are prepared to sacrifice in innumerable ways in overcoming significant forms of adversity together. But such deep forms of attachment are not necessary; it is sufficient for solidarity to be grounded in forms of identification that are merely *de dicto*.[51]

This account of the relation between love and solidarity also allows us to highlight the special sense that solidarity embodies a form of *equality* among participants. As we have seen, solidarity requires a commitment to sharing one another's fate in ways relevant to our overcoming adversity. We can go further: When we act in solidarity with one another, we take the ground of our solidarity as structuring each of our lives in important ways. This pushes us,

---

51 Many thanks to Barry Maguire for discussion on this point.

as I mentioned above, to seek common understandings – *and* recognition of common differences among us – regarding what *being a worker*, *being a woman*, *being a citizen*, and so on, ought to mean for us. It also leads us into common action against adversity, in which we are prepared to share one another's fate. When we deliberate and act together, deference and servility is considered inappropriate.

When we interact, what matters is that we are *workers*, not that you are an engineer and I am a factory worker; what matters is that we are *fellow nationals*, not that I am a poet and you are a banker; what matters is that we are reciprocally dependent on the *societal division of labor*, not that I am a doctor and you are a janitor; what matters is that we are *cancer survivors*, not that you are Black and I am White; what matters is that we are members of Extinction Rebellion, not that you are South African and I am Chinese. Societally accepted distinctions in rank or esteem or privilege among us are exposed as arbitrary; it would be a form of disrespect to fellow solidaries to take them as relevant. This may take work; it may be all too easy for familiar patterns of hierarchy to reassert themselves in our common action. But solidarity requires us to resist them.[52] This will have, then, important implications for how we are to conceive of the demands of solidarity: we ought, in our joint action, to conceive of any hierarchy between us as merely an instrument for pursuing our goal, and to be judged on that basis, rather than as reflecting some independent criterion of social status, rank, privilege, or esteem.[53]

It is important to note that the egalitarian structure of solidarity need not deny intersectionality. When we focus on what unites, rather than what divides us, this could be mere commitment to a cause; it need not bring any sense of our essential identity as, say, women. And even if given instances of solidarity among women – continuing with the example – do emphasize what brings women together as addressees of particular forms of oppression, this can be against a background of a deep and genuine recognition that the structure of this oppression will be inflected differently according to one's other identities and commitments (for more on this point, see section 3).

---

52 On this point, see hooks 2015b, esp. ch. 4; Mohanty 2003, esp. ch. 4.
53 I will return to this point in section 2, when discussing Kolers 2016.

1.3 Distinguishing empirical from normative uses

We are now in a position to distinguish empirical from normative concepts of solidarity, on one hand, and concepts and conceptions of solidarity, on the other. So far, the concept of solidarity I have outlined is purely descriptive.[54] As long as the profile of commitments, intentions, and other attitudes I have outlined is satisfied, even members of the Mafia or a terrorist cell can be acting in solidarity. Solidarity can, that is, exist among groups that we believe should not exist because they pursue immoral ends. The concept of solidarity outlined can therefore serve as a basis for empirical study of whether and what kind of solidarity exists among members of any group.

It is at this point that we can introduce a further nuance.[55] Several components of my schema are best understood as variables that range over different kinds of *significant adversity*, ways of *sharing others' fate*, and types of *identification* (I leave it open whether other components of the schema – say, *commitment* to overcoming adversity, or *trust* – are best understood as variables or left as constants).[56] This opens the possibility of defending more specific concepts of solidarity – each of which fixes the values of each of these variables in different ways. For example, an empirical study of nationalist solidarity might assign *way of life* to the variable

---

54 In her important monograph on solidarity, Sally Scholz argues that the broader notion of solidarity has three components. First, it specifies a relation between the individual and the group of which the member is a part. Second, solidarity must represent some form of unity among members of the group; there must be something, that is, that 'binds people together'. Third, solidarity 'entails positive moral obligations' (Scholz 2010, p. 19). Solidarity is therefore, on this account, essentially moralized. There can be, by implication, no genuine solidarity between terrorist groups or White nationalists. See also Gould forthcoming.
55 I adopt a similar strategy as MacCallum in his famous article on freedom. See MacCallum 1967.
56 The schema for solidarity given above is, that is, what Millikan calls a *substance template*: it indicates the kinds of things we ought to look for and study in instances of solidarity. The schema helps us to *identify* rather than merely *classify* a given social form as an instance of solidarity. 'Animal' is a substance template: once we know something is an animal, we know that we can ask about how it gets around, what its metabolic rate is, whether it is a vertebrate or not, and so on – things it would make no sense to ask, for example, of chairs. See Millikan 2000, ch. 3.

identification, combatting the oppressors/preserving the nation by public resistance/language policy to the variable *significant adversity, obligations of mutual aid and support* to the variable *sharing others' fate*, and so on. With such a more specific concept of solidarity in hand, the researcher could then verify whether and to what extent solidarity exists among members of a given nation. A study of socialist solidarity in the workers' movement would, of course, proceed very differently, assigning different values to each variable. In this way, we can also generate novel concepts for new contexts of collective action (as we will do when we consider the five main traditions in which solidarity has developed as a key concept).

This structure can also explain the possibility of more local disagreements[57] among different interpretations of the general concept for a specific group or set of similar groups. In a study of French nationalism, for example, two empirical researchers might disagree regarding whether *way of life* is in fact the basis of French national solidarity, or whether, say, *shared participation in national institutions* (and hence *identification based on role*) provides a better characterization. Here the disagreement might be explained as a response to the fact that both researchers are, let us assume, aiming to capture the specific character of French national solidarity. The overarching concept of solidarity can provide additional structure to their disagreement; it can, for example, aid them in specifying exactly which variable or set of variables is the focus of their disagreement. If there is substantive disagreement over specifications of two different concepts to be used in empirical study of a particular case, then we say that researchers have two different (empirical) *conceptions* of solidarity for that group.[58] If the two are non-competing, then we

---

57 For an instructive discussion of different forms of canonical and noncanonical disagreement over concept usage, see Plunkett and Sundell 2013b, 2013a. Plunkett and Sundell, it should be noted, do not use the concept/conception distinction in the same way as I do.
58 The distinction between concept and conception I use here, though much more general, is compatible with Rawls's usage in Rawls 1999, p. 5. The idea of a negotiation over which of two different specifications of an overarching concept of solidarity might be more useful in a particular context of inquiry could be explained, although I don't press the point here, with Plunkett and Sundell's notion of a 'metalinguistic negotiation' (Plunkett and Sundell 2013a). If we think of the social kind as picked out

say that they are simply using two (non-competing) *concepts* of solidarity. In the latter case, there would be no point to the disagreement, as might be the case if one researcher were testing an empirical hypothesis about the relationship between solidarity and levels of support for the welfare state, and France was only one case among many, whereas the other was a historian aiming to explore the changing character of French national solidarity over time. The disagreement becomes substantive and meaningful, that is, only in light of the theoretical aims of the researchers, the object of study, and with respect to one or more of the variables isolated in the overarching formula defining the concept. Note that this leaves open the possibility that two researchers in a dispute might not *really* be disagreeing even though they believe they are; what matters is whether their theoretical aims and object of study really do only leave space for at most one of the concepts in dispute.

The account also gives structure to the development of *normative* accounts of solidarity. Note that the main variables mentioned in the formula for the overarching concept of solidarity refer to *operative* reasons.[59] Fellow solidaries *take themselves* to have reasons, grounded in identification, to join together to overcome significant adversity; they also *take themselves* to have reasons to be committed to the cause, not to bypass each other's will, to share one another's fates, and to trust one another. A normative account of solidarity for a given group or set of groups seeks to identify when actors *really do* have reasons grounded in identification to join together, *really do* have reasons to be committed, to trust, to share one another's fate, and so on. A normative conception of solidarity for the EU, for example, would aim to specify what kind of identification (if any) gives EU citizens and residents reasons to join together to accomplish various ends, what kinds of reasons (or perhaps obligations) citizens and residents have to share one another's fates in the accomplishment of those ends, what reasons people have to trust one another, what level of commitment is required, and so on. The overarching concept

by the overarching concept, the idea of a metalinguistic negotiation over more particular uses is, I believe, compatible with content externalism. Cf. Cappelen 2018, ch. 15.
59 I draw the distinction between 'operative' and 'genuine' reasons from Scanlon 1998, p. 19.

of solidarity provides a framework for articulating such a normative account, and helps to identify possible sources of disagreement, and to diagnose when disagreement is merely verbal or otherwise illusory.

The distinction between concepts and conceptions can do the same work as it did when we were comparing different empirical accounts of solidarity.[60] Suppose that two political theorists are developing accounts of solidarity for the EU, but one is looking at what solidarity requires in the area of external policy and the other in the area of economic and monetary union. While there will undoubtedly be overlap in the values they assign to each variable in the general definition of solidarity, it is unlikely that there will be real disagreement, given the different focus of each account. Here it would be appropriate, therefore, to speak of two different, non-competing (normative) *concepts* of solidarity. It would be otherwise if it were two theorists developing accounts of solidarity for the *same* context, say, solidarity in refugee and asylum policy. In this case, assuming disagreement regarding the specification of one or more of the variables, we would speak of a divergence in *conceptions* of solidarity. Should one argue, for example, that member states must share each other's fate by accepting a fair allocation of refugees because they share a Christian way of life, and the other because they each identify with their role in reproducing common institutions, they would be disagreeing substantively regarding the variable, *reasons arising from mutual identification* but not necessarily *sharing others' fates* or *overcoming significant adversity*. Similar things, of course, could be said for normative accounts of solidarity that seek to specify the obligations of workers to participate in strikes, or men to participate in the feminist movement, or citizens and residents to come to each other's aid in the wake of a natural disaster.

In section 3, I will develop a normative conception of identification, in each of its guises, as a basis for solidarity; this will, among other things, allow us to put the distinction between empirical and normative conceptions into use. But, before we do so, I will seek to employ the general account to make sense of solidarity's history. This is important since, as I mentioned in the introduction, the historical,

---

60 Cf. Forst forthcoming on the relation between concept and conceptions of solidarity.

political, and social uses of solidarity have formed the concept into a *practice* – a lived system of norms, rules, and expectations that gives rise to new self-understandings, new concepts, and new possibilities for collective action and social relation within complex, modern societies.

2 History

I ended the previous section by saying that our twofold concept of solidarity – identification plus a special, more demanding form of committed joint action – can aid us in *making sense* of solidarity's history. But what do I intend by *making sense*? The uses and meanings of solidarity throughout its history are multiple and varied. As I mentioned in the introduction, so varied are they that many often wonder whether there is anything distinctive or worth preserving in the term, or whether it can simply be reduced to some other notion, such as sympathy, charity, support, justice, or fellow-feeling. Others worry that it is merely an empty bit of rhetoric piped in to give a noble caste to one's political or social program. This is too hasty. While the history of the term and its corresponding practices are rich in diversity and heterogeneity, there is also, I want to claim, an underlying unity that explains why the term and the practices it drives, are so resilient; why, that is, they resonate with us as both distinctive and normatively compelling. The aim of the present section, then, is to capture that underlying unity while also giving the tools to allow for variation across time. If the account is successful, it should strengthen our confidence that solidarity is the normatively rich, descriptively powerful, and politically salient practice that many today take it to be. In this section, we focus on the term's historical uses; and in the final two, on its normative ones.

There is also another reason to explore the history of the concept. As I mentioned in the introduction, it could be that current usage fails to track both the underlying phenomenon and what is valuable and normatively compelling about the practice. It could also be that current usage, under the warm hue cast by the term, has incorporated related notions that do not fit well under its rubric. By excavating the original concept and its role during its emergence and early development, we will be able to reflect more clearly on whether we should treat the new usages as suggesting a new and revised concept that we should adopt, or whether they muddy the phenomena that make solidarity into the valuable social kind it was and continues to be.

In brief, I will argue that solidarity names an egalitarian, mutualistic, and cooperative practice among strangers, whose aim is to overcome significant forms of adversity in an era when traditional social ties – of, for example, kinship, guild, and church – have weakened. Solidarity is, as we have already seen, omnilateral and symmetrical as well as transformative and critical. Even in the context of the welfare state, solidarity requires a recognition that collective action is necessary to overcome adversity. Solidarity always aims, that is, to change the order of things.[61] If we run together various forms of humanitarianism and charity with solidarity, it becomes easy to miss the distinctive normative character of our guiding notion.

Solidarity is, furthermore, a peculiarly modern concern.[62] While one can trace the term to its roots in Roman law – where an obligation *in solidum* was a joint contractual obligation in which each signatory declared himself liable for the debts of all together – its use as a term denoting a type of broadly social (rather than narrowly legal) relation becomes prevalent only in Europe – and especially in France

61 I thank Jared Holley for discussion on this point.
62 I say that the concept of solidarity is *modern*. But does that mean that I don't believe solidarity exists before the modern era? No. As I have already highlighted, there is a difference between solidarity as the social kind and SOLIDARITY as a concept. The social kind, understood as a distinctive form of action, is probably as old as humanity itself. But the concept describing it acquires salience and significance in the modern era for the reasons I have cited. It is only in the modern era that it becomes theorized as an object of particular social concern. It then becomes what Hacking calls an 'interactive kind': once it enters into general usage, it transforms the kinds of possibilities for solidarity that there are in politics, and the meanings and opportunities associated with it. We can say that the 'thin' social kind has existed for centuries, but, as the concept enters usage and debate, the category itself acquires new layers, opportunities, and possibilities. For analogues, see Hacking 1999; Mallon 2016. As I mentioned in the introduction, an analogy is the phenomenon of sexual harassment – a phenomenon that has existed for centuries but only becomes theorized and conceptualized in the 1970s, which transforms the meanings and possibilities for action and reaction associated with it. See the history recounted, e.g., in Brownmiller 1999.

– during the early nineteenth century.⁶³ Why then? As any cursory glance at the major early texts (e.g., Saint-Simon, Fourier, Renaud, Leroux, Comte) would reveal, the language of solidarity emerges as a response to growing anxiety regarding the expansion of commercial society, large-scale industry, and the perceived collapse of traditional communities.⁶⁴ From this perspective, it is no surprise that language of solidarity emerges in *France*, where the upheavals of the Revolution and its aftermath had first placed the ideal of republican *fraternité* firmly on the map. If societies are to hold together in the presence of emerging class conflict and the centrifugal, individualistic pull of markets, then something must replace the old ties of rank, guild, family, and traditional religious practice.⁶⁵ That something was thought to require a social bond between strangers, a form of identification strong enough to give individuals the sense of being connected to a larger whole on which they depend, and which in turn disposes each to share in the good and bad fate of all the rest. For this early French context, I will focus on Léon Bourgeois – where the term becomes a basis for an entire political program – and Émile Durkheim – where the term 'solidarity' becomes a central category of his sociology.

Earlier calls to solidarity – in 'mutual aid' societies, the first industrial strikes, myriad pamphlets, and the early socialists and sociologists – were synthesized and given a more systematic cast with the emergence of 'solidarism', the movement that gave the early French Third Republic its 'official philosophy'.⁶⁶ In 1896, Léon Bourgeois – prime minister of France from 1895 to 1896 – published what would become the programmatic manifesto of the movement in a pamphlet entitled *Solidarité*.⁶⁷ Steering a course between the laisser-faire, individualist 'economism' of Herbert Spencer and the oppositional, revolutionary politics of socialism, Bourgeois invoked solidarity to characterize the bond that ought to tie together all citizens of a modern industrial republic. Bourgeois begins his pamphlet

63 On this history, see, e.g., Wildt 1999.
64 See, e.g., Blais 2007; Stjernø 2005.
65 See also Tönnies 1980.
66 Célestin Bouglé writes, 'Solidarism is becoming a kind of official philosophy for the Third Republic', cited in Blais 2007, p. 26, my translation. For the history of solidarism, see especially Blais 2007; Hayward 1961.
67 Bourgeois 1902.

with the unity that characterizes more sophisticated organisms in nature. Every such organism has specialized parts – each performing different but complementary functions – that work together to maintain and reproduce life. The more differentiated the parts, the more complex the system that unites them, and hence the 'higher' they are in the order of nature. Bourgeois calls the bonds that make the separate parts in any organism into a unified system *natural* solidarity.

But, Bourgeois continues, the reciprocal, specialized dependence implicit in the natural division of labor also exists, in a different form, in the life of all modern societies. There are two essential differences. The first difference is that societies are made up of individuals possessed of reason and will, and so the laws of nature are not sufficient to ensure that the parts will coordinate to sustain and reproduce the life of the whole. The second difference follows directly from the first. Because the coordination necessary to maintain and reproduce a society depends on the reason and will of individuals, the laws that govern that reproduction must also work via those very same faculties. The laws governing *social* solidarity are, therefore, necessarily *moral*.

What *mores* ought to govern the division of labor understood in its widest sense as the division of roles in any society, and so, ultimately, the distribution of the benefits and burdens of joint production (*la répartition des profits et des charges*)? Bourgeois writes that we must look for an answer, not at human beings as isolated monads (as the laisser-faire economists do), but at the moral implications of the very reciprocal dependence that constitutes society in the first place. Once we do so, we will see that every individual within the societal division of labor owes the vast preponderance of what they are able to obtain from that society – for example, through their talents and abilities, or through the knowledge they acquire from that society – to two sources. They owe a debt, first, to past generations and, second, to contemporaries who, in the present, reproduce and advance the institutions, knowledge, resources, and societal conventions from which they gain (almost) all that is theirs.

> [Because of man's dependence on the societal division of labor] a necessary exchange of services exists between each and all. The free

development of his faculties, of his activities, in short, of his very *being*, can only be realized, for each individual, as a result of the concurrent contributions of other men's faculties and activities. This free development can, furthermore, only reach its full extent as a result of the accumulated contributions of the past.

There is therefore a debt owed by each to all the rest, in virtue of the contributions and services rendered by all to each.[68]

To make the notion of a social debt more precise, Bourgeois points to the idea of a 'quasi-contract' that is prior to all contracts, and prior to all social association. It is not, however, a social contract understood as a historical contract between isolated individuals to create a government or state. It is, rather, an explicitly justificatory device intended to model the fact that each individual, whatever their role in society, is ultimately a being of equal moral status.[69]

The idea of a quasi-contract is then used to determine the distribution of benefits and burdens in society, and hence to specify the social debt that each owes to all. What distribution of benefits and advantages would individuals choose, in an initial position of equality in which they didn't know their place in that society, to govern their life together?[70] Against the laisser-faire economists, Bourgeois concludes that the chosen distribution would ensure greater protection for the needy. And against the socialists, he concludes that it must protect private property and advancement by merit. Only if such a distribution is realized through common institutions can true, moral solidarity be realized. According to Bourgeois,

> There where necessity has placed individuals in relationships whose terms men have had no prior chance to discuss, the only law that can fix these terms must be an interpretation and representation of the accord that would have been agreed had the parties been freely and equally consulted prior to their relationship. […] The *quasi-contract* is nothing but the contract that each party would have consented to prior to their association. […] The resulting distribution of benefits of this double debt [debt to contemporaries and to the past] will be

---

68 Bourgeois 1902, p. 137, my translation.
69 See also Bourgeois's discussion of equal moral worth at pp. 109–10.
70 Bourgeois's formulation bears a striking resemblance to Rawls. For Rawls on the difference principle as a principle of 'fraternity', see Rawls 1999, pp. 90–1. Cf. the illuminating discussion of solidarism as distinct from liberalism in Kohn 2018.

fair only if all the parties are considered equal, that is, equal as persons who have a right to deliberate and consent. Reasons to favor or disfavor any particular person as anything other than a free and equal party to the contract will be banned. [...] Without this prior equality of worth and right, the quasi-contract could not be considered a contract that each party would have agreed to as free and equal.[71]

The use of the 'quasi-contract' as a way of modelling underlying equality has an important upshot for our account. What makes the quasi-contract binding, given that there was never an original consent to the terms, are the facts of interdependence – of cooperative contribution and benefit – that underlie political and social association. But Bourgeois is clear that, to realize the moral demands of interdependence in institutional life, individuals must also recognize themselves in their role as cooperative producers. Citizens must perceive the basis of their *natural* solidarity as the foundation for a *moral* solidarity. Solidarity therefore requires that citizens *identify* with one another on the basis of their *role* in sustaining and reproducing the division of labor. The object of social education, Bourgeois writes, should be

> to place each individual in that frame of mind in which he sees that he is an *associate*, to create in every one of us a *social being*, to give us the habit to behave *socially*, that is, to be mindful, to whatever extent is possible, of our debt to others in every one of our actions, and especially in every transaction in which what we produce is exchanged with what others produce.[72]

The recognition of the *quasi-contract* as binding is meant to follow, that is, from a recognition of how much each person's ability to benefit from use of their talents relies on the contributions of myriad others in a vast formal and informal division of labor. If they receive much less than they are owed (once everyone's basic dependence on the entire system is taken into account), they are correct in feeling exploited; if they receive more than they are due, they should feel the weight of a debt that they are not repaying.

This brief reconstruction of Bourgeois's view already gives us two sets of distinctions that will be useful as we move on. First, social

---

71 Bourgeois 1902, pp. 132–4, 8, my translation.
72 Bourgeois 1902, p. 182.

solidarity refers to the unified character of a society bound together by two characteristics. It is bound together, via its division of labor, by the reciprocal dependence of its constituent elements (similar to the unity of a sophisticated natural organism bound together by the reciprocal dependence between its specialized organs). But social solidarity requires more than the mere existence of a functioning division of labor. It *also* requires a particular set of attitudes towards its constituent division of labor and a particular way of organizing that division. The bonds that make unity possible are, as we have seen, *moral* rather than *natural*. A society that has a complex division of labor but where individuals fail to identify with one another as contributors and beneficiaries of cooperative production fails to exhibit the solidarity that is latent in its structure and organization. So on this reading, solidarity refers, at the most basic level, *both* to the differentiated unity that exists between those who depend on one another to achieve a set of important common ends, *and* to the unity of those who *identify* with one another on the basis of their respective roles and are *committed* to sharing one another's fate as participants in that joint project.

Second, solidarism suggests a threefold distinction between the *grounds* of solidarity, namely the complex division of societal labor and the reasons of identification and reciprocity it generates, the *object* of solidarity, namely the discharge of the 'social debt' through institutional reform, and the *scope* of solidarity, namely the members of the interdependent society. Put in terms of our formula from section 1, the solidarist concept of solidarity assigns *role interdependence* to the variable *identification, interest-based conflict, individualism*, and *class struggle* to the variable *significant adversity*, a *progressive tax system* and *social insurance* to the variable *shared goals*, and *discharging the social debt* to the variable *sharing others' fate*.

The connection between the division of labor and solidarity is associated by us today – though it was not at the time – with Émile Durkheim's 1893 doctoral thesis, *The Division of Labor in Society*. Though Bourgeois does not appear to have read it,[73] there is a great deal of convergence between Durkheim's conception of (organic) solidarity and Bourgeois's pamphlet. The ideas contained in both,

---

73 Bourgeois was mainly influenced by Alfred Fouillée's writings on solidarity. See Blais 2007.

as Marie-Claude Blais discusses in her history of solidarity in France, reflect the current of enthusiasm for solidarism and for new advances in cellular biology in the late nineteenth century.[74] In that early work, Durkheim draws a distinction between *mechanical* and *organic* solidarity. Characteristic of premodern societies with a limited division of labor, mechanical solidarity is realized when people identify with one another on the basis of a 'collective consciousness' constituted by shared norms, rules, and sentiments.[75] In our terms, mechanical solidarity requires identification with others on the basis of a *way of life*. Durkheim writes:

> In fact we all know that a social cohesion exists whose cause can be traced to a certain conformity of each individual consciousness to a common type. [...] Indeed under these conditions all members of the group are not only individually attracted to one another because they resemble one another, but they are also linked to what is the condition for the existence of this collective type, that is, to the society that they form by coming together. Not only do fellow-citizens like one another, seeking one another out in preference to foreigners, but they love their country. They wish for it what they would wish for themselves, they care that it should be lasting and prosperous, because without it a whole area of their psychological life would fail to function smoothly.[76]

In these passages, it is clear that solidarity is not, for Durkheim, merely another name for social cohesion; it refers, rather, to one of its important causes. Solidarity refers, moreover, not just to a set of attitudes – including 'attraction' to others based on a shared way of life – but also to the collective action required to sustain and reproduce the shared way of life and the collective consciousness that defines it. The collective consciousness is reinforced and maintained, Durkheim argues, through the ritual and repeated collective punishment of norm violators. Without such punishment, society would fall apart.[77] This is why, as Durkheim often emphasizes, repressive law is the fundamental *expression* of mechanical solidarity.

---

74 I thank Rouven Symank for discussion, including the massive influence of Louis Pasteur on the intellectual life of the *belle époque* in France.
75 Durkheim 1984 [1893], pp. 63–4.
76 Durkheim 1984 [1893], p. 81.
77 Durkheim 1984 [1893], pp. 80–1.

Repressive law institutionalizes the collective punishment needed to reproduce and sustain the collective consciousness, and hence the social cohesion of the group. In our terms, the *ground* of solidarity is identification with others on the basis of a shared way of life; the *object* of solidarity is the reproduction of the collective consciousness; the *joint action* that is constitutive of solidarity is collective punishment, whose aim is to overcome the *significant adversity* threatened by crime, betrayal, dissent, revolt, and opposition;[78] and the *willingness to share another's fate* is represented by the lack of differentiation between members (who are as prepared to die for one another as they would be to die for their near and dear[79]).

Where mechanical solidarity is based on similarity, organic solidarity is based on differentiation. The more complex a society becomes, the more its division of labor grows. At the same time, and as a result, the collective consciousness slackens, and individuality expands. In its place, a new solidarity is required to maintain social cohesion. This solidarity, too, is expressed in the law. But it is not repressive, or penal, law that predominates, but what Durkheim refers to as restitutive, or cooperative, law. As the division of labor grows, so does the law required to coordinate it: this is why we witness an impressive expansion of civil law in the administrative, contractual, property, tort, family, corporation, and labor domains. With expanding differentiation of roles comes rising individuality: the collective consciousness is no longer able to provide a stable ground of solidarity. Solidarity, Durkheim claims, must follow from the very interdependence that constitutes the division of labor itself. Solidarity must be based, that is, on the essential interdependence of our roles just like the interdependence of functions in an organism. The whole panoply of civil law, however, only serves to integrate and coordinate the system; it is solely a source of 'negative' solidarity. Durkheim writes:

> [T]he rules relating to 'real' rights and personal relationships that are established by virtue of them form a definite system whose function is not to link together the different parts of society, but on the contrary to detach them from one another, and mark out clearly the barriers separating them. Thus they do not correspond to any positive social tie. The very expression 'negative solidarity' that we have employed

---

78 Durkheim 1984 [1893], pp. 67–8.
79 Durkheim 1984 [1893], p. 153.

is not absolutely exact. It is not a true solidarity, having its own existence and specific nature, but rather the negative aspects of every type of solidarity. The first condition for an entity to become coherent is for the parts that form it not to clash discordantly. But such an external harmony does not bring about cohesion. On the contrary, it presumes it. Negative solidarity is only possible where another kind is present, positive in nature, of which it is both the result and the condition.

What is this positive component? What is the ground, object, and nature of this new, organic solidarity?

The answer lies in the public morality that must develop alongside the division of labor in order to stabilize and reproduce society. Durkheim writes:

> Men cannot live together without agreeing, and consequently without making mutual sacrifices, joining themselves to one another in a strong and enduring fashion. Every society is a moral society. In certain respects this feature is even more pronounced in organized societies. Because no individual is sufficient unto himself, it is from society that he receives all that is needful, just as it is for society that he labors. Thus there is formed a very strong feeling of the state of dependence in which he finds himself: he grows accustomed to valuing himself at his true worth, viz., to look upon himself only as a part of the whole, the organ of an organism. Such sentiments are of a kind not only to inspire those daily sacrifices that ensure the regular development of everyday social life but even on occasion acts of utter renunciation and unbounded abnegation. For its part society learns to look upon its constituent members no longer as things over which it has rights, but as co-operating members whom it cannot do without and towards whom it has duties.[80]

At the heart of this morality, as it was for Bourgeois, is a recognition that the benefits one derives from exercise of one's specialized role depend on the contributions of myriad others to an overall system of which one is a part. This recognition, Durkheim tells us, is often sufficient to inspire 'acts of utter renunciation' as a way of honoring one's debt to society.

The morality that governs organic solidarity is clarified when Durkheim turns to describe what can go wrong – what, that is,

80 Durkheim 1984 [1893], p. 178.

leads to *deficits* in solidarity (and what to do about them). One way in which things can go wrong – the predominant way, especially if we consider the labor conflicts which came to a head with the Paris Commune (1871) and the Long Depression (1873–92) in France – is through class conflict. This conflict upsets the smooth integration of the differentiated parts required for society to function. Durkheim notes three causes of such conflict – each one of which requires a similar solution. The first cause is *anomie*, the loss of direction and orientation that can accompany specialization. Anomie is the primary social danger accompanying the growing depth and extent of the division of labor, and threatens the sense in which we are essential contributors to the success of society as a whole:

> Every day [the worker] repeats the same movements with monotonous regularity, but without having any interest or understanding of them. He is no longer the living cell of a living organism, moved continually by contact with neighboring cells, which acts upon them and responds in turn to their action, extends itself, contracts, yields and is transformed according to the needs and circumstances. He is no more than a lifeless cog, which an external force sets in motion and impels always in the same direction and in the same fashion.[81]

The second cause is *force*, the sense of injustice that arises from a feeling that one's work is not valued according to its worth and one's own merits – the sense, in short, that one is exploited. Such grievances, Durkheim notes, are especially strong when premodern elements of caste persist in modern conditions. The third cause is *disuse*, or the aimlessness, resentment, and lack of focus that comes from not having enough work. In each case, Durkheim argues, the citizen comes to lose a grip on his larger place in reproducing the whole; as he turns inwards, his grievances seem to him larger and his duties to others less pressing; he is less fulfilled by his labor, seeing it no longer as a reflection of his nature; mistrust takes root; he no longer sees his potential employers as cooperative partners, but begins to see them as enemies.

Durkheim's proposed solution is clearest in the Second Preface to the *Division of Labor*, added in 1902. He argues there that the state alone cannot guarantee the conditions necessary for maintaining

---

81 Durkheim 1984 [1893], pp. 289–90.

organic solidarity against the threats we have just discussed to its survival. The state is 'too remote' and 'general' in its operation.[82] Instead, he argues that only the

> professional grouping is a moral force capable of curbing individual egoism, nurturing among workers a more invigorated feeling of their common solidarity, and preventing the law of the strongest from being applied too brutally in industrial and commercial relationships.[83]

By 'professional grouping', Durkheim means that the various industrial branches of an economy would be grouped into *corporations* (modelled on the feudal corporation). Unlike unions, corporations would be constituted by both employers and employees, and would have the power to regulate wages, conditions of work, appointments, and promotions; they would also have the authority to coordinate with other branches and with government. The effect of such groupings would be to recreate organic solidarity where it was most under pressure:

> Within a political society [e.g., a corporation], as soon as a certain number of individuals find they hold in common ideas, interests, sentiments and occupations which the rest of the population does not share in, it is inevitable that, under the influence of these similarities, they should be attracted to one another. They will seek one another out, enter into relationships and associate together. Thus a restricted group is gradually formed within society as a whole, with its own special features. Once such a group is formed, a moral life emanates from it which naturally bears the distinguishing mark of the special conditions in which it has developed. It is impossible for men to live together and be in regular contact with one another without their acquiring some feeling for the totality which they constitute through having united together, without their becoming attached to it, concerning themselves with its interests and taking it into account in their behaviour.[84]

The idea is that, in grouping together in smaller, functionally organized units – tradesmen with tradesmen, bankers with bankers, and so on – individuals would regain their sense of contributing to society while, at the same time, giving everyone a felt stake in the justice

---

82 Durkheim 1984 [1893], p. 27.
83 Durkheim 1984 [1893], p. 11.
84 Durkheim 1984 [1893], pp. 17–18.

and fairness required to reproduce it. In our terms then, the *ground* of organic solidarity is identification based on professional role within the division of labor; *joint action* requires organizing society into corporations, running each corporation, and regulating the division of labor justly; the *object* of joint action is the peaceful reproduction and maintenance of society in the face of the *significant adversity* represented by class conflict and division; the *scope* of solidarity is all those involved in the division of labor (Durkheim is keen, here, to emphasize that this division of labor is increasingly international[85]); and the *disposition to share one another's fate* is represented by the willingness to sacrifice self-interest ('egoism') for the good of the whole, which includes securing just conditions of work for each organ of society.

The second main context in which the language of solidarity develops is socialism.[86] This tradition, reproduced in workers' movements throughout the past two centuries, is more familiar to us, so I will spend less time discussing it. The socialist tradition grows out of the same post-revolutionary soil as solidarism, including most importantly the early utopian socialists (chief among them Saint-Simon and Fourier).[87] However, unlike solidarism, socialism called for class-based action against the bourgeois owners and organizers of capital. It was, that is, *oppositional*. Solidarity is the name of the unity between those who recognize one another as the objects of pervasive exploitation, who together create the essential conditions in which modern societies flourish, and who have a common enemy against whom the struggle must be waged, namely the capitalist. Ralph Chaplin's 'Solidarity Forever' – often sung at union meetings and socialist gatherings – evokes this sensibility well:

> It is we who ploughed the prairies, built the cities where they trade,
>
> Dug the mines and built the workshops, endless miles of railroad laid;
>
> Now, we stand outcast and starving, 'mid the wonders we have made.

---

85 Durkheim 1984 [1893], pp. 315–16.
86 For a useful history of solidarity in the socialist tradition, see Stjernø 2005, which is especially good on the role of solidarity in the major twentieth-century European social and Christian democratic parties.
87 An important related school of thought is anarchism as elucidated in writers such as Bakunin and Kropotkin.

The shared experience of exploitation and the shared action necessary for joint social production (as in ploughing the prairies and building the cities), in turn, provide the grounds for obligations of mutual aid and sacrifice. As Karl Kautsky, one of the most influential Marxists in the late nineteenth century, writes in the *Class Struggle*, which was the German Social Democratic Party's official commentary on the proposed Erfurt program of 1891:

> But as soon as the workers discover that their interests are common, that they are all opposed to the exploiter, it takes the form of great organizations and open battles against the exploiting class. [...] And when [these elevating tendencies] have once wakened full class-consciousness in any group of workers, the consciousness of solidarity with all the members of the working-class, the consciousness of the strength that is born of union; as soon as any group has recognized that it is essential to society and that it dare hope for better things in the future, – then it is well nigh impossible to shove that group back into the degenerate mass of beings whose opposition to the system under which they suffer takes no other form than that of unreasoned hate.[88]

It is important, as we will see later on, that unity among workers is grounded in the structural position of the worker in society; it is not, therefore, tied to his or her particular occupation, or indeed, nationality (hence the labor movement's internationalism). In 1871, in a speech given in Amsterdam after a congress of the First International, Marx says:

> Citizens, let us think of the basic principle of the International: Solidarity. Only when we have established this life-giving principle on a sound basis among the numerous workers of all countries will we attain the great final goal which we have set ourselves. The revolution must be carried out with solidarity; this is the great lesson of the French Commune, which fell because none of the other centers – Berlin, Madrid, etc. – developed great revolutionary movements comparable to the mighty uprising of the Paris proletariat.[89]

---

88 Kautsky 1910 [1892], ch. 5, sec. 5–6. See also Wildt 1999.
89 Marx 1978, p. 522. Given its association with the 'utopians', it is revealing that neither Marx nor Engels ever used 'solidarity' as a term in any of their systematic writings. Where they did use the term was in their speeches and letters in defense of the workingmen's associations that were springing up everywhere in defense of socialism.

Once again, it is useful to distinguish the grounds, scope, object, and content of solidarity. The ground of solidarity in the socialist tradition is, depending on one's interpretation, identification with one another either on the basis of the *role* shared by workers in joint production (as in the Chaplin quote) or on the basis of a *condition* they share as exploited.[90] The joint action required of the worker is participation in the workers' movement, including the union and party; the *object* of solidarity is, in the final instance, the overthrow of capitalism, which is intended to overcome the *significant adversity* posed by poverty, coercion, and exploitation. And the *willingness to share another's fate* is contained in the obligations of loyalty and reciprocity involved in the struggle against the oppressors (for example, not breaking the picket line).

The third school of thought is liberal nationalism, where references to solidarity flourish in the wake of 1848. For the nationalist, solidarity is anchored in shared identification with an 'imagined community' where membership is defined not in terms of class or social position, but in terms of an underlying way of life characterized by common folkways, mores, and a shared history of struggle. In 1882, Ernest Renan gave a seminal lecture in which he claimed that the nation is an expression of a 'great solidarity (*une grande solidarité*), constituted by a sense of the common sacrifices that have been made and that one is disposed to make again'.[91] And Giuseppe Mazzini, whose version of liberal-republican nationalism was to have such a great influence on nationalist movements across the world, writes in 1871:

> The individual's means and his thirty or forty years of adult life are but a tiny drop in the vast Ocean of existence. As soon as he becomes aware of this, he ends up discouraged and abandons the entire undertaking. If he is a good man, he will now and again engage in simple charity. If he is evil, he will isolate himself in complete selfishness. But give this man a Country [*patria*] and establish a link of solidarity

---

90 For earlier proto-socialist elaborations of the idea that mutual dependence elicits group consciousness and commitments to sacrifice, see Sewell 1980 on guilds, corporations, and mutual aid societies in France until 1848, and Hayward 1959.
91 Renan 1882, p. 29 available at http://fr.wikisource.org/wiki/Qu'est-ce_qu'une_nation_%3F (accessed May 15, 2023).

[*solidarietà*] between his individual efforts and the efforts of all subsequent generations; place him in association with the labors of 25 to 30 million men who speak the same language, have similar habits and beliefs, profess faith in the same *goal*, and have developed specific tools for their work as required by the general conditions of their land, and the problem will change for him at once: his strengths will be greatly multiplied, allowing him to feel up to the task.[92]

On this understanding, the nation is understood primarily as a project in which each participates over time and across generations. Charles Taylor gives a similar reading:

> The difference is that patriotism is based on an identification with others in a particular common enterprise. I am not dedicated to defending the liberty of just anyone, but I feel the bond of solidarity with my compatriots in our common enterprise, the common expression of our respective dignity. Patriotism is somewhere between friendship, or family feeling, on one side, and altruistic dedication on the other. [...] But particularity enters in because my bond to these people passes through our participation in a common political entity. Functioning republics are like families in this crucial respect, that part of what binds people together is their common history. Family ties or old friendships are deep because of what we have lived through together, and republics are bonded by time and climactic transitions.[93]

Patriotism (or nationalism – I am not here drawing a distinction) is therefore not simply a passive belonging, but a belonging that requires joint action both to defend and to reproduce it.[94] For the liberal nationalist, in short, identification with fellow nationals on the basis of a shared way of life is the *ground* of solidarity; the *object* of solidarity is the defense and reproduction of the nation understood as a *patria*, which requires a standing commitment to overcoming the *significant adversity* posed by (mostly) external threats. The *joint action* that is constitutive of nationalist solidarity,

---

92 'Nazionalismo e Nazionalità' (1871) in Mazzini 2009, p. 63. It is relevant that the younger Mazzini had been an exile in France and Switzerland in the 1830s, where he was introduced to the circle of Saint-Simonians then in Paris, including Pierre Leroux. For this history, see Faucci and Rancan 2009.
93 C. Taylor 1989, p. 166.
94 On this point, see also Miller 1995.

in turn, is the continuous contribution, through one's daily social, political, and cultural activities, to the group project understood as a common good. And, finally, the *willingness to share one another's fate* is represented by the disposition to stand by one's fellow nationals and to aid them when in difficulty, even to be willing to die for them when necessary.

The fourth school of thought is Christianity. The Christian tradition, most prominent in Catholic social thought but also in some forms of Protestantism, is grounded as an ideal of human fellowship in which each human being is considered as *imago dei* and hence as deserving of the same love that joins God and man. Pope John Paul II, who in many ways has done the most to secure a place for solidarity in the Catholic tradition, writes

> Solidarity is undoubtedly a Christian virtue. [...] In the light of faith, solidarity seeks to go beyond itself, to take on the specifically Christian dimension of total gratuity, forgiveness and reconciliation. One's neighbor is then not only a human being with his or her own rights and a fundamental equality with everyone else, but becomes the living image of God the Father, redeemed by the blood of Jesus Christ and placed under the permanent action of the Holy Spirit. One's neighbor must therefore be loved, even if an enemy, with the same love with which the Lord loves him or her; and for that person's sake one must be ready for sacrifice, even the ultimate one: to lay down one's life for the brethren.[95]

Solidarity, for the Catholic, is grounded in universal love. The basis for this love flows from identification with others on the basis of a shared experience of human suffering, which is a necessary result of a condition that we all share, namely that we are mortal products of original sin. The focus of Christian love is therefore the relief of suffering in all its forms – a sacrifice which, modelled on the life of Christ, aspires to a reconciliation with God. In a sermon delivered on Wawel Hill in Krakow on October 19, 1980, Józef Tischner, who was influential in Poland's solidarity movement, said:

> With whom, therefore, is our solidarity? It is, above all, with those who have been wounded by other people, with those who suffer pain that could be avoided – accidental, needless pain. This does not preclude

---

[95] *Sollicitudo rei socialis* (1987), §40.

solidarity with others, with all who suffer. However, the solidarity with those who suffer at the hands of others is particularly vital, strong, spontaneous.[96]

On this reading, solidarity is a commitment to aid the suffering grounded in identification with other human beings, who are viewed as engaged in a common struggle against sin and vulnerability. We commit to helping others because they share with us a common condition and experience. This understanding of solidarity is also at the heart of the Christian Democratic political tradition, especially those aspects that emphasized the social responsibilities of the Christian.[97]

There is, however, another strand within the Christian tradition that emphasizes a different form of identification: Christian solidarism. In *Ethics and the National Economy* (1917), its founder and most prominent advocate, Heinrich Pesch (1854–1926), writes:

> Christianity teaches us that people, despite all individual and also social differences in occupation and ownership, are nevertheless *socii*, i.e., comrades, precisely by virtue of those differences. They are dependent on each other and bound together by a *solidaristic community of interests* in all of their industrial relationships as masters and journeymen, as employers and workers, and in the human race overall, which is the great universal family of nations.[98]

On this corporatist understanding, it is not just the shared experience of human suffering, or the understanding of the human being as *imago dei*, but a recognition of the interdependence of human beings in society that grounds a demand to share one another's fate. On this picture, we are meant to recognize how both our flourishing and our suffering are a result of mutual influence and mutual reliance in and through the multiple associations to which we belong; in response, we have obligations to share others' fates by coming to others' aid and by limiting the harm we do. In the 1967 encyclical *Populorum Progressio*, on global development and the inequality between rich and poor nations, Pope Paul VI writes:

> We are the heirs of earlier generations, and we reap benefits from the efforts of our contemporaries; we are under obligation to all men.

---

96 Tischner 1984 [1982], pp. 8–9.
97 See, e.g., Van Kersbergen 2003.
98 Pesch 2004 [1918], p. 104.

Therefore we cannot disregard the welfare of those who will come after us to increase the human family. The reality of human solidarity brings us not only benefits but also obligations.[99]

The passage unmistakably resonates with the French solidarist tradition discussed above. As is widely recognized, John Paul II was also deeply influenced by this strand of Catholic social thought (and its realization in Leo XIII's *Rerum Novarum*).[100] In *Sollicitudo rei socialis*, he writes:

> It is above all a question of interdependence, sensed as a system determining relationships in the contemporary world, in its economic, cultural, political and religious elements, and accepted as a moral category. When interdependence becomes recognized in this way, the correlative response as a moral and social attitude, as a 'virtue,' is solidarity. This then is not a feeling of vague compassion or shallow distress at the misfortunes of so many people, both near and far. On the contrary, it is a firm and persevering determination to commit oneself to the common good; that is to say to the good of all and of each individual, because we are all really responsible for all.[101]

On this reading, the ground of solidarity is, as in Bourgeois and Durkheim, an identification based on our *role in the division of labor*, which includes a recognition that our participation in an unjust social order perpetuates suffering, and makes us accomplices. The doctrine goes hand in hand with the Church's teaching on subsidiarity, in which local associations – including perhaps most importantly the family – have ethical priority to more general, encompassing associations, such as the state.[102] More general and encompassing associations should intervene in the affairs of the

---

99 §17.
100 See, for example, the helpful discussion on the 'solidarity of interdependence' in Potter 2009. See also Doran 1996, pp. 92ff; Beyer 2014, pp. 12–13.
101 *Sollicitudo rei socialis*. (1987), §38.
102 The doctrine of subsidiarity receives its most important expression, after a brief mention in *Rerum Novarum*, in Pope Pius XI's *Quadregismo Anno* (1931). It is also worth noting that two of the most prominent advocates of Christian solidarism and subsidiarity after Pesch, Oscar Nell-Breuning and Gustav Gundlach, were also very influential in shaping German Christian democracy in the postwar period. See, e.g., Koslowski 2000.

lower only to help or aid them in the accomplishment of their tasks. On this understanding, the response to individual suffering must be collective; it cannot be done by individuals acting alone, but by each body, at each level of generality, working together as a unit to preserve the common good. As Pope Francis noted in a follow-up catechism to his COVID-19 encyclical *Fratelli Tutti*, 'there is no true solidarity without social participation, without the contribution of intermediary bodies: families, associations, cooperatives, small businesses, and other expressions of society. Everyone needs to contribute, everyone.'[103]

The emphasis on a commitment to collective action in response to identification with others as vulnerable, interdependent, and *imago dei* is most evident in the Catholic liberation theology that developed in the 1970s and 1980s in Latin America.[104] According to the Salvadoran Jon Sobrino, for example:

> Those who enter into solidarity with the poor ... recover their human dignity by becoming integrated into the pain and suffering of the poor. From the poor they receive, in a way hardly expected, new eyes for seeing the ultimate truth of things and new energies for exploring unknown and dangerous paths.[105]

The non-poor must fight *alongside* rather than *for* the poor; this requires the non-poor to divest themselves of privilege and join the struggle by first winning the trust and reliance of the least well-off. According to Paulo Freire, whose influence on liberation theology was vast, a pedagogy

> must be forged *with*, not *for*, the oppressed (whether individuals or peoples) in the incessant struggle to regain their humanity. This pedagogy makes oppression and its causes objects of reflection by the oppressed, and from that reflection will come their necessary

---

103 'Heal the World: Subsidiarity and the Virtue of Hope' (September 23, 2020), www.vatican.va/content/francesco/en/audiences/2020/documents/papa-francesco_20200923_udienza-generale.html (accessed May 15, 2023). I thank Meghan Clark for discussion and pointers.
104 It is worth noting that liberation theology had an important influence on Pope John Paul II's writing of *Sollicitudo*. In that encyclical, for example, he endorses the 'preferential option for the poor'. See Beyer 2014, p. 14.
105 Sobrino 1994, pp. 98–9 quoted in Potter 2009, p. 145.

engagement in the struggle for their liberation. And in the struggle this pedagogy will be made and remade.[106]

The liberation theologists are at one in the belief that oppression cannot be overcome, as it were, from the top down. As Gustavo Gutiérrez writes in the seminal text *Theology of Liberation*,

> The process of liberation requires the *active participation of the oppressed*; this certainly is one of the most important themes running through the writings of the Latin American Church.[107]

Oppression must be overcome through an awareness among the poor that their situation is a result of social organization, rather than as a result of the natural order of things, and can be overcome by collective action. From this point of view, the most dangerous obstacles in the way of liberation are ignorance and silence.

Once again, we can use our set of distinctions to make sense of the overall Christian doctrine. The *object* of Christian solidarity is reconciliation with Christ; the *grounds* are identification with other human beings on the basis of a shared *experience* of human suffering, of our *condition* as *imago dei*, or of our interdependent causal *role* in reproducing suffering. These grounds give us reason to act together to overcome the *significant adversity* of human suffering in all its forms. The *scope* of solidarity extends across all of humanity. And, finally, we ought to be prepared to 'shoulder one another's burden', through works of aid, succor, and communication, which together constitute a *willingness to share another's fate* in our terms.

The fifth school of thought is associated with more recent social movements such as the civil rights movement, feminism, disability, and LGBTQ movements. Each of these movements shares the oppositional character of socialism, but each has a different understanding of what the grounds and object of solidaristic action are. According to bell hooks, for example,

> We understood that political solidarity between females expressed in sisterhood goes beyond positive recognition of the experiences of women and even shared sympathy for common suffering. Feminist sisterhood is rooted in shared commitment to struggle against

---

106 Freire 1993 [1970], p. 48.
107 Gutiérrez 1973, p. 127.

patriarchal injustice, no matter the form that injustice takes. Political solidarity between women always undermines sexism and sets the stage for the overthrow of patriarchy. Significantly, sisterhood could never have been possible across the boundaries of race and class if individual women had not been willing to divest of their power to dominate and exploit subordinated groups.[108]

The usage is clearly oppositional, but instead of aiming to overthrow *capitalism*, the feminist movement aims to overthrow *patriarchy*. And just as the socialist requires the worker to divest themselves of the power and privilege of their particular position among workers, hooks calls on all women to forgo forms of class, racial, and status privilege and power that might divide them. And just as the socialist invokes the injustice of workers' domination and exploitation by the capitalist as a basis for identification, hooks invokes the injustice of women's subordination and subjugation by men.

Other social movements, such as Black nationalism, are also oppositional, but the basis of identification is distinct. For the Black nationalist, the basis of identification that provides the ground of solidarity is not merely sharing a condition, namely oppression; it also includes sharing *a way of life* centered on shared history, mores, and folkways. An important strand (though not the only strand) of Black nationalism – one that was especially prominent in the1960s and 1970s – holds that high-sounding appeals to the possibility of integration in the name of a universal fight against injustice cannot ground a robust solidarity among Blacks.[109] A deeper, widespread engagement with a distinct culture is also needed. According to this form of nationalism, Blacks (in America) constitute a distinct, and distinctly cultural, nation-within-a-nation whose origins lie in Africa. Enriched and shaped through decades of opposition to and struggle against slavery, Jim Crow, and post-Reconstruction betrayal, Black experience in the US provides a 'residuum of ethnic group consciousness' that defines the contours of African-American culture.[110] Nationalists argue that, though at the moment inchoate

---

108 hooks 2015a, p. 15; see also hooks 2015b, p. 47.
109 For the development of modern Black nationalism, and its distinctness from the 'classical' period, see Robinson 2001; Moses 1988. See also the study of Black nationalist attitudes in Dawson 2003.
110 Cruse 1967, pp. 14–16.

and marginalized, Black culture calls for development and expression (for example, in the arts, music, literature, and theatre); without it, and the sense of collective identity and pride it secures, Blacks cannot securely win their freedom in a fundamentally hostile American society. In a speech announcing the establishment of the Organization of Afro-American Unity (1964), Malcolm X quoted from its charter (which he had penned along with a group of others):

> 'Afro Americans must unite and work together. We must take pride in the Afro American community, for it is our home and it is our power, the base of our power ...' Lastly, concerning culture and the cultural aspect of the Organization of Afro American Unity. 'A race of people is like an individual man; until it uses its own talent, takes pride in its own history, expresses its own culture, affirms its own selfhood, it can never fulfill itself. Our history and our culture were completely destroyed when we were forcibly brought to America in chains. And now it is important for us to know that our history did not begin with slavery. We came from Africa, a great continent, wherein live a proud and varied people, a land which is the new world and was the cradle of civilization.'[111]

Some Black nationalists have not only fought for social, cultural, and economic autonomy from White America[112] but also fought for political-territorial separation. With respect to the latter, some have advocated a separate Black state within the US, while others have supported the founding of an autonomous nation on the African continent.[113] Like the (European) nationalisms discussed above, a uniting feature of Black nationalism, despite these differences, is that a distinct identification based on a shared *culture* is required to foster and sustain Black solidarity in the face of oppression.

And, finally, someone like Martin Luther King, for example, appeals to forms of solidarity whose essential features resonate with elements of socialism, in its oppositional character and widespread support for the labor movement, *and* Christianity. In the 'Letter from a Birmingham Jail', for example, Martin Luther King invokes a universalist and Christian form of mutualism and interdependence:

---

111 Malcolm X 1992, p. 80.
112 See, e.g., Rivers 1995.
113 Most prominently, Martin Delany and Marcus Garvey. See Moses 1988.

I am cognizant of the interrelatedness of all communities and states. I cannot sit idly by in Atlanta and not be concerned about what happens in Birmingham. Injustice anywhere is a threat to justice everywhere. We are caught in an inescapable network of mutuality, tied in a single garment of destiny. Whatever affects one directly affects all indirectly.[114]

And, in a speech to the Illinois American Federation of Labor and Congress of Industrial Organizations in 1965, King invoked the Christian idea of a 'brotherhood of man' to call for a coalition between the civil rights and labor movements:

> The two most dynamic movements that reshaped the nation during the past three decades are the labor and civil rights movements. Our combined strength is potentially enormous. [...] If our two movements unite their social pioneering initiative, thirty years from now people will look back on this day and honor those who had the vision to see the full possibilities of modern society and the courage to fight for their realization. On that day, the brotherhood of man, undergirded by economic security, will be a thrilling and creative reality.[115]

But, once again, in all such social movements and in spite of significant differences in their characterization of each of the central aspects of solidarity, solidarity refers to the mutual sacrifice and joint action demanded by an identification with one another on the basis of a way of life, condition, role, set of experiences, or cause.

Note that each of the five traditions I have considered also bears the other features of solidarity discussed in section 1. In each case, solidarity is understood to embody a commitment *among equals*.[116] In each case, those acting in solidarity take themselves[117] to have an

---

114 Available at http://kingencyclopedia.stanford.edu/kingweb/popular_requests/frequentdocs/birmingham.pdf (accessed December 9, 2022).
115 For Martin Luther King's support for the labor movement and his views on economic justice, see Honey 2018; Shelby and Terry 2018.
116 Cf. Zhao 2019, p. 8, who, citing the possibility of paternalistic and hierarchical relations of solidarity, denies that equality and symmetry are necessary conditions.
117 I remind the reader that here we are discussing solidarity in its *descriptive* guise. What matters, then, are the reasons, attitudes, dispositions, and principles that participants *avow* and *display*, not whether those principles (like equality) are actually realized. Whether they are actually realized in practice is a *normative* issue that can be taken up in a separate, critical

equal standing with respect to one another, whatever their other roles, positions, backgrounds, beliefs, interests, or values. In a solidary action, everyone is meant to count equally. Attitudes of servility and submissiveness are considered out of place.[118] This does not preclude the existence of authority, or leadership, within a solidaristic group. Those who wield power and authority are considered delegates or representatives of the group; deference is due because of their special epistemic position or practical abilities, or because they have been selected through a fair procedure, not because they are of higher rank.

Furthermore, according to each of our traditions of thought on solidarity, relations among solidaries are *symmetrical*. As a committed form of joint action grounded in identification, solidarity is *omni-* rather than *unilateral*. Each stands for all, and all stand for each. At the heart of solidarity is therefore *reciprocity* (I return to this below, in sections 3 and 4). This does not mean that every act of concern and aid must be reciprocated, that everyone be in a position to reciprocate, or that all contribute in the same way; all that is required for a given instance of collective action to be a form of acting in solidarity is that participants identify with one another on one or more of the bases we have discussed, are mutually committed to overcoming adversity together, have a standing disposition to share one another's fate, and trust one another to meet the expectations embedded in their solidary activity.[119] To what degree each *ought* to contribute, given the circumstances and the more general background, is a separate, normative issue (see next two sections for the normative evaluation of different grounds of solidarity).

In an important and illuminating account of solidarity, Avery Kolers characterizes solidarity as both *asymmetrical* and *deferential*,

---

moment. Does the movement in question, say, *genuinely* realize the demands of equality it avows? Do people really have *genuine* reasons to identify on the basis concerned? (See the next two sections, 'Grounds' and 'Value', for discussion on the normative evaluation of solidarity). I thank Tom Parr for discussion.
118 Cf. Rawls, who writes: 'fraternity [which we interpret here as solidarity] is held to represent a certain equality of social esteem manifest in various public conventions and in the absence of manners of deference and servility' (Rawls 1999, p. 90).
119 On the role of reciprocity in solidarity, cf. Miller 2017, p. 63; Forst forthcoming.

rather than symmetrical and egalitarian.[120] Kolers argues that paradigmatic cases of solidarity involve one group, S, *deferring* to an object group, G, but not vice versa. According to Kolers,

> [solidary action] is not principally justified by appeal to goals, nor do we choose sides on the basis of shared goals. To the contrary, when S is in solidarity with G, it is G, not G's ends, that S endorses or values. S is disposed to adopt *whatever* goal G sets for the action or as a political aim. For instance, insofar as they are in solidarity, heterosexual persons who support the right of same-sex couples to marry do so not because they individually want same-sex marriages to be possible, but because the LGBTQ community treats that as an important goal.[121]

Paradigmatic instances of solidarity involve members of (out)groups (e.g., heterosexuals) committing themselves to do whatever members of a disadvantaged (in)group (e.g., homosexuals) require to overcome injustice. Importantly, on this picture outgroup members commit to the *group*, rather than to any aim pursued by the group. As a heterosexual, I do *not* act in solidarity by committing directly to fighting heterosexism alongside members of the LGBTQ community; rather, to act in solidarity, I must commit to the LGBTQ community as such, and so to whatever members tell me I need to do to promote their cause, whatever cause that is.

One advantage of this view is that it captures an important moral aspect of coalitional social movements in which more privileged (out) groups act as allies of less privileged (in)groups who are fighting injustice. As has often been noted, the trouble with such coalitions is that members of privileged groups often tend to be blind to the way in which privilege colors and sometimes distorts their efforts to support the aims of the movement.[122] Outgroup allies can sometimes reproduce, unconsciously, wider structural patterns of power and exclusion as they fight alongside ingroup members; they can perpetrate, for example, forms of epistemic injustice in seeking to impose their own agenda or ideals onto the wider

---

120 Kolers 2016.
121 Kolers 2016, p. 58.
122 Compare critiques of 'second-wave' feminism as being too White, (unconsciously) exclusionary, and middle class. See, e.g., Zakaria 2021; Spelman 1988; Crenshaw 2017; hooks 2015a.

movement.[123] Kolers' work reminds his readers that genuine solidarity requires that members of outgroups put aside their particular concerns, ideals, prejudices, and so on, and *listen*.[124] They must be prepared, in turn, to accept their relative epistemic limitations vis-à-vis members of ingroups who have not only 'skin in the game' but also a vivid lived experience of the forms of injustice they are fighting. And they must also be prepared to defer out of respect for the disadvantaged: whether or not the disadvantaged have better epistemic access to truths about the struggle, etc., the privileged ought to defer out of respect for what is at stake for the disadvantaged.[125]

There are, however, three main problems. First, once deference of an outgroup member to an ingroup is made paradigmatic of solidarity in general, it becomes difficult to account for the idea of *solidarity* among Blacks *as* Black, or among women *as* women. Kolers attempts to include ingroup solidarity by saying that each member in such cases defers to the *group's* aims.[126] So there is still deference of individuals to a group, only in this case, the individuals defer to the very group of which they are members. This, however, looks misleading. What members of ingroups are doing is deferring *to each other*, symmetrically, in deciding *together* what to do *as a group*, not deferring to a *tertium quid* – 'the group' – from which they take their marching orders. Putting the attitudes of *outgroup* members at the core of solidarity as a phenomenon, furthermore, has the odd effect of foregrounding, in any discussion of solidarity, the structure of relations between outgroup and ingroup members, rather than ingroup members among themselves.

Second, while deference is often required, especially when outgroup members participate in a collective struggle alongside ingroup members, why make deference a conceptually necessary condition for being in solidarity in the first place? This seems to rule out forms of solidarity in which participants act together in more loosely and democratically organized ways. Third, the account

123 On this point, see, e.g., Clark forthcoming.
124 See also Deveaux 2021, pp. 204ff.
125 I thank Barry Maguire for discussion. For more on the idea that solidarity can be objectionably exclusionary and, indeed, illiberal, see Sangiovanni forthcoming.
126 Kolers 2016, p. 62.

of deference seems too strong. It might be true that one may defer to certain members within a movement, but this will be because there are independent reasons for giving them authority to decide (including reasons of respect for what they have at stake), not because one is committed to them *whatever they may decide to do*.[127] It seems more plausible, for example, that heterosexuals supporting the LGBTQ community do so because they value the *ends* that the community seeks to pursue (e.g., ending gender-based oppression), not – except in very special cases involving LGBTQ friends or family – because they value the *individuals* as such ('whatever ends they may pursue') who constitute the community. And it seems more plausible, then, to say that we defer to certain members of a group (e.g., the leaders) because such deference is more likely to advance the cause against gender-based oppression, because we will be more successful in coordinating our ends, because the individuals are in a better epistemic position to know the struggles they face and what is required to overcome them, or because of respect for what they have at stake, than because we are committed to the leaders *as individuals*.[128]

Christianity can also be read as rejecting the idea that solidarity must be symmetrical. The Catholic tradition, in particular, has often been unclear whether there is a difference between charity, *caritas* – understood as love of one's neighbor on the basis of our common, fallen humanity – and solidarity. This is evident in the Tischner citation from above, where he goes on to cite the Good Samaritan as an example of solidarity. And it is even evident in Pope John Paul II, who, in the very same encyclical (*Sollicitudo rei socialis*) in which he expounds his solidarity of interdependence, writes 'Those who are more influential, because they have a greater share of goods and common services, should feel responsible for the weaker and

---

127 On deference, see also the instructive discussions in Gould 2020, p. 131; Deveaux 2021, p. 205.
128 For more on this distinction, recall the discussion of love as a *de re* attitude and solidarity as (most commonly) *de dicto*. Note that for cases in which there is asymmetry (with or without deference) – where, say, one group is disposed to share the fate of another group but not vice versa – then I say this is not *solidarity* but *support for a cause*. I say more about this below.

be ready to share with them all they possess.'[129] Charity (*caritas*) and mercy (*misericordia*) are prototypically unilateral: there is the giver of aid, forgiveness, succor, and support, and the receiver who is suffering and in need. The relation is asymmetrical. Above I provided an interpretation of the Catholic texts – influenced by Christian solidarism – that insists instead on a distinction between charity and solidarity. Solidarity, on this understanding, is necessarily egalitarian, social, collective, and grounded in an awareness of interdependence. Charity is not. On this alternative interpretation, the Christian identifies with those in need as engaged in a *joint struggle* – where human beings (both oppressed and non-oppressed) are conceived of as *fighting together* to overcome the suffering of the human condition. She sees a fundamental symmetry between those who are in a position to aid and those in need – those in need identify with the struggle, and with other participants on the basis of their mutual commitment. According to this alternative reading, there is a key distinction between charity and solidarity even within the Christian tradition.[130]

There are some further theoretical and evaluative reasons that support this reading. First, even from within a solely Christian perspective, if solidarity is just the same as charity, then why use the term at all? Making it the same as charity drains it of its distinctive meaning.[131] But, second, it also disconnects solidarity from its history. As we have seen, the reading of solidarity as a public, symmetrical, and egalitarian form of acting together against significant adversity – a form of acting that is, in turn, grounded in diverse forms of *de dicto* identification – unifies its history, and makes sense to us as diverse and anonymous inhabitants of modern, industrial cities, states, and regions. This understanding also makes better sense of

---

129 See also *Populorum Progressio*, which often speaks of the need of the rich nations to come to the aid of the poor, but without any mention of the need to engage the agency of those in need, including by acts of renunciation, mutual understanding, and communication (recall liberation theology), and through education aimed at joint rebellion against oppression (recall Freire).
130 See also Rippe 1998, p. 358, although, for Rippe, solidarity still remains primarily uni- rather than omnilateral.
131 See also Bayertz 1999a, p. 19; West-Oram et al. 2016, p. 2; Gould 2007, p. 157.

the *value* of solidarity for us, which is deeply bound up with the history of egalitarianism as a collective struggle. Recall that at the heart of solidarity is both an outward demand – as we face the public – and an inward expectation – as we look on one another – to be *treated as equals*. Charity, even understood as grounded in a form of identification with the human rather than merely in a general moral duty, does not capture the cooperative nature of this value or fit with its historical importance to us.[132] (I return to a fuller explication of the value of solidarity below, which will serve to complete this argument.)

One may still want to object. Surely, one might say, we can stand in solidarity with prisoners by protesting on their behalf, whatever their attitudes toward us happen to be. But is it so obvious? If the prisoners believe, say, that our protest is pointless, do not want our support, are not committed to acting together, and are not disposed to share our fate (were, say, the roles to be reversed or we to need

---

132 With respect to the distinction between charity and solidarity, it is worth remarking on the early and influential discussion of solidarity in Pierre Leroux's 1840 *Doctrine de l'humanité*. Known at the time as a Saint-Simonian but also somewhat mystical socialist, Leroux defends a religion of humanity grounded in an account of the solidarity of the human species. What is useful for our purposes is his attempt to argue that, while Christianity is a religion of solidarity – after all, it, too, represents a faith in the unity of the human in Christ – it must be superseded by a religion of humanity. The discussion turns on his rejection of Christian charity as a foundation of human fraternal love. Where Christianity goes wrong, he argues, is that it leads to a denial of self-love, and hence of something necessary for individual freedom. In Christianity, the stark opposition between self-love and the command to love one's neighbor leads to forms of self-denial that are pathological and extreme. Furthermore, Leroux argues, Christian charity is founded on pity, and hence on inequality. It presupposes and reinforces an imbalance of power, which is in direct contradiction with the altruism that is supposed to drive it. The solution is to ground, Leroux argues, love of another in love of oneself through an act of identification of oneself, as a human being with needs and desires, in others, and of others in oneself. This renders solidarity, he writes, 'organizable' by secular society, rather than relying on an otherworldly love of God. See Leroux 1845, pp. 157–75. Leroux writes: 'Pity may be the perversion of compassion, but its alternative is solidarity.' See also Hannah Arendt, who writes: 'It is out of pity that men are "attracted toward *les hommes faibles*" but it is out of solidarity that they establish deliberately and, as it were, dispassionately a community of interest with the oppressed and exploited' (Arendt 1990 [1963], p. 88).

their aid in *our* action on their behalf), then we cannot be acting in solidarity *with them*. To believe otherwise is to mistake support for a cause or resistance to an injustice or humanitarian aid as solidarity. We already have concepts to express what we are doing; what does calling such support 'solidarity' add? On the other hand, if the prisoners are prepared to coordinate with us in resisting their condition, have a standing disposition to share our fate as protesters 'on the outside', and trust us to do our part as we trust them to do theirs, then we are acting in solidarity because and insofar as we are acting *together* (on the basis of identification with a cause) to better their conditions.[133]

There are, of course, more borderline cases. Suppose that we are protesting on the outside, and the prisoners on the inside, but neither of us knows that the others are so doing. And suppose that all our other conditions were satisfied such that, *if we were to know of their protest and they of ours*, then we would be acting in solidarity. In this case, we would, if we could, organize together with them and be prepared to share their fate, and they would, if they could, organize with us and be prepared to share our fate. Our solidarity here is *latent*. We are acting in solidarity on the outside, and they are acting in solidarity on the inside, but our actions have not yet joined up.[134] We can say that our action, in these circumstances, is organized not just to *support* the prisoners, but *in their name*: we recognize that their chances of organizing and mobilizing are slim,

---

133 A good example are the protests of the Silent Sentinels against Woodrow Wilson's lack of support for women's suffrage. On October 20, 1917, police arrested a large group of women (including Alice Paul, one of the leaders of the movement) and sent them to the Occoquan Workhouse, where they were eventually beaten after going on hunger strike. Many on the 'outside' protested, including Dudley Field Malone, who resigned his post within the administration in solidarity with the women, and wrote a public letter to the president. For this history, see www.newspapers.com/clip/32859084/dudley-field-malone-resigns-1917/ (accessed February 5, 2023) and Stevens 1920.

134 This is a result of the fact that for us truly to be *acting together* (in *any* case), there must be something close to common knowledge; indeed, all the main accounts of joint action, including Bratman 2014; Kutz 2000b; Gilbert 2000; Tuomela 2013; Searle 1990 include a variant. I here revise, then, what I held in Sangiovanni 2013 in a discussion of resistance groups that do not know of each other's existence.

given their conditions, but we would organize collectively if we could and we do what we can to make such collective agency possible; on the other side, they also would welcome our support and do what they could to organize and coordinate with us. For these reasons, our action still counts as in solidarity with the prisoners, even though the solidarity remains only latent. It becomes *actual* when our actions join up in a single joint action, and we are each disposed in all the relevant ways.

The same analysis is relevant when we speak, for example, of solidarity with refugees.[135] Refugees, in most cases, are not an organized social movement or group pursuing a shared goal to fight their condition.[136] Is there a sense, then, in which we act in solidarity with refugees when we protest our governments' policies? Just as in the case of the prisoners, our protest is a *latent* form of solidarity if it is undertaken *in the name of the refugees*, as a result of the fact that refugees, that is, are not able, given their circumstances, to organize and mobilize against our governments' policies. As a form of latent solidarity, our action (just as in the case of the prisoners) has to be geared toward and make room for the participation of refugees where and when this is possible. It must be designed to enable their participation in a truly collective agency.[137] On this understanding, we do not act *for* the refugees but always aim to act *with* them. At the same time, they must welcome our action and do what they can, within their constrained conditions, to organize and coordinate with us. Once again, if our action does not take this form – if, for example, we merely act to fight the injustice but make no effort to act together with the refugees, or if the refugees only take a distant interest in what we are doing – then it is not even a latent form of solidarity, but merely support for a noble cause.

We can say similar things with more straightforward cases of charity. Merely sending money to earthquake survivors is not solidarity, for all the same reasons. Once again, why not call such actions

---

135 I am indebted to discussion in Owen 2021.
136 There are, however, important cases in which refugees *do* succeed in organizing. See the collection of essays in Bradley et al. 2019. Many thanks to Catherine Lu for the reference.
137 For the importance of this requirement, see Deveaux 2021, ch. 6; Land 2015.

humanitarian? What does calling them instances of solidarity add?[138] I concede that much of our contemporary usage – which does allow for such unilateralism – parts ways here;[139] considering the history of solidarity, I believe this usage is a vestige of the Christian elision between charity and solidarity. If I am right, then there is a case for abandoning it. Doing so would help to keep in clear view the distinctive value of solidarity – recall its essentially cooperative and egalitarian character – and maintain a connection to its history – recall, for example, that solidarity resonates in an age where the centrifugal forces of markets grow and traditional sources of social connection wane. In these conditions, solidarity names a practice of collective agency and transformative mobilization. Unilateral, humanitarian aid does not capture either element.

One might wonder, relatedly, whether recognition of mutual responsibility to others on the basis of belonging to a real or imagined community is sufficient for solidarity.[140] On this view, joint action against adversity is not part of the core concept of solidarity. But,

---

138 In an insightful discussion of solidarity, Van Parijs forthcoming claims that the difference between charity and solidarity is that the latter (but not the former) is based on the thought that 'I help you because I assume that I could have been you – even though I know that I am not you and may also know that I shall never be in the sort of trouble in which you are now'. But most Christian accounts of charity, indeed, most forms of humanitarianism, emphasize the same thing: it is in virtue of our shared vulnerability, or shared suffering as fallen human beings, that we owe others our aid. 'There but for the grace of God go I' is a prototypically Christian thought. If this is right, then what distinguishes, on this reading, solidarity from charity? I have suggested the difference is that solidarity necessarily involves *joint struggle* in a way that a mere disposition to aid on the basis of an underlying identification – as in the earthquake case – does not. See also note 119.

139 Onora O'Neill, for example, distinguishes solidarity *with* (unilateral) and solidarity *among* (omnilateral) in O'Neill 1996, p. 201. See also A. E. Taylor 2015, who distinguishes *expressional* (i.e., unilateral) from *robust* solidarity (i.e., omnilateral).

140 Van Parijs forthcoming, for example, writes: 'What is distinctive of solidarity, I submit, is the symmetry captured by the expression "mutual responsibility", responsibility for each other as members of some (more or less imagined) community. When I help you out of solidarity, I do so because you are "one of us", because "I could have been you", because, in this sense, I "identify" with you.' For a similar view, see Mason 2000, p. 27.

as I have argued, this is too broad. My picking up my brother at the airport – and hence discharging a mutual responsibility based on belonging to the same family – would count as an instance of solidarity. And so would returning a lost wallet to its owner.[141] Conceiving of solidarity in this way would make it indistinguishable from the general class of responsibilities that flow from special relationships like family, friends, and communities. It would therefore make it less useful in illuminating the social phenomenon underlying the distinctively modern, omnilateral, and transformational character of solidarity over the past two centuries.

So far, we have used the formula defended in section 1 to make sense of solidarity's history. We have used the term, for the most part, in its interpretive guise rather than its normative one. We have yet, that is, to *evaluate* any of these instances of solidarity, or to assess whether any of the grounds evinced provide *genuine* reasons to act together in the first place. This is the aim of the next two sections.

3 Grounds

I have argued that solidarity is a form of acting together to overcome significant adversity grounded in identification. We act solidaristically when, that is, (a) we identify with one another on the basis of a shared way of life, cause, set of experiences, condition, or role, (b) we are, as a result, committed to doing our part in overcoming significant adversity and to setting aside, in a range of cases, narrow self-interest in its pursuit, (c) we have a settled, reliable disposition to come to others' aid in support of our goal, and are disposed not to bypass one another's wills in that pursuit, and (d) we trust one another with respect to (b) and (c) (where trust is reliance plus a normative expectation that others will indeed be committed and come to our aid when necessary). In section 2, we saw that this characterization can make sense of the paradigmatic cases of solidarity (viz. solidarism, socialism, nationalism, Christianity, and social movements such as feminism and civil rights). On this reading, solidarity does not name an emotion, such as fellow-feeling, and it

---

141 I draw this example from Van Parijs forthcoming.

cannot be reduced to mere support for a noble cause (e.g., donating money to Oxfam). It is also omni- rather unilateral: acts of charity, altruism, or humanitarian aid do not, as such, count as instances of solidarity. Solidarity, furthermore, cannot be merely passive: the dispositions and commitments mentioned above must be dispositions and commitments displayed in a form of irreducibly joint action. We cannot *be* in solidarity unless we *act* in solidarity.

In this section, I want to ask: What counts as right reasons for acting in solidarity with others in the sense described? My focus will be on the role of identification in giving us grounds for acting in solidarity with others. It is often said that my identification with you *as a woman* or *as a worker* or *as an African-American* or *as a French citizen* or *as an antifascist* can provide me a reason, or even an obligation, to act in solidarity with you. But why? And under what conditions? I am not interested in the empirical question about whether people are, or are not, motivated to act in solidarity by appealing to their identification with others under one or more of such descriptions. I am interested in whether this appeal has normative force, and why. In this section, therefore, we turn from the interpretive and descriptive to the more explicitly normative. In the penultimate subsection, I indicate some reasons to think that identification is, in fact, not just a commonly avowed ground for acting in solidarity but also paradigmatic of it.[142] Once again, if the argument regarding possible grounds of identification gives us a useful framework for thinking through some of the normative issues that arise in reflection about solidarity, it should also serve to support the overall argument.

3.1 Way of life

Let us begin with sharing a way of life.[143] The paradigmatic form of solidarity that emerges from identification with others based on a shared way of life is nationalism. The nationalist believes that there is a territorially defined public culture that binds together a

---

142 This discussion also serves to respond to Kolers' worry (Kolers 2016, pp. 59–60) that my original discussion, in Sangiovanni 2015, lacks an account of the 'pro-attitudes' (beyond mere commitment to a goal) that characterize solidarity.
143 On the idea of a way of life, see Mason 2000, pp. 22–3.

group of people across generations.¹⁴⁴ The public culture defines a readily identifiable set of commonplaces and fixed points of historical reference, is often based on a common language and linguistic tradition (in literature and music, for example), and gives rise to a set of mores and folkways that are reproduced in everyday life. The nationalist, on this reading, need not seek statehood, but they do seek to govern and determine themselves.¹⁴⁵ Suppose that I identify both with being Sioux and with other Sioux in the epistemic, affective, and normative senses outlined above. When and why should this fact give me reasons to act in solidarity together?

The most obvious reasons would apply in circumstances where our way of life – which we value as an important part of practical identity – is under threat. This threat could come from many quarters. To illustrate: One of the most important for Native American peoples, including the Sioux, is the threat posed by unlawful expropriation of ancestral lands by colonial governments. We should, we say, join together in solidarity to fight the threat.¹⁴⁶ At the very least, this is a prudential reason to act in solidarity: joining together allows us to preserve something that each of us values and that none of

144 See, for example, Miller 1995.
145 Cf. Coulthard and Simpson 2016, pp. 6–7.
146 See, for example, the struggles of the American Indian Movement throughout its history to address injustice against native peoples in Banks and Erdoes 2005. More recently, see the protests against the Dakota Access Pipeline build on Standing Rock Sioux land in www.nytimes.com/2016/11/02/us/north-dakota-oil-pipeline-battle-whos-fighting-and-why.html (accessed February 14, 2022). See also the account of 'grounded normativity' in Coulthard 2014; Coulthard and Simpson 2016, pp. 254–5; and the account of the structural injustice of colonialism in Lu 2017. I thank Jared Holley for a helpful discussion on anticolonial solidarities in general. In my terms, anticolonial solidarities have most commonly (though not exclusively) been based on a *way of life* (especially in the context of the anticolonial nationalisms of the 1960s and 1970s) and/or on a *condition* as structurally dominated by settler powers (especially in the context of the *transnational* solidarities typical of the pan-movements, such as Pan-Africanism and the various cross-national movements for Indigenous rights, such as the Red Power movement); allies in these struggles then count as acting in solidarity on the basis of identification with a *cause*. See also Coulthard's engagement with Fanon in Coulthard 2014, in which he discusses the importance of revitalizing and reclaiming Indigenous *ways of life* as a mode of prefiguring a postcolonial future.

us could defend alone. There is also an important sense in which, because we identify our well-being with the well-being of the group, failing to act in solidarity is also a failure of integrity. The way of life defines who we are; not to show up is a form of self-betrayal. But the normative force of the reason is not merely prudential. We would also be right in feeling let down or even betrayed should one of our number not join the struggle. Why? What is the basis of the normative expectation that other members should join the struggle?

One might appeal here to a general duty to fight injustice. The problem is that this doesn't pick out those with whom one identifies. Everyone has such a duty. Everyone, on that basis, has a reason to join or, at any rate, help in the struggle. If someone did join for that reason alone, then one would be joining others on the basis of identification with a *cause* rather than on the basis of identification with a *way of life*. Non-Sioux could join for those reasons (I will return to identification with a cause and its relation to what Lawrence Blum calls *outgroup* solidarity[147] below).

One might appeal instead to the way of life itself – to what, in our example, it means to be Sioux in the first place.[148] The idea here is that a mutual readiness to come to each other's aid against an oppressor, mutual trust, and a willingness to set aside self-interest in overcoming significant adversity are among the core values constitutive of the Sioux nation – which include, in addition, the special character of our attachment to land and earth, the bonds of community and loyalty, our distinctive sense of shared history and ancestry, the feeling of at-homeness that belonging brings, and the pride and honor attached to membership. To identify as Sioux then requires you also to join in solidarity when necessary. Otherwise, you are not an authentic Sioux. There are two main problems with this view. First, it makes solidarity a requirement of membership without explaining to us *why* it is such a requirement.[149] Without

---

147 Blum 2007.
148 See also Simmons 1996 for a convincing critique of the argument that we can have special obligations to other members of social groups, when and because such membership is a constitutive part of our identity.
149 This, it strikes me, is also a problem with arguments in favor of associative obligations that take the same shape as Scheffler 1997. Scheffler argues that, if special relationships didn't require participants to give each other's interests priority, they would lack the value that we (correctly) attribute

further argument, this makes the solidarity that is claimed as constitutive of Sioux identity look arbitrary and unmotivated. Second, it rests the case on appeal to authenticity. But why is being more authentic a reason to feel betrayed? At most, it can motivate the charge that the individual is betraying *themselves*, but it cannot serve to show that they are betraying other Sioux.

A more nuanced argument is the following. Let us suppose that the special character of our attachment to land and earth, our bonds of community and loyalty, our distinctive sense of shared history and ancestry, the feeling of at-homeness that belonging brings, and our pride and honor in membership are values that both you and I recognize are realized by membership in the Sioux nation. We can then say that, *without* a mutual readiness to come to each other's aid against an oppressor, *without* mutual trust, and *without* a willingness to set aside self-interest in overcoming significant adversity, we will never be able to sustain those values. Solidarity is here conceived of as an instrument necessary to protect what we value. But what is the normative force of this argument? It is tempting to say that it is simply the force of the requirement that if you will the end, you are under a rational requirement to will the necessary means.[150] There are two problems. First, on this reading, your refusal to join should be understood as an instance of narrow irrationality – like willingly failing to take your ticket to board the plane – rather than

---

to them. Therefore, recognizing the value of special relationships implies that we have special responsibilities. Could one use this form of argument to claim that members who have reason to value the Sioux nation must act in solidarity when required to overcome adversity? The success of the argument would turn on whether it could be shown that membership of the Sioux nation would lack value if members didn't recognize such mutual obligations. But the prior question must surely be: Why would membership of the Sioux nation be impoverished *without* a recognition of the moral demands of solidarity? The trouble is that the answer to this question would seem to presuppose an argument explaining why demands of solidarity are, indeed, a requirement, which is what we are trying to show in the first place.

150 Cf. Tommie Shelby, who writes: '[An obligation to resist racial injustice] would follow from the principle that if one wills the end, one also wills the necessary means, provided of course these are morally permissible. If such a position is sound, then blacks who fail to commit to black solidarity are open to criticism' (Shelby 2009, p. 214).

an instance of letting down others. This seems to miss the moral import of the demand to commit. Second, the failure to commit doesn't seem like a failure of means–ends rationality. To see this, consider that it is open for someone to respond: 'As long as *you* join in solidarity with others in fighting the oppressors, I don't need to; so failing to join is not an instance of narrow irrationality at all – indeed, it strikes me as the eminently prudent thing to do.'

This possible response makes evident what the moral force of the demand to join really is. When you, as an identifying Sioux, decline to join, you *free ride* on the attempts of others to salvage what is of value to all of us. Your failure is a failure of reciprocity for what others have sacrificed, or propose to sacrifice, to maintain the way of life that you also value. Suppose you join but then persistently fail to come to other solidaries' aid in the pursuit of the struggle; here, too, we can say that your failure constitutes a form of free-riding. When others are disposed to come to each other's aid, this not only makes our overcoming mutual adversity more likely to succeed, but it also increases mutual trust (which includes, recall, reliance), which, in turn, makes cooperation more likely to endure in the face of hardship.[151] These are public goods that benefit you as an identifying and participating member of the Sioux; in failing to be similarly disposed, you accept the benefits without providing a fair return.

The account, I believe, generalizes beyond nationalism to other ways of life. Sharing a way of life as Catholics, or even as, say, mountain climbers, can, when adversity threatens, create both prudential *and* moral reasons for joining together in solidarity. It is important, however, that the moral pressure to join in solidarity stems only indirectly from sharing a way of life *as such*: the main source of moral pressure comes from considerations of fairness, from, that is, the benefits that fighting against adversity brings to those who share the way of life. This does not imply that identification is unimportant. Identification explains the investment one has in

---

[151] Note that the argument from fairness would also apply to a non-Sioux who lives among the Sioux, and whose way of life is also threatened by government expropriation. Should she decline to join, she would also be free-riding, and so also be criticizable on that basis. On fair play, see also note 153.

the way of life, and hence a good part of the benefits one derives from it; without those benefits, the argument from fairness would cease to apply. If one, for example, is a fellow national but does not identify with others on that basis, and one does not otherwise benefit from the way of life that national belonging realizes,[152] then the argument from fairness will cut little ice.[153] Identification is, then, best understood as an enabling (though not necessary) condition for the argument from fairness to apply, but does not by itself generate the moral pressure to join in solidarity with others. I return to this point below, when comparing different grounds of solidarity, and when discussing whether there are reasons for identification in the first place.

3.2 Role

In this subsection, I turn to reasons for solidarity grounded in sharing a *role*. A role is a position defined by social or legal convention to

---

152 I return to cases of this kind below, when discussing alienation.
153 This is a standard fair play case in which an individual sincerely and correctly believes the costs are not worth the benefits of cooperation (and hence where there is no independent reason why turning down the benefits would be illegitimate). On the importance of the condition that the costs be worth the benefits, see Simmons 1979, pp. 320–1. Note, however, that I modify Simmons' defense of fair play in two ways. First, the belief that the costs are not worth the benefits must be not only *nonculpable* (i.e., the person's beliefs cannot be a result, say, of avoiding gathering evidence) but also *correct* (the person's beliefs that the costs aren't worth the benefits must be true). If the person falsely but nonculpably believes that the costs are not worth the benefits, then the person is a free-rider, but has an excuse. On this modification, see Arneson 1982; see also Simmons 2001, pp. 32–3. Second, there must be no independent reason why turning down the benefits would be wrong (e.g., if turning down the benefits would unilaterally impose unreasonably large costs on others, or if turning down the benefits, although not unilaterally harmful, could not be suitably generalized). On the importance of generalizability, see Cullity 1995. Note that, on this modified view, voluntary acceptance of benefits is *not* required for fair-play obligations to apply (whether such obligations are, in addition, *enforceable* is a different matter). Voluntary acceptance, that is, is not required when the belief in the costs/benefits is false, or when the refusal of the benefits would not be generalizable or impose large costs on others. I discuss and further defend these modifications in Sangiovanni ms.a.

accomplish a task or set of tasks within a larger, often institutional, division of labor. Husband, teacher, worker, and machinist are examples of roles. Appeals to solidarity on the basis of role are common, especially within the workers' movement (though, as we will see, the basis for solidarity in the workers' movement can also be understood as grounded in shared *condition* rather than merely a shared role). Take Ralph Chaplin's 'Solidarity Forever', a union classic:

> It is we who ploughed the prairies, built the cities where they trade,
>
> Dug the mines and built the workshops, endless miles of railroad laid;
>
> Now, we stand outcast and starving, 'mid the wonders we have made.[154]

The identification with each other as workers is grounded, on this understanding, in the role we play with respect to the product of capitalism: *we* make what is essential to our civilization; the capitalist is but a parasite, who exploits our labor and leaves us destitute. We ought, then, to band together in solidarity to fight against the system that oppresses us. Note that the basis is not sharing a cultural identity or way of life: there is little that, say, the hairdresser and the waste collector need to have in common by way of culture or way of life to be in solidarity. It is also not experience: again, hairdressers and waste collectors may experience their roles (or the oppressive hand of capitalism) in very different ways. And, while workers may come to share a cause if they band together, the basis of identification is simply being a worker, *prior* to joining together in solidarity.

It is helpful to introduce, at this point, the distinction between sharing a *role* and sharing a *condition*. This is because it is possible to interpret the worker's movement in either way. If identification is based on workers as *producers*, then the grounds for mutual sympathy, understanding, and shared normative orientation typical of *de dicto* identification is the *role*. If, on the other hand (or in addition), identification is based on workers as *oppressed* or *exploited*, then the grounds for sympathy, affirmation, understanding, and shared normative orientation is the *condition* shared by workers.

154 Ralph Chaplin, 'Solidarity Forever'.

This is important, since there will be variation in the way in which different categories of workers are oppressed, and variation in their role vis-à-vis the reproduction of capitalism.[155] The character of the reasons for joining together will also be subtly different, depending on which type of identification is emphasized. It is unclear, in particular, how the role of worker as such within socialism can provide grounds for joining together. Workers are not joining together in the name of their role as producers or to protect a shared project they are engaged in (what would the project be – the reproduction of capitalism?); the role understood in this way is, after all, the cause of their oppression. The ground for joining together in solidarity is better understood as the *condition* that workers find themselves in, namely, the condition of labor-based exploitation. This also makes better sense of the grounds of their mutual sympathy, affirmation, and understanding, and makes it clear that the pressure to generate a shared normative orientation will come from a need to understand the sources and character of their oppression, rather than a shared understanding of their role as producers (independently of their oppression). We will return to oppression as a source of identification below.

Clearer examples of identification based on role, and of the solidarity that might emerge from them, are sectoral roles. The basis of identification, in such cases, is the role understood as the basis of joint *project* that is valued and affirmed by its participants (contrast the role of worker in the socialist movement, which is often not valued and affirmed as such). Take medicine, for example. Medicine is a profession that has a long history and a rich structure of shared norms and standards.[156] Most doctors think of themselves as playing a part in a larger practice that serves to promote health and fight illness. They think of themselves as contributing in a vast division

155 An interesting, almost paradigmatic, example of worker-based solidarity is the Polish union Solidarnosc. It is somewhat unusual in this context because Solidarnosc, while beginning in the shipyards of Gdansk, became a movement representing 'society' (*spoleczenstwo*) against an alien, totalitarian state power. In this case, it was the oppression suffered by citizen-workers at the hands of the *nomenklatura* that provided the basis of identification. See Ash 2002; Michnik 1985.
156 For the emergence of medicine as a profession (in which it is often contrasted with medicine as a business or guild), see Haakonssen 1997.

of labor that, when viewed as a single profession, serves those final ends. The final ends of medicine, in turn, structure doctors' everyday deliberation and collaboration with other doctors. Doctors are not only responsive to what other doctors are doing, but seek to ensure that their efforts are coherent across smaller-scale pursuits, say, within a hospital. And the administrators of a hospital, in turn, seek to coordinate their activity with other hospitals within a health system, and that health system in turn is part of a larger, global pursuit of the same ends. The shared orientation to such final ends is the basis for the mutual sympathy, affirmation, understanding, and normative deliberation among doctors.

Identification, as we have said, is not yet solidarity. Among doctors, identification can become solidarity when there is some form of adversity that threatens the shared project animating doctors. A good example is the series of junior doctor strikes in the UK in 2016. Junior doctors were offered a new contract by the Conservative government that, among other things, would have the effect of increasing the number of weekends that doctors would be forced to work (at a lower net pay) and would have an adverse impact on those more likely to work part time, and hence on women. Doctors worried that such long hours were not only unfair, but also likely to diminish the quality of service due to fatigue; the adverse effect on part-time workers was also said to make the gender pay gap worse. What reasons did doctors in general – not just junior doctors – have for joining and supporting the strikes, and hence for acting in solidarity?

Again, one source of reasons is the injustice borne by junior doctors. But, as before, this is a general reason flowing from a natural duty, and applies to anyone in a position to contribute (including non-doctors). Among doctors – including senior doctors – who identify with the project that unites them, there is an important prudential reason: to protect the project from being undermined by a hostile and misguided government. The reason is prudential because the success of the project of the whole, and of doctors as participants in the project, contributes to doctors' well-being. If we are senior doctors, identification with medicine as a profession, and with other doctors on that basis, guides and structures an important part of our life, and defines not only who we are but also how we want others to perceive us. When we fight on behalf of the junior doctors, we therefore also fight for ourselves (even if, as senior doctors, we have no direct personal stake in their success). If we fail to turn up, then, there is an important sense in which we betray *ourselves*; there is an important sense in which we can be criticized, as a result, for lacking integrity.

But *morally*, just as was the case for way of life, the mutual sympathy, affirmation, understanding, and normative orientation that are constitutive of identification do not, on their own, provide any reasons for joining in solidarity. The strongest reasons come, rather, from considerations of fairness: should a junior doctor (or, indeed, any doctor who identifies with the project) fail to support their colleagues, they would be free-riding on the efforts of others to protect what is of value to them. Only a doctor that, as a matter of justice, correctly supports the government's proposed contract – or has independent, overriding reasons for not striking – would be justified in not acting in solidarity with her colleagues.[157] If she *nonculpably* (but falsely) believes that the government's contract is worth supporting, then, though a free-rider, she has an excuse: her failure to support the strike, though mistaken, makes her a wrongdoer but not blameworthy.

Another important source of identification grounded in project-based roles is *citizenship*. Understanding the sense in which citizens can identify with one another on a basis other than cultural belonging or way of life is key, I believe, to the idea of, as it is often called, civic or social solidarity. It is often said that welfare state institutions, for example, are products of solidarity, or governed by a principle of solidarity, but it is just as often unclear what is meant.[158] If solidarity is understood as simply a willingness to share resources, or a commitment to social justice, then it is too unspecific. There are many instances of sharing resources that do not count as instances of solidarity, and identifying solidarity with social justice dissipates the theoretical and practical interest of solidarity as a value *distinct from* social justice. The distinctive nature of civic solidarity, however, can be preserved if we understand it as grounded in the identification of citizens with one another. But on what basis? The nationalist

---

157 On fair play, see note 153.
158 On welfare state solidarity and its relation to justice, see also Bayertz 1999a, pp. 21–6.

will say that the identification that binds citizens together is an identification based on a shared way of life. But there is another way that I want to defend here, that does not ground civic solidarity in identification rooted in *sharing a culture* but in *sharing authorship of a set of institutions*.[159] As in our other examples, the moral pressure to act in solidarity will depend on the presence of identification, but be ultimately derived from demands of fairness. On this view, solidarity *supports* demands of justice by grounding such demands in the nature of civic identification, rather than in general, natural duties to support just institutions. (I return to the relationship between justice and solidarity in the next section.)

Citizens who identify with their role as citizens conceive of their joint participation in reproducing, reforming, and authoring common institutions as providing normative orientation. The argument is an analogue of Bourgeois's case for solidarity as interdependence. Where Bourgeois emphasizes our myriad contributions, through work, to the joint social product, this account emphasizes a more fundamental contribution to the basic structure that makes our contribution through work to the joint social product possible in the first place. We recognize, as citizens, that it is not only through our state's official political acts – its legislative, executive, and adjudicative output – but also through our support of informal conventions and norms that we collectively author the basic institutions that both constrain and enable individuals' pursuit of the good life. When citizens identify with one another *as citizens* in this sense, they recognize that their ability to generate a marginal product of labor, or to invest in productive resources, and thereby to gain, depends on the contributions of millions of others in a complex division of labor that is backed by a set of basic social and political institutions.[160] They therefore recognize that their public, civic, economic, cultural, and political activity has a cumulative effect on the prosperity of the state as a whole, and are disposed to seek an understanding of how their coordinated actions impact on the prospects of other citizens. When things go well, their collective achievements as authors contribute to their own sense of well-being; when things

---

159 See also Stilz 2016.
160 I make this argument in the context of the global justice debates at greater length in Sangiovanni 2007.

go poorly, they perceive their own lives as less flourishing as a result.

While there is, of course, profound disagreement about the character and requirements of the values and ideals that underlie common institutions, citizens who identify share a readiness to define them through deliberation (and sometimes more open conflict); this process of reflection, deliberation, and conflict reflects a disposition to see common institutions as their own, as reflecting their collective deliberation and disagreement. Indeed, it is more often than not the characteristic lines and modes of *dis*agreement – rather than areas of consensus – that form the focus of identification among citizens. This is a direct result of the fact that identification is not, on this understanding, grounded in a shared culture or in a shared set of values, but in the exercise of shared agency as a people.[161] Citizens recognize that their peers come from multiple, sometimes only thinly overlapping cultural backgrounds.[162] Their attachment to common institutions is founded on what they *do* together, which defines, in part, who they *are*. (Note that nationalists have it the other way around: who we *are* should define what we *do* together.)

Solidarity becomes a demand of citizenship, then, when citizens recognize that sustaining and reproducing common social and political institutions requires commitment to overcoming, together, the adversity created by imperfect markets; legacies of racism, sexism, colonialism, and other forms of arbitrary exclusion and oppression; poverty and (especially work-related) illness; vulnerability to foreign interference, disruption, and economic dependence; pandemics; and so on. Solidarity also requires mutual trust, which, in this context, implies a tolerance for difference and a recognition that sustaining a common life requires respect for (sometimes foundational) disagreement, and a willingness to meet others halfway.[163] Solidarity, finally, demands a disposition to come to each other's aid in overcoming adversity, which, in this case, can be interpreted as a willingness to divide the joint social product fairly and in a way that recognizes the contributions of each to the functioning of the whole.[164] As

---

161 Cf. Jodi Dean's conception of reflective solidarity in Dean 1995, p. 123.
162 See also Miller 2017, p. 68.
163 On meeting others halfway, see the Introduction to Banting and Kymlicka 2017.
164 Recall Bourgeois 1902. For more discussion, see Kohn 2018.

before, there are two sources of rational pressure at work here. First, there is prudential pressure from our identification with the project; to fail to act in solidarity with others with whom we identify is then a failure of integrity. But there is also moral pressure from a sense of fairness: should citizens who identify fail to act in solidarity with others – by failing, say, to support policies that divide the social product fairly, or to be disposed to engage others with tolerance and respect, or to do their part in maintaining, reproducing, and reforming common institutions that are just or nearly just – they would not only be contributing to injustice but also free-riding on the efforts of others to maintain the public good.[165]

One might think my rendering of civic solidarity bears some similarity to constitutional patriotism.[166] There is a crucial difference. According to the constitutional patriot, what binds individual citizens into a people is a shared commitment to constitutional principles and values, such as justice and liberty – where, importantly, this commitment takes particular historical forms in different polities according to their specific histories and political cultures. By contrast, on my account, civic solidarity is based *not* on a shared affirmation of principles and values, but on the basis of a horizontal identification with other citizens (and, indeed, residents) for the role they play in authoring and reproducing common institutions. Often such shared authorship will involve a shared commitment to values and principles but it need not. As I mentioned previously, it is possible for there to be deep disagreement about which such principles and values ought to govern our cooperation; as long as there is a shared intention to continue political and social life together, and there continues to be horizontal role-based identification, commitment to overcoming significant adversity, dispositions to share one another's fate, and trust, then there is enough for civic solidarity.[167]

---

165 On conditions for fair-play obligations to apply, see note 153.
166 See, e.g., Habermas 2001; Ingram 1996; Müller 2007.
167 Cf. Levy 2005, p. 107: '[The inhabitants of a political community] are not what nationalists falsely claim co-nationals to be: members of some pre- or extra-political social whole that can make its will felt through politics … They are not the particular subset of humanity united by allegiance to some particular political ideal, at any level of abstraction; even if most people had sufficient political knowledge and sufficiently coherent views to qualify as holding an ideal, politics contain a perennial diversity of such

So far I have focused on *project*-based roles like medicine and citizenship. But there are also non-project-based roles that can provide a basis for identification and also, ultimately, solidarity.[168] I will focus on two. The first are *activity*-based groups like fraternities and sororities (such as the Alpha Kappa Alpha's), social and sporting clubs (such as a rowing club), and communal organizations (such as a masonic lodge). Most clubs and societies are not organized around a project but around an *activity* or set of activities. Membership in the society brings with it an organizing set of norms, expectations, rituals, and values that govern interaction within the society. I classify such groups as grounded, ultimately, in a *role* because the basis of identification is *participation* in the activities of the group. This is why identification – and by extension solidarity – is generally stronger among more active members. A good example of solidarity involving such groups is the mobilization of Alpha Kappa Alpha (AKA) sorors on behalf of a fellow sister, Kamala Harris. The AKAs (along with other Black sororities and fraternities) did an enormous amount of background work to get out the vote in the 2020 US presidential election. While Black (and feminist) solidarity undoubtedly played a large motivating role, so did sisterhood[169] (and so did, more indirectly, membership in *a* Black sorority or fraternity, whose founding principles go hand in hand with activism and anti-racism).[170]

The second are *relationship*-based roles. Being a parent, for example, is a role, though it is not based on a project: there is (except in very special cases) no project of parenthood which all parents take themselves to be participating in. Rather, parenthood is a social role defined by a position within a culturally inflected division of

---

ideals … There is no polity made up entirely of liberals or social democrats or civic republicans, and each of those is found in more than one polity.' The account of civic identification I defend in the text, which relies only on our role as collective authors, does not fall prey to this criticism.
168 I thank Siba Harb for highlighting to me the importance of making this distinction.
169 Where sisterhood is understood here as referring to members of a sorority rather than to women as such.
170 www.npr.org/sections/codeswitch/2020/11/09/933117256/in-harris-black-sororities-and-fraternities-celebrate-one-of-their-own?t=1611592108610 (accessed April 15, 2023).

labor (on this reading, even non-biological caregivers, for example, can be parents). And, of course, parenthood can be a powerful source of identification. Seeing someone, for example, struggling to keep themselves sane while trying, and failing, to balance work and family responsibilities can easily trigger each of the epistemic, affective, and normative components of identification we discussed earlier. And it can also provide a basis for acting in solidarity with other parents when the government cuts subsidies for childcare.

3.3 Condition and experience

In this subsection, I discuss identification based on *condition* and on *experience* together. This is because the differences between the two are subtle and often confused. To illustrate the idea of a solidarity grounded in shared experiences, I gave the example of *being a cancer survivor*. In this subsection, I change example to engage an important illustration of contemporary solidarity, namely the idea of *sisterhood*, or solidarity among women *as* women. Is sisterhood best grounded in identification with a way of life, set of experiences, condition, or cause? Answering this question will also show how our distinctions between possible forms of identification can be used for a normative evaluation of different conceptions of solidarity. This is relevant *inter alia* when we take the internal perspective of a group seeking to establish a 'we' as a basis for acting in solidarity: What forms of identification should provide the basis for our solidarity? Which ones shouldn't? (Note that there could be more than one ground – indeed, there could be, among different members, different and overlapping bases for acting in solidarity.) While I focus on sisterhood in this subsection, it should be clear that the account could be used to illuminate other examples, too.[171]

It seems uncontroversial today to assert that, given diversity among women, the basis for sisterhood should *not* be shared experiences

---

171 See Shelby 2009 for an account of how identification based on a condition (in our terms) rather than on a way of life or a set of experiences can ground a powerful form of Black solidarity. Cf. Gooding-Williams 2009, pp. 189ff, 238; Marin 2018. See also the illuminating discussion in Deveaux 2021, ch. 4, on how a shared condition (and shared understanding of that condition) can ground solidarity among the poor.

of womanhood. This has, by now, become a staple of the feminist literature: the experiences of Black, working-class, Egyptian, Irish, lesbian, trans women (including the intersections among any of these categories) will be vastly different – so different that it would be exclusionary and divisive to base identification and, in turn, a politics of solidarity on a canonical list of such experiences. Trying to come up with such a list will, more often than not, turn out not to represent something universal about women but something altogether more partial, namely the perspective of those privileged few who have the power and access to forge and disseminate the list as 'canonical' in the first place.[172] For many feminists, the response is to acknowledge (rather than repress) the radical diversity among women (including the ways in which race, class, sexuality, nationality, and gender intersect[173]), and to build solidarity on commitment to a cause.[174] According to bell hooks, for example,

> We understood that political solidarity between females expressed in sisterhood goes beyond positive recognition of the experiences of women and even shared sympathy for common suffering. Feminist sisterhood is rooted in shared commitment to struggle against patriarchal injustice, no matter the form that injustice takes.[175]

---

172 For seminal contributions on this point, see, among others, Lorde 2009, pp. 219–20; King 1995; Spelman 1988; Crenshaw 1990.
173 For a useful overview of recent debates on intersectionality, see Carastathis 2014. See also Collins 2019.
174 See, e.g., 'The Master's Tools Will Never Dismantle the Master's House', in Lorde 1984, pp. 111–12 and 'Difference and Survival', in Lorde 2009, p. 201.
175 hooks 2015a, p. 15. Cf. de Beauvoir 2012 [1949], p. 18, who writes, 'The proletarians have accomplished the revolution in Russia, the Negroes in Haiti, the Indo-Chinese are battling for it in Indo-China; but the women's effort has never been anything more than a symbolic agitation. They have gained only what men have been willing to grant; they have taken nothing, they have only received. The reason for this is that women lack concrete means for organizing themselves into a unit which can stand face to face with the correlative unit. They have no past, no history, no religion of their own; and they have no such solidarity of work and interest as that of the proletariat. They are not even promiscuously herded together in the way that creates community feeling among the American Negroes, the ghetto Jews, the workers of Saint-Denis, or the factory hands of Renault. They live dispersed among the males, attached through residence, housework, economic condition, and social standing to certain men – fathers or husbands – more firmly than they are to other women.'

Solidarity: nature, grounds, and value 83

Ending patriarchal injustice, on this picture, requires an acknowledgment that such injustice will take different forms in different circumstances, and that sisterhood requires coming to terms with the way that race, class, nationality, and so on, can divide and exclude women among themselves.

This way of framing the question raises a puzzle. If the best way to understand sisterhood is to see it grounded in commitment to a *cause* or *coalition* against injustice, then what distinguishes, if anything, solidarity among *feminists* and solidarity among *women*? After all, men can (and should be) feminists. Men can (and should) recognize the marks of patriarchal injustice and fight against it. Emphasizing a common commitment to fighting patriarchal injustice gives rise to a solidarity grounded in identification based on a *cause* (on which more below). But, once any kind of common experience (or common essence) is rejected as uniting women, what role is there for a politics of solidarity grounded in identification among *women*? What kind of identification, if any, ought to ground *sisterhood* among women *as* women?

Referring to critiques of the category *woman* as united by a set of shared experiences (of the same kind I mentioned above), Iris Marion Young writes:

> I find the exclusively critical orientation of such arguments rather paralyzing. Do these arguments imply that it makes no sense and is morally wrong to talk about women as a group or, in fact, to talk about social groups at all? It is not clear that these writers claim this. If not, then what does it mean to use the term *woman*? More importantly, in the light of these critiques, what sort of positive claims can feminists make about the way social life is and ought to be? I find questions like these unaddressed by these critiques of feminist essentialism.[176]

I mention Young at this point because I find her discussion of what might unite the type *woman* illuminating as a possible basis for

---

176 Young 1994, p. 717. See also Zack 2005, p. 7 and Alcoff 2005, p. 143: 'What can we demand in the name of women if "women" do not exist and demands in their name simply reenforce the myth that they do? How can we speak out against sexism as detrimental to the interests of women if the category is a fiction? How can we demand legal abortions, adequate child care, or wages based on comparable worth without invoking the concept of "women"?'

identification and solidarity among women as women – a basis that, in turn, promises to be less vulnerable to the diversity and exclusion critiques briefly alluded to before.

According to Young, women as a group form what she calls a *series*. A series is united neither by a set of intrinsic properties possessed by all members of a group, nor by a shared recognition of constituting a group, nor by a shared set of goals or experiences; it is united, rather, by a relation between persons and a set of socially conditioned material objects around which they orient their activity. The group of bus riders – who orient their activity around objects like bus stops, buses, and so on, and the norms, expectations, and patterns of behavior surrounding them – constitute a series. Similarly, radio listeners – who orient their activity around the radio and the norms, expectations, and patterns of behavior enabling and conditioning radio listening – are a series. And so are women. The primary material object around which women are expected to orient their activity is the sexed body. This is not the body understood as possessing a vagina, clitoris, breasts, and so on. Rather, it is the body as conditioned by social rules and expectations.[177] Young mentions menstruation, lactation, pregnancy, and childbirth as examples. Each of these activities is not just a brute biological fact but shaped by social practices that condition possible meanings and opportunities. The norms, expectations, and patterns of behavior surrounding the body, in turn, give rise to a range of further socially conditioned physical objects (such as clothes, cosmetics, tools, spaces, and so on), and hence further social practices. Together these reinforce two overarching social structures that position women as subordinate to men: heterosexuality (who desires and who is desired, who possesses and who is possessed) and the sexual division of labor (who does what, where, and how).

On this picture, women are those individuals marked out by the system of objects and social practices as occupying a particular position vis-à-vis men. The category *woman* is defined, that is, by

---

177 One might wonder here whether another exclusion is in the wings: what about trans women? But even in this case, one might argue, in defense of Young, that trans-women as women are also expected to comply with the social rules and expectations that have built up around the sexed female body. This threatens further forms of exclusion and subordination if they cannot meet those expectations. See, e.g., Hall 2009.

the relation of individuals to gendered social structures rather than by any intrinsic properties they share. Young is keen to emphasize that a particular individual's *response* to how the structure positions her/him will be as variable as you like. Some will resist and challenge the positioning and expectations, others may internalize them, others will waver and become alienated. And, even more importantly for our purposes, some individuals' response to the structure will be further conditioned by other aspects of their circumstances, including race, class, nationality, sexuality, and so on. There is no expectation, then, that women's (or men's) particular experience of the structure will be the same. What *is* the same is *subjection* to the structure, which is reproduced through myriad daily interactions, characteristic scenarios, institutionalized forms of behavior, expectation, and habit, and so on.[178]

The analysis of women as a series also provides a possible basis for identification among women grounded in a *condition* shared by women: subjection to a subordinating gendered social structure. This does not imply, as we have seen, that women who identify in this way with one another have had the same *experience* of such subjection. Here we can draw contrast to identification among cancer survivors, which *is* based (we are imagining) on sharing a set of experiences. Identifying with others as a cancer survivor is identification that presupposes that others with whom one identifies have had cancer. The common experience is what motivates mutual sympathy, understanding, and an attempt to make sense together of that experience. But, as we have seen, making particular experiences the basis of identification among women is unnecessarily exclusionary, given the wide diversity of ways in which women experience their subjection to a gendered social structure. Identification based on *condition* promises to avoid these problems. Subjection to an oppressive social structure is like subjection to a system of law: two different individuals can be subject to the law – can be addressed by the system – without experiencing the weight of the law in the same way.[179]

178 Cf. Haslanger 2012, p. 239.
179 Cf. Haslanger 2012, p. 239: 'So women have in common that their (assumed) sex has socially disadvantaged them; but this is compatible with the kinds of cultural variation that feminist inquiry has revealed, for the substantive

Notice that I shifted above from speaking of the concept *woman* (in my elaboration of Young's account) to the possibility of identification among women as women. The two ideas can come apart. One may, indeed, come to believe – as many feminists do – that there is *no* unified concept *woman*, or that the concept is unified, but not by the idea of oppressive subjection to a gendered structure. It would still be possible, on the picture I have drawn, to identify with other women who *are* oppressed by the gendered system on the basis of their shared condition.[180] There is, that is, no necessary congruence between the concept *woman* and the basis for identification among women. To illustrate: suppose you believe it is *possible* for there to be *non-oppressed* women – women who are not subordinated vis-à-vis men.[181] It is, on this view, not a necessary part of being a woman that one is oppressed. It might nonetheless be true that, in *our* world, all women are (contingently) oppressed, and come to identify with each other on that basis.[182]

An intersectionality theorist may object that it is a mistake to say that there is a *single* gendered social structure. Each person, depending on their circumstances, is addressed by the gendered social structure in a fundamentally different way – so different that there is no sense in speaking of it as a single system. A Black woman's body, for example, will be gendered and positioned vis-à-vis men in different ways than a White woman's body, the body of a working-class woman in a different way than an upper-class woman's, and so on. The objector concludes that it would be just as arbitrary and inevitably exclusionary to identify with other women, who are positioned so differently, on the basis of a common *condition* as it would be to identify on the basis of a common *set of experiences*.[183]

---

content of women's position and the ways of justifying it can vary enormously. Admittedly, the account accommodates such variation by being very abstract; nonetheless, it provides a schematic account that highlights the interdependence between the material forces that subordinate women, *and* the ideological frameworks that sustain them.' See also Alcoff 2005, p. 148.
180 On this point, see Mikkola 2007, pp. 375–80.
181 Cf. Stone 2007, pp. 160–3 on Haslanger. And see also Stoljar 1995, p. 281.
182 I thank Jude Browne for helpful discussion.
183 Crenshaw 1990, p. 1299; Spelman 1988, p. 167. See also Stone 2004.

This is, I believe, a difficult objection to meet successfully. In a Youngian spirit, one might respond to the objection in the following way: Just as it would be mistaken to say that an *employed* and an *unemployed* immigrant within a single society are subject to entirely different systems of law, it is a mistake to say that *White* and *Black* women are subject to entirely different gendered structures. Within a single society and system of law, employment law and immigration law are *interlocking* and *overlapping*.[184] To be sure, there is no way to understand how unemployment affects immigrant rights without understanding how immigration and welfare law *interact*. However, although the employed and the unemployed immigrants' legal rights will differ in basic ways (including their rights to stay, their right, in some cases, to access welfare, and so on), there are other ways in which they are addressed in the *same* way by immigration law (including their rights to access emergency care, their rights to appeal immigration decisions, and so on). Drawing the analogy, we can say that the same is true of Black and White women in, say, the US. While it is certainly true that Black women's bodies are positioned by the gendered social structure in different ways than White women's bodies, there are many dimensions of the gendered social structure that address Black and White women in the same way. The objects, norms, expectations, and practices of the gendered social structure address Black and White women, across many dimensions, *in common* (which is not to say that their *experience* of that subjection will be the same). That common subjection, the response concludes, can be a basis of identification among women *as* women, just as the common subjection to immigration law of an employed and unemployed immigrant can be the basis of their resistance to that law *as* immigrants.

I am not sure what to make of this kind of response, since it will certainly meet with the following counter: the response begs the question about whether there really is only *one* gendered system of subjection with different manifestations (analogous to a complex system of law with different parts), or rather many more such systems (analogous to different systems of law each with its own internally complex structure). Indeed, it is difficult to come up with examples

---

184 Cf. the Combahee River Collective on the interlocking character of oppression (Combahee River Collective 1983 [1977]).

that survive the objection: norms and practices regarding beauty, the sexual division of labor, the way heterosexuality is enforced, and so on, all *do* seem to address Black and White women differently (and upper- and lower-class women, and women of different religious backgrounds). One cannot, I believe, adjudicate between the two views by employing solely empirical criteria. Adjudicating requires asking: What is the *point* – politically, socially, and ethically – of insisting on one or the other reading? If one believes that the struggle for woman's liberation needs more solidarity among women *as* women, then one might be attracted to the Youngian view.[185] If, on the other hand, one believes that, historically, the call for sisterhood has been exclusionary, partial, blinkered, and divisive, and that it is more important to focus on fighting injustice than to seek an elusive common ground, then one will more likely opt for the intersectional–coalitional view. For our purposes, we need not come to a conclusive view; it is enough if we see how a politics of solidarity founded on identification among women on the basis of a shared condition (rather than a shared set of experiences, or a shared cause) *might* proceed.

We can now step back and, as in the other cases we have discussed, ask: Does identification based on a shared condition (or set of experiences) give us reason to act in solidarity? We need to consider two aspects of solidarity for a full answer. The first is whether and why identification on the basis of condition or experiences gives us reason to join together to overcome adversity. The second is whether and why identification on these bases gives us reason to come to each other's aid in the face of adversity. As before, I am not doubting that identification makes individuals *more likely* to join together to fight adversity and to come to each other's aid. I am asking whether this is more than an irrational bias toward those who are 'like us', whether, that is, we have any special, identification-based reasons to join together and come to each other's aid.

With respect to the first aspect, identifying with one another on these bases implies, as we have seen, that the set of experiences or condition has an important and guiding place in our life. It is an important part of who we are. So when adversity threatens, it

---

[185] Cf. Schor 1994; Riley 1988.

threatens us *as cancer survivors*, or *as oppressed*. We have, as a result, prudential reasons to join together to fight the threat. This is true even if we have no direct personal stake in a particular form of adversity (suppose, say, that some form of legal adversity is faced by oppressed members of our group in a different country), since our identification implies that we associate our own well-being with the well-being of the group. We are better off when and because all members of our oppressed group (or all cancer survivors) are better off. By fighting together, then, we protect something that we value together. As we have seen above with the Sioux and the doctors, we also have *moral* reason to join together to fight adversity when and because others have already begun to do so. If we stay back, we are free-riding on their efforts.

With respect to the second aspect, my identification with others, as we have seen, makes me more attuned to other solidaries' needs, and more emotionally responsive to their suffering. This makes it more likely that I will come to their aid in ways relevant to our common struggle. But does the fact that I empathize give me any moral reason to give their needs special attention? It strikes me that it does not.[186] Empathy attunes us, and so will make it more likely that we will aid, but it does nothing to give our solidaries' needs any moral priority. However, the fact that the shared set of experiences or a shared condition defines a socially salient group that defines who we are, and that structures and guides our life, gives us, in the same way as before, *prudential* reasons to aid others with whom we identify. By contributing to other members' good, I contribute to the good of the group, which is a key part, in turn, of my own good.

There is, however, also a closely related *moral* reason to do so, which is evident when we consider that the disposition to mutual aid characteristic of solidarity is also a public good. When we, as identifying members, are prepared to aid one another in the pursuit of our collective goals, we will be better able to overcome the adversity that threatens us. Mutual aid will also promote trust, which, in turn, will reinforce identification; mutuality creates, that is, a virtuous circle. Therefore, if I fail to aid others in ways necessary to accomplish

---

186 See also Jodi Dean's critique of what she calls 'affectional solidarity' in Dean 1995, pp. 116–17.

our ends, then I will be, as in the other cases we have discussed, free-riding on others. Others can criticize me for benefiting from a practice that is necessary for our success in overcoming adversity – a success that, as someone who identifies with others on one or more of our bases, I welcome and endorse.

So far we have discussed oppression as a shared condition that can form the basis of identification within a group. Another, more general, shared condition that is perhaps the most proximate to solidarity is sharing a *common fate* or *destiny*. We share a common fate when we have been thrown together by adverse circumstances. We have already seen one example: being in a train wreck together. In the next section, we will consider another: being prisoners of war together.[187] Rainer Bauböck provides a powerful case for thinking of solidarity within the EU as founded on sharing a common fate.[188] In the eurozone crisis of 2009–12, for example, the fate of Germany, along with all other eurozone countries, was inevitably tied to the fate of Greece. This was a direct result of the nature and degree of interdependence between European nations. Sharing a fate is a powerful basis for the sympathy, normative orientation, and mutual understanding that constitutes identification. This kind of case is proximate to solidarity because the basis for identification among those who share a fate is the fact that they each face the same adversity. If they organize to overcome it, are disposed to come to each other's aid in that struggle, and begin to trust one another, then their collective action becomes an instance of solidarity. The basis of their identification is, then, also the object of their solidarity.

3.4 Cause

Identification with others on the basis of a cause is the most straightforward of our sources. We identify with others on the basis of a cause when we each share commitment to that cause, and know that we all share it. Our mutual commitment provides a basis for

---

187 On common fate as a basis for social identification, see Brewer 2003, pp. 36–7.
188 Bauböck 2017.

mutual understanding, sympathy, and normative orientation as we try to work out the best way of promoting our cause.[189] Solidarity naturally emerges from such identification whenever our cause requires defense. We join together to promote our cause against the adversity that threatens it. 'I am a Berliner' is, for example, an act of identification with West Germans in Berlin on the basis of a cause. When conjoined with a commitment to share the fate of West Germans against Soviet expansionism come what may, and as a statement of collective resolve against the Soviet Union (embodied and realized via NATO), it also becomes an act of solidarity.

Note that identification with others on the basis of a cause is, while perhaps less durable, the least restrictive of our bases: we need not share a way of life, role, set of experiences, or condition to share a cause. Indeed, while sharing a cause can be the basis for solidarity, sharing a cause can also be a *product* of solidarity in each of our examples. When junior doctors, Blacks, citizens, the Sioux, and so on, band together to fight adversity, they promote a common cause together. In addition to identifying on the basis of role, experiences, condition, or way of life, then, those engaged in solidarity can also identify on the basis of the particular cause that has motivated them to action (to fight the government, overcome racial injustice, fight inequality, and so on). This provides a further ground for commitment, trust, and mutual aid that is lacking with those who identify, but do not join the struggle.

Identification on the basis of a cause also explains how members of outgroups can join in solidarity as allies with members of ingroups. When you join the junior doctors' strike against the government, though you are not a doctor, you act in solidarity with junior doctors; when you, as an Asian-American, protest injustice at a BLM event,

---

189 For an insightful account of solidarity grounded in this form of identification, see Scholz 2010. See also Kolers 2016, ch. 2, who argues that, although solidarity is 'not action taken for political ends but action taken on others' terms', it should not be confused with loyalty. Loyalty requires deference to the group *as such*, solidarity is deference to the group *in virtue of a deeper commitment to fighting injustice and oppression*. In our terms, then, Kolers' account of solidarity is an instance of identification, ultimately, with a cause.

you act in solidarity with Blacks;[190] and so on.[191] You do not act as a result of your identification as a doctor or as Black, or even as a result of an identification grounded in a shared fate, but as someone who identifies with a cause. While it would be reasonable for members of ingroups to be less trusting of outgroup allies,[192] trust can be won through being reliable and committed over time. As trust grows, so does the mutual sympathy, understanding, and coordinated normative orientation constitutive of cause-based identification.

3.5 Reasons to identify in the first place

So far, I have assumed that individuals identify in one or more relevant senses; I then explored when and why reasons of solidarity arise. We might wonder: Can there be reasons for identifying *in the first place*? If so, what kind of reasons are they? These reasons are best assessed by considering what is at stake when someone feels alienated from the way of life, role, set of experiences, condition, or cause that determines their membership in the social group. In this kind of case, we assume that one is already a member of the relevant group (either by choice, as in the medicine example, or nonvoluntarily, as in the racial group examples). We set up the question in this way because we are not asking whether there is reason to *adopt* a role, cause, or way of life in the first place, which would bring in independent concerns that are not relevant to our inquiry.

To see the variety of considerations in play, consider these possibilities:

> *Doctor* (role). Jane, though a doctor, does not take practicing medicine to have a very large role in her life, feels no particular emotional

---

190 See, for example, the Asians 4 Black Lives movement. They describe their aims here: https://medium.com/@asians4blacklives/asians-4-black-lives-uplift-black-resistance-help-build-black-power-b01ef091cc0c (accessed May 6, 2022).
191 As we have seen in sections 1 and 2, it is important that, for such outgroups to act in solidarity, the attitudes of mutual support, commitment, and cooperation have to be reciprocal. If joining the common action is unwelcome by those for whom one acts, then one cannot be said to be acting in solidarity.
192 On this point, see Gooding-Williams 2009, p. 190.

attachment to it, and does not put the enlarged epistemic perspective that comes with her skills and experience to any other use than in completing her day at work. She sees that medicine is a worthwhile activity, of course, but her attachment to the profession and to her fellow doctors *qua* doctors does not extend much further than that. It is a job. She does not do more than is strictly required by her contract, and she takes no interest in strikes and the like unless they have a narrow impact on her own life.

African-American (condition). Jerome, though Black, does not take being Black to be very important in his life, and he does not identify with other Blacks as Black. He finds the concept of race alienating and based on false beliefs about genetics and biology. He also does not find the idea that there is a Black culture plausible, and does not believe that focusing on a shared condition as 'oppressed' is very helpful as a basis for collective action. Indeed, he finds that the best way to overcome racial injustice is through a program of 'racial uplift' pursued via individual ingenuity, hard work, and grit.[193]

Environmentalist (cause). Kate has been an environmental activist all her life. But now she finds herself alienated from it as a cause. She has grown cynical; she believes that it is too late, since the world is warming too fast for anyone to make any difference. She severs her ties to all the environmentalist groups and activities that had been central to her life before today. She still sees that environmentalism is a worthy cause, but she now believes it is hopeless.

Catholic Worker (way of life). John has lost his faith. He was active in his faith, going to church, developing his understanding of the Holy Spirit, and so on, until now. He has a crisis of faith that leads him to stay away from church, to stop going to confession, to cease seeing his Catholic friends, and to no longer feed the poor and homeless at the local Catholic Worker. He also no longer shows up to Worker protests against racial injustice, war, and inequality. He feels guilty about it. He feels he should rediscover his faith and struggles to find a way back.

Cancer survivor (set of experiences). Larissa has breast cancer, which is now in remission. But she would prefer not talking about it with anyone. She feels that the pressure from other cancer patients to identify as a 'cancer survivor' rings false. She doesn't feel she has any

---

193 Jerome is loosely modeled on the Black conservatives described in Dawson 2003, pp. 281ff.

special attachment to others just because they happen to have had similar experiences in suffering a horrible disease.

What reasons might each individual have, if any, to identify? There may be, to be sure, *prudential* reasons. It may be the case, for example, that it would be good for Jane, Kate, Jerome, John, and Larissa to reorient their lives affectively, normatively, and epistemically in light of their shared role, way of life, and so on, and to identify with others on that basis. Their life might be more flourishing as a result. Whether or not they have such reasons will depend on the further circumstances of their life, and there is little in general that we can say. There may be general prudential reasons, of course, for any human being to identify *with something* – given the profound role that such identification usually plays in a human life and given the nature of our sociability – but such general reasons will rarely play a role in motivating anyone in particular. But whatever prudential reasons apply, there is little further normative pressure – other than the proffering of advice – that we can put on someone on this basis.

It might be thought, given the personal and intimate nature of identification, that there are *no* non-prudential reasons to identify with other members. This is a mistake: there are, I will argue, sources of normative pressure on individuals to identify that do not come merely from prudential considerations. In evaluating each scenario, we must be attentive to both the reasons each takes themselves to have (I will refer to them as a person's *operative* reasons) and compare them to the reasons they *genuinely* have (a person's reasons as such).[194] In the case of Jerome and Kate, for example, the reasons for feeling alienated do not stem from purely prudential considerations about what would make their life go better. Rather, their alienation stems from either moral judgments about what justice requires or from pragmatic judgments about the best means to achieve given ends (or both). For example, Jerome agrees that Blacks are subject to racial injustice; he just has very different ideas about what might best promote the cause. These are his operative pragmatic reasons, reasons he takes himself to have about the best means to a given end. He may be wrong about this. If he is wrong, then he *does* have reason to identify with other Blacks as oppressed, since this

---

194 For this usage, see, e.g., Scanlon 1998, p. 19.

is the best way to achieve racial justice (which he continues to believe is worthwhile). Notice that it is much the same with Kate, the environmentalist, who takes herself to have pragmatic reasons to abandon the cause, but may be wrong about them, given her continuing commitment to stopping climate change. In each case, then, there can be non-prudential reasons for them to revise their pragmatic beliefs in a way that would give them reasons to continue identifying.

Jerome, unlike Kate, may also have moral reservations. He may feel that, even if he were to agree that racial solidarity is necessary to overcome injustice, most Blacks who identify with one another on the basis of their oppression do not merely have *different* ideas about the nature, causes, and consequences of racial injustice, but radically *incompatible* ones that would make their joint pursuit of justice impossible. Again, he may be wrong. Whether he *is* wrong turns on substantive empirical and moral questions about racial injustice and about the appropriate degree of toleration for disagreement within the broader group. If he is wrong on either account, then there is normative pressure on him to change his attitudes toward other Blacks. If he is wrong, then he has, that is, (genuine) reasons to be more empathetic, to do more to promote a common perspective on the causes and consequences of oppression, and to take the joint struggle against injustice more seriously than he is currently doing. If he does have such reasons, he also has, *a fortiori*, the same reasons to act in solidarity with other Blacks as we discussed above in standard non-alienated cases. Kate's situation is analogous: she may also have moral reservations about identifying with other environmentalists on the basis of the cause if she believes other environmentalists have come to have radically incompatible ideas about climate change. And, just like Jerome, she may be wrong in her judgments.

To be sure, even if Jerome recognized the reasons to change his attitudes, this may not be enough to bring him to a full identification with other Blacks, just as it may not be enough to restore Kate to full identification with other environmentalists. Identification, as we have seen, has normative, epistemic, and affective dimensions. But all three together may not be forthcoming. Both Jerome and Kate could end up in a situation like John, the Catholic Worker. John believes that he has conclusive reasons to seek out and understand his fellow Workers, but he lacks the desire. He lacks the desire because he lacks the belief required for his faith. Although he sees that he has reason to believe, these reasons do not motivate him to believe.[195] He just can't quite summon the faith that is the foundation of his identification; without his faith, that is, he finds he no longer identifies with other Catholics in the normative, epistemic, or affective senses. In these kinds of cases, the person is divided against themselves. John may still be criticizable if he does not act in solidarity when this is needed and expected of him, given that he still sees all the reasons that support his identification as a Catholic Worker, and hence all the ways in which he still benefits from their activities.[196] This only *may* be the case, however, because it might also be true that, given the magnitude of his personal crisis, it would be unfair to expect more of him. He could be excused, as it were, rather than justified in his refusal.

But what if Jerome, Kate, and John were to entirely lose their interest in racial justice, environmentalism, and Christianity? What if, that is, they no longer took themselves to have reason to pursue any of these things? For all three, there would now be general reasons to identify that flow from natural duties to support justice-promoting endeavors. These are reasons, as we have seen before, that apply to anyone. It may be that Jerome, Kate, and John can best realize this duty by identifying with anti-racism, environmentalism, and Christianity, respectively. This might be the case because of their special, past connection to each of those groups – a connection that might make them more effective in discharging the duty successfully. But this is entirely contingent. It may be that, in virtue of their profound alienation, none should realize the general duty through the paths they once did; they would be *less* effective, were they to try. In that case, their energy would be better spent elsewhere. Or they may feel that they would justifiably prefer to discharge that duty in other ways, given their alienation. There is very little, I believe, that one could say if they chose to do so.

In assessing this more thoroughgoing alienation, does it make a difference that Jerome is a member of a *nonvoluntary* group (African-Americans), and Kate and John are not (environmentalists and

---

195 On the possibility of akratic beliefs, see Scanlon 1998, p. 36.
196 Cf. Miller 2017, p. 66 on 'as if' solidarity.

Christians)? Even though Jerome would gladly dissociate himself from Blacks as a group (since, recall, he believes that the concept of race is a vestige of a racist past that has no use today), he cannot do so. The way race is socially constructed prevents him from dissociating himself. Kate's (and John's) situation is different. When Kate ceases to believe in the environmentalist cause, and ceases to associate with other environmentalists, she ceases to be an environmentalist. The same thing is true of John (given standard understandings of Christianity). Leaving aside past ties that they have in virtue of their past memberships, they are now just like any third party. Does this difference in their situation make any difference to their respective reasons to identify? No. Note that fellow environmentalists, Christians, and Blacks are likely to feel let down by Kate, John, and Jerome. They will feel let down because they expect that those who identify as members of the group will continue to do so, since their contribution is needed for the success of the causes in which they participate. But these expectations, though understandable, do not, I believe, create any special normative pressure to continue identifying.[197]

Can identifying African-Americans rightly say to Jerome that he will continue to benefit from their collective efforts, in virtue of his being Black, in a way that Kate and John no longer benefit after they have abandoned environmentalism and Christianity? It strikes me that, once we ask this question, the grounds for fair play have shifted, with important consequences. In the previous scenarios, we were assuming that, were Jane, Jerome, and John to have recognized the moral and strategic reasons that applied to them, they *would have* come to identify with the members of their social group. Here we are supposing that, even were they to have recognized the moral and strategic reasons that applied, they still would *not* have come to identify. This is because, in our scenario, each of the three has lost interest in the cause *as such*. They might recognize the moral

---

[197] There is an old story that the women in Kant's village would set their clocks by noting when he passed by their houses on his evening walk. They surely have a reasonable expectation, given his regularity, that he will go out on his walk every night. They can justifiably rely on him to do so. But it would be absurd to claim that, should he decide to stay in one evening, he would be betraying their trust or otherwise letting them down. For this example, see Simmons 1996.

and strategic reasons as important ones for *others* who identify, but not themselves. In this case, if fair-play considerations apply, they must apply *not* in virtue of the benefits of *identification* but in virtue of other, more indirect benefits. The benefits to Jerome would come *not* from identification with a cause that he identifies with in principle, but from merely being Black; similarly, Jane and John benefit now merely as members of the general public. These fair-play considerations are much weaker because the benefits are narrower. To be sure, Jerome benefits *as Black*, and so more than a member of the general public. But still the benefit is indirect and no longer mediated by the structure of his identifications (and the reasons supporting those identifications). And so it is with John and Jane. They might, then, have general moral reasons to *support* collective efforts, but they now lack moral reasons to *identify*.

The cases of Jane (the doctor) and Larissa (the cancer survivor) are subtly different in virtue of the fact that the source of their identification is not as intimately bound up with struggles against injustice. With respect to Jane, does she have reason to identify with her fellow doctors? What kind of fault, if any, is her failure to do so? To be sure, she is less public spirited than her peers, and less invested in her profession. Prudentially, she may have reason to take more of an interest. Her public-spiritedness would also be praiseworthy in itself. (But is there really any requirement for her to be public spirited *with respect to her profession*? Wouldn't she be just as praiseworthy were she to show that spirit in other areas of her life?) Does she have any other reason to regret her alienation from her work? Once again, fair-play considerations are relevant. Her success in her profession – dependent on the flourishing of the profession as a whole – depends, it seems reasonable to assume, on more than doctors merely 'doing their job'. It requires doctors to be engaged in steering and guiding the profession and in maintaining its ethical, professional, and administrative standards as well as adapting them to changing circumstances. A practice guided by a common project supported by doctors who identify with their role and with each other as occupants of the role makes everyone, including Jane, better off. Given her reliance on the profession as a project, it seems much less plausible for Jane (when compared to Jerome and Kate) to sincerely and correctly hold that those benefits are not worth the cost. Furthermore, it can't be argued that Jane, who has options to being a doctor, doesn't accept those benefits voluntarily.[198] Fair-play considerations give her reasons, if not obligations, to take her profession and its standards more seriously, to orient her work around those common standards, to seek out and engage other doctors on the project, and to do to her part in shaping them. While (objective) reasons to believe, desire, and act intrinsic to identification then apply to her, even if she were to accept them, she may still find herself alienated. In that case, she will be in a situation like John's.

Larissa's case is, I believe, different. Given her views about her own cancer, there is very little reason for her to identify with other cancer survivors (again, leaving aside any prudential considerations). She may benefit from the organizing work that other cancer survivors do, but her benefiting will be indirect. Here it is plausible for her to say that, though she benefits, the organizing work, while laudable, is not worth the cost to her of contributing. She does not rely on other cancer survivors' identification in the way that Jane relies on other doctors' identification.

The conclusion we should draw is that reasons to identify once alienation has set in are scarce. In one sense, this is as it should be: identification is an intensely private and intimate matter. It is through our identifications that we become who we are, or discover who we would like to be. It would be surprising if there were many sources of non-prudential reasons for identifying with a cause, role, way of life, set of experiences, or condition. Once again, this is as it should be: if there were too many reasons to identify – especially if we think of reasons to identify that extend beyond cases of alienation – then we would be quickly overwhelmed.[199]

3.6 Is identification a core condition?

So far, I have only discussed when and why identification can provide reasons to act in solidarity with others. I have not argued that such identification is paradigmatic of solidarity; for all I have said so far,

---

198 On the role of voluntariness in fair play, see note 153.
199 See Viehoff forthcoming for a lucid account of the way in which we would be overwhelmed if the demands of solidarity were to come from too many sources.

it could be that there are core instances of solidarity that are not grounded in any kind of identification. In this subsection, I want to suggest that identification on the basis of one or more of the grounds discussed characterizes all core cases of solidarity.

The argument proceeds by trying to find the most likely cases of solidarity *without* identification. It strikes me that the most plausible such test case is the following. In summer 2020, Jeff Bezos posted a message of support for BLM on the Amazon website, followed by an e-mail exchange in which he defended his decision against an angry customer (who, in a familiar refrain, claimed that all lives matter, not just Black lives). Did Bezos act in solidarity with BLM? Let us suppose that the BLM movement (or the vast majority of its adherents) welcomed the message (so there is no question of symmetry), and would come to Bezos' aid should he need it in ways related to the joint effort. But let us further suppose that Bezos is cynical in his support: he does not really identify with the cause that BLM represents. He merely supports it because it will be good for business if people believe he is sincere. He will, as a result, be willing to sacrifice narrow self-interest where this will be public and serve to prove his sincerity, and be willing to pay some short-term reputational costs to secure the long-term advantage as he sees it. We might imagine that this was the case when he wrote the response to the angry customer. Suppose, finally, that his gamble fails, so that he ends up *hurting* his business even in the long run. From the outside, it will be impossible to tell whether he is sincere or not; he is effective at masking his operative reasons; and indeed it looks particularly plausible that he is sincere, since his gamble has failed to pay off. In this case, he does everything that an identifying participant in the movement would do, but for cynical reasons. Did he act in solidarity? No. Genuine identification is paradigmatic, whether it be identification with a cause, role, way of life, set of experiences, or condition.

But, one might wonder, isn't it possible to act in solidarity with others – by meeting conditions 1 to 4 from section 1 – but *fail* to identify with other solidaries on *any* basis? To be sure, one might think, acting in solidarity *usually* goes along with identification on the basis of a cause, role, way of life, condition, or set of experiences, but this need not *always* be the case. Take John, the Catholic Worker. He believes he has reasons to identify with other Catholic Workers on the basis of his faith and his commitment to faith-based justice, but he feels alienated. He has lost his faith and hence his enthusiasm regarding Worker activities. But suppose he still shows up, trusts the others to do their part, maintains his disposition to aid fellow Workers when necessary, and so on. Or suppose there is someone, Paula, who meets conditions 1 to 4 for a given struggle against adversity – the Catholic Worker, or BLM – but doesn't take that struggle or its group-based causes to be very important in her life; she lacks the normative, epistemic, and affective orientation toward the struggle or other participants that is intrinsic to identification.

These are limit cases that show something important: cases of solidarity that do not involve any identification are hard to come by. It strikes me that John's case *can* be classified as an instance of solidarity precisely because he sees he has reason to identify, even if he can't bring himself to actually identify. It is the exception that proves the rule. If we suppose that Paula in addition to failing to identify also sees no reason to identify with other participants in the struggle, then it strikes me as less plausible to say that she is acting in solidarity. Indeed, we may reasonably wonder why she goes out of her way to participate in the group's activities, given that she *doesn't* identify. She may say that she does so because justice requires some action, and this is the group whose struggle she has adopted, but any other group would have done just as well. If this is the case, I think we have reason to doubt whether she is truly acting in solidarity, or just in support of a worthy cause. Indeed, if other members knew of her reasons, they might also have reason to doubt her commitment. But even if we resist this conclusion, we can grant that the case is unusual, and seems indeterminate precisely because it only *partially* satisfies the paradigmatic conditions.

3.7 Sharing interests or values

One might reasonably wonder, at this point, why I haven't mentioned shared *interests* or *values* as potential grounds of solidarity.[200] The

---

200 Cf. Feinberg 1974, p. 234, who argues that a strong community of interest is a necessary condition. The idea of sharing interests and values is ubiquitous in the recent literature on solidarity. See, e.g., Bayertz 1999a, p. 8, who mentions shared interests alongside shared convictions, feelings, and history.

reason I haven't is that they don't strike me as precise enough to warrant inclusion alongside the other grounds I have discussed; indeed, any case of shared interests or values that strikes us as relevant can be captured more informatively by one of our other grounds. It is often said, for example, that workers' solidarity is grounded in their shared interests. Now, in one sense, this is true, but it does not really distinguish between interests shared in virtue of sharing a role, set of experiences, or condition. Sharing any of those further properties will give one shared interests, but they will do so in very different ways. Furthermore, if sharing interests as such can give grounds for acting in solidarity, and for identifying with one another, then it will become easy to confuse interest groups for solidarity groups. But interest groups – which are formed precisely to protect shared interests, such as the interests of consumers or pensioners – are not solidarity groups, precisely because they lack the identification among participants (e.g., affective, normative, and epistemic attitudes) and the willingness to share another's fate in ways relevant to the shared goal. Eliminating the idea of a shared interest as central helps, that is, to clarify things.

I hope it is clear that similar things can be said with respect to sharing values.[201] We might share all kinds of values, but that fact alone will not, except when one of our other bases is at play, normally give rise to identification, or, a fortiori, to acting in solidarity. Of course, sharing a *cause* or an *aim* will often reflect shared values, and I need not deny that. Furthermore, recall that, as we have seen, sharing values is not always necessary: people can act in favor of a cause they share, or act together to overcome significant adversity, even if on the basis of very different values or in the presence of

---

At a general level, Bayertz 1999a, p. 3 defines solidarity as containing a factual element – what he refers to as some 'common ground' (including shared interests, convictions, feelings, and history) – and a normative element – namely positive obligations to aid others. But, if this is right, then any special obligation, say, among friends, family, parties to a contract, and so on, would count as an obligation of solidarity. The definition also makes it unclear whether the obligations must be genuine to count as solidarity: does the common ground between members of a White nationalist party give them obligations to aid one another in their struggle?

201 Cf. May 1996, p. 44.

serious disagreement on values.²⁰² Failing to share values (or interests – think of privileged outgroups who identify on the basis of a cause) does not preclude solidarity.

4 Value

So far, I have discussed the normative specification of each of the variables in the general definition of solidarity. But we can also ask: Why and when does acting in solidarity have value?²⁰³

Solidarity will often, of course, have *instrumental* value. As we have seen, when we are moved by considerations of solidarity, the joint actions and institutions that are the focus and result of our action will be more stable and robust in the face of foreseeable obstacles and unavoidable setbacks. And, when the attitudes constitutive of solidarity are common knowledge, trust and therefore reliance among participants is likely to grow, as is their willingness to share one another's fates.²⁰⁴ This much seems uncontroversial. But does acting in solidarity have any *non*-instrumental value? I believe it does. Before we proceed, however, we need to be clear about what kind of non-instrumental value I will be discussing.

Sometimes the idea of non-instrumental value is associated with the idea that something must possess its value *impersonally*.²⁰⁵ If something is non-instrumentally good, that is, it must be good *simpliciter* – we are led in this way to imagine whether that thing

---

202 On this point, see also Miller 2017, p. 64.
203 Here I intend to explore the *non-specific* value of acting in solidarity. We might also wonder what the value of acting in solidarity in specific contexts might be, but that would vary according to the context, so I focus on the general case. Cf. Carter 1999, to which I am indebted.
204 David Miller lists a range of other instrumental benefits of solidarity in Miller 2017, pp. 66–7.
205 The *locus classicus* for this view is G. E. Moore 1993 [1903]. For an argument against the idea that there is such a thing as impersonal goodness, or goodness *simpliciter*, see Kraut 2011. Although I find the argument convincing, I need not be committed to it here. It is enough if I can show that solidarity is non-instrumentally good for us, and leave the question whether it is also good *simpliciter* aside.

would be good completely independently of any human interest – rather than good *for* someone or something. Furthermore, if something is good *for* someone or something then it must be good because it is *useful* for that someone or something: knives are good for cutting (by which is meant that knives are useful for cutting), flour for baking, arrows for shooting, nourishment for growth. Therefore, the argument goes, whenever something is good for something else, this must be because it contributes to it, and if it contributes to it, then it is a means to it. It makes no sense to say, on this view, that something can be *non-instrumentally* good *for* something or someone. When we say that friendship is good *for* us we must mean that it is good because of its effects on our flourishing or well-being or happiness. On this picture, friendship contributes to well-being as a means to an end, and so instrumentally.

But this is a mistake: things *can* be non-instrumentally good for us. The mistake lies in missing that something can contribute to flourishing without being a *means to* flourishing. It can simply be constitutive of flourishing. Water is good for a plant because it is useful: without it, a plant cannot flourish. But the vigor and growth of the plant is good for it not in the sense that it instrumentally contributes to its flourishing. Rather, its vigor and growth make their contribution constitutively: they are what its flourishing consists in. We can say the same for goods like love, pleasure, knowledge that reflects one's interests and passions, the appreciation of beauty, and health.[206] Each of these is good for us (when they are good for us[207]) not instrumentally, but constitutively. The presence of them does not lead to something else, namely our flourishing. Rather, our flourishing just consists in a certain arrangement of the goods of

---

206 I do not argue here for a substantive account of human flourishing as an account of well-being, which would take us too far afield. For such accounts, see Foot 2001; Kraut 2007; Thompson 2008. Other accounts of well-being, such as ideal-desire theories, are also compatible with the general account defended here.
207 All of these goods, that is, can sometimes be bad for us, depending on what else is true of our lives. Pleasure can sometimes be bad for us, just as love can. But when the conditions are right, each of these things makes their contribution to our flourishing constitutively. So, we might say, their value for us is conditional but constitutive. I say more about this below.

which it is made, just as something's being a statue just consists in a certain arrangement of the lump of clay of which it is made. Indeed, one way of showing that something is non-instrumentally good is to show that it contributes (constitutively rather than instrumentally) to our flourishing. This is what I will argue about solidarity: solidarity is non-instrumentally good, but it is non-instrumentally good *for* us, by which I mean that, in the right conditions, solidarity makes our life better.

Suppose that we will surely die at the hands of our oppressors. Do we simply let ourselves be killed, or do we die fighting together? Here our joint struggle has, let us suppose, no instrumental value whatsoever. It does nothing to promote our general cause, which is by now lost. We can even suppose that no one will ever come to know of our last battle against the oppressors. This kind of case serves to bring into relief the fact that, when we act in solidarity, we do not merely act so to *realize* the cause or to promote one another's flourishing. Rather, we act *for the sake of* each other and the cause. When I act for the sake of a cause or for the sake of another, my action is guided by more than just its instrumental significance to the realization of an end. My action is, we can say, *expressive* of my commitment both to the cause and to others; when I die fighting I manifest and make plain my double commitment. The question then becomes: What value does such expression have? Solidarity has non-instrumental value because the actions that are expressive of its constitutive attitudes, commitments, and sacrifices (conditions 1 to 4) instantiate non-instrumental values such as valor, trust, mutual commitment, and reciprocity.

The expressive account of the value of solidarity therefore shares a feature with a purely individual action of the same general kind. The non-instrumental value of an individual's struggle against some adversity can also, that is, be explained by the first expressive consideration just canvassed, namely the commitment to a worthy cause, and the valor required by its pursuit. But acting in solidarity adds another feature: in struggling *together*, we not only express our commitment to a worthy cause and the valor of our pursuit but also the worthiness of our commitment to sacrifice *for one another*. Our valor has non-instrumental worth, but so do our mutual commitment and the reciprocity that it brings with it.[208] G. A. Cohen characterizes exactly the kind of reciprocity I have in mind in this way:

> [In communal (or perhaps solidaristic would be more appropriate here?) reciprocity] there is indeed an expectation of reciprocation, but it differs critically from the reciprocation expected in market motivation. If I am a marketeer, then I am willing to serve, but only in order to *be* served: I would not serve if doing so were not a means to get service. Accordingly, I give as little service as I can in exchange for as much service as I can get ... A non-market cooperator relishes cooperation itself: what I want, as a non-marketeer, is that we serve each other ... To be sure, I serve you in the expectation that ... you will also serve me. My commitment to socialist community does not require me to be a sucker who serves you regardless of whether ... you are going to serve me, but I nevertheless find value in both parts of the conjunction – I serve you *and* you serve me – and in that conjunction itself: I do not regard the first part – I serve you – as simply a means to my real end, which is that you serve me.[209]

When I act to serve you, and you act to serve me, it is the *conjunction* of the former and the latter that has (non-instrumental) value, rather than merely the former in addition to the latter, taken separately. Again, recall the essentially relational character of solidarity: as a form of joint action, solidarity is made up of the symmetrical network of I–you relations and attitudes described above.

On the Cohen reading, the reciprocity constitutive of solidarity has value independently of its effects. But, leaving aside the other values instantiated by solidarity, *why* should we value solidaristic reciprocity *as such*? At first glance, one might think that the value of such reciprocity is exhausted by the fact that it contributes to the achievement of goals that would otherwise be unreachable. But I think Cohen is right to suggest that there is something more (although he does not explore what it might be).

---

208 See also Zhao 2019, pp. 12–13 who argues that solidarity is non-instrumentally good because it expresses an 'attitude of community' toward others. Bommarito 2016, similarly, argues that solidarity can be non-instrumentally valuable when and because it not only 'manifests concern for others' but also aids in the development of such concern through habit and re-enactment.
209 G. A. Cohen 2009, pp. 42–3.

To unpack why solidaristic reciprocity has non-instrumental value, it is instructive to return to the history of solidarity. Recall the role that solidaristic reciprocity plays as a counter to the fragmenting, divisive, and alienating forces unleashed by the rise of modern industrial societies. The anomie, isolation, and market egoism of modern society destroys the quality of traditional civic and social relations. Solidaristic reciprocity, it is hoped, could serve to replace the old ties with new ones. Solidaristic reciprocity becomes, then, not just a means of realizing objectives that we would otherwise be incapable of achieving, but also constitutive of a new kind of social unity among strangers – a unity grounded in a sense of collective resolve and joint responsibility. This social unity has, at its core, a common recognition that our individual flourishing inevitably depends on the actions of myriad others in an extensive division of labor, and hence that the flourishing of all is necessary for the flourishing of each. This aspect of solidarity is evident, as we have seen, in each of the main sources of our thinking on solidarity, namely solidarism, socialism, liberal nationalism, Christianity, and the social movements of the twentieth century.

We can deepen this account of social unity by considering it in light of Rawls's discussion of a well-ordered society as a social union of social unions. In those passages, Rawls draws a distinction between what he calls private society and social union.[210] Private society is the society established by the pursuit of self-regarding ends organized by common rules that work to the benefit of everyone. Market society is a paradigm (as is Hegel's notion of civil society). The value that marks such cooperation is efficiency: by following common rules, everyone is able to do better for themselves than they would have otherwise. Each actor views the scheme as a way of getting the best outcome for themselves. Cooperation is purely instrumental. In a social union, by contrast, participants see common rules as establishing the basis for a shared project in which each contributes to a collaboratively achieved and valued end. This end, Rawls says, is valued for its own sake. Examples include games, where the shared end is a 'good play of the game', as well as the arts and sciences, where the collaborative ends that are the

---

[210] Rawls 1999, pp. 456–79.

product of the shared activity are complex and articulated over many generations.

The shared ends have non-instrumental value, but, Rawls argues, so does the very cooperation involved in producing and reproducing the activity that sustains those ends. The cooperation itself is non-instrumentally valuable because and insofar as it allows us to participate in the complementary excellences of others. Because of the complexity of all worthwhile human endeavors, no one person can realize all of the excellences of all of the valuable activities open to us. We must choose which excellences to develop over a life. In seeing our shared ends realized through the mutual learning, coordination, and adjustment of our talents and abilities with those of others, we rightly[211] take pleasure in the complementarity of our talents. We take pleasure, that is, in the fact that everyone's good is affirmed by the contribution of each, and in the fact that our cooperation permits the realization of activities that could never have been realized by any one of us alone.

But there is another aspect to the value of cooperative activity (one not noticed by Rawls). It strikes me as uncontroversial that the value of truly joint activity is *conditional* on the ends having some value. But it would be wrong to conclude that, therefore, we value the activity required to produce the ends merely instrumentally. Hume gives us an apt example in the case on the individual: we do not value simply attaining the solution to a difficult mathematical problem; we also relish the difficulty of thinking through and solving the problem ourselves. We face and overcome a challenge; we rightly take pleasure in the exercise of the capabilities that enable us to solve the problem.[212] Our agency is reflected, invested, and embodied in both the work and the solution; the work and the solution represent not only our skill but also the deeper values and commitments that led us to it; we see *ourselves* in them. Our knowledge of the solution, though valuable as an end, would not have the same meaning for

---

211 *Nota bene*: We take pleasure in the activity because of its value, rather than the other way around. The pleasure is a reflection of its value. We do not, that is, believe the activity is good merely because of the pleasure it gives us.
212 Hume 1978 [1793], pp. 449–52. See also Frankfurt 1999, pp. 90–1; Owens forthcoming.

us were it simply given to us. The working through therefore doesn't have merely instrumental value, but also *non-instrumental* value. The non-instrumental value of the activity is, however, *conditional* on the value of the end.[213] If the end were trivial or uninteresting or otherwise not worth pursuing, then the activity – challenging though it might be for us – would be *much less* non-instrumentally valuable than when it is in the pursuit of something interesting or truly difficult.

We can clarify the structure of this argument with the idea of an organic unity. An organic unity exists whenever a unified whole – a whole, that is, that possesses more structure and internal complexity than a mere collection of items – has a value that is greater than the sum of the values of its parts taken independently. Knowledge of the stars, for example, has (non-instrumental) value; it is, in our terms, good for us for its own sake. And so does the ardent pursuit of knowledge for its own sake. But notice that the latter would be much less good for us were it to lead to *ignorance* and *falsehood* or were it directed to knowledge that is *trivial*; by contrast, the value of the pursuit is immeasurably heightened when it leads to *genuine* knowledge that is also *significant*.[214] Furthermore, the knowledge alone would be less good for us if we possessed it *without* actively seeking or wanting to possess it (or, indeed, if we wished we didn't have it).[215] In such cases, the whole *ardent-pursuit-of-knowledge-where-the-knowledge-acquired-is-genuine-and-important* has greater value for us than the value of the knowledge itself (taken independently) plus the value of the ardent pursuit of knowledge

---

213 Cf. Korsgaard 1996, pp. 263–4.
214 I adopt here the conditional interpretation of organic unity distinguished in Hurka 1998. This account is different from the one recommended by Moore, where the value of the parts remains constant in an organic unity, i.e., where the *whole* is the carrier of (greater) value (G. E. Moore 1993 [1903], pp. 79ff). See also Nozick 1983, pp. 413ff. It is, however, important to note a significant difference between the account of value I have offered and the account in Nozick, Hurka (and Moore). For the latter three, the non-instrumental value at stake is *impersonal*; they are interested in the good *simpliciter*. For me, it is *personal*; I am interested in what is good-for-us. This is why I have used our *involvement* and *engagement* in the ends we pursue to explain the non-instrumental value of that pursuit.
215 For this point, see Parfit 1984, pp. 501–2.

(taken independently). And so it is with the Humean example we just considered. Solving a truly difficult and interesting math problem has (non-instrumental) value. Ardently pursuing a solution to a math problem also has (non-instrumental) value. But when the ardent pursuit succeeds, and is in the service of a truly challenging problem, the value of the pursuit is much greater than it otherwise would have been.

The truly joint activity of a social union has the same structure. The pleasure we take in our endeavor, as an activity, is the same as Hume's working through a difficult mathematical problem. But in social union, the activity acquires another, cooperative, dimension. We not only see our own individual skills, commitment, and values reflected in the work we do as individual participants, but we also see our skills, commitment, and values transformed and mutually adjusted through the you-and-me reciprocity discussed above. The working through is now on an entirely different scale. It is not, however, merely a matter of scale. Once our skills are developed and exercised collaboratively, we also begin to relish the mutual accountability to others that our collaborative pursuit requires.[216] We acquire obligations to others; we rely on one another; we begin to trust each other; we develop and apply standards to each other that are intrinsic to our activity and the norms governing it. The mutual obligations and mutual subjection to shared norms are welcomed as a reflection of our joint commitment to the ends we pursue together. When our cooperative activity is successful, we then rightly take pleasure in the realization of our *collective* agency: just as in the individual case, we see *ourselves* (as a unitary 'we') reflected in the outcomes we realize. It then makes sense to say that we not only identify with each other, but also with our successes and failures *as a group*.

It strikes me that solidaristic reciprocity has the same properties; indeed, solidaristic reciprocity seems like a paradigm example of social union. The mutual recognition at the heart of our identification with one another – whether as, for example, workers, citizens, women, fellow nationals, or human beings – triggers a demand to act together to overcome our shared adversity. In acting together, we realize the

---

216 For this point, I am indebted to Owens forthcoming.

force of our joint resolve, and rightly take pleasure in the commitment, complementarity, and trust that has made it possible for us to do much more than what any one of us could have done alone. At the same time, we see our collective agency invested and reflected in the activity required to realize our joint ends. We take pleasure in the complex exercise of those reciprocal, mutually adjusted, and mutually reinforcing capabilities that have enabled us to overcome forms of adversity that would have been impossible to overcome alone.[217] The collective activity of overcoming, then, just like the mathematical working-through, comes to have non-instrumental value. While this value is conditional on the worthiness of our ends, it is still valued for its own sake.

But, one might wonder, if solidaristic reciprocity has non-instrumental value, then does that commit us to saying that solidarity among the Mafia also has non-instrumental value? No. On the picture I have just painted, the non-instrumental value of the trusting, cooperative you-and-me reciprocal activity constitutive of solidarity is, as we have seen, *conditional* on the value of the ends it promotes. If the ends are wicked – as we are assuming the ends of the Mafiosi are – then the solidarity enacted to realize them becomes disvaluable as well. This goes for all forms of solidarity bent to wicked ends: racist groups, terrorist cells, xenophobic nationalists, and so on. While they count as forms of solidarity if all our conditions are met (and they *take themselves* to have reasons to identify with one another in overcoming some significant adversity), their solidarity has negative value. This is as it should be: imagine a world in which the Mafiosi disrupt an entire political order, and do so in solidarity, and a world in which they disrupt the political order, but without solidarity. Is the former in any sense better than the latter (though both are bad, all things considered)? If anything, it seems that the former is *worse* than the latter. Solidarity's non-instrumental value is *amplified* by whether it promotes good, or bad, ends: if solidarity's ends are good, then the non-instrumental value is all the greater;

---

217 Cf. the value of unity-in-diversity as discussed in Nozick 1983, pp. 415–16, where he argues that the degree of organic unity increases as a function of the internal diversity and complexity of an entity, on one hand, and its degree of unity, on the other. See also the instructive discussion of the unity of value in Wenar 2023.

if they are bad, then its non-instrumental value is all the worse.[218] Solidarity in the service of a valuable end is an organic unity.

4.1 Comparison to justice

I want to close this section with a reflection about the relation of solidarity to justice – a reflection that will, at the same time, also allow us to highlight the distinctiveness of the concept I have outlined.[219] Solidarity is both broader and narrower than justice, whether we understand justice as the domain of institutional morality (as, for example, Scanlon does[220]) or of enforceable duties (as Kantians usually do[221]). It is broader in five senses. First, it can involve reasons to act that may be neither enforceable nor institutional; indeed, sometimes we may have reasons to act in solidarity with others that, while pre-emptive of a wide range of lower-level concerns, are

218 Many thanks to Juri Viehoff for discussion on this point. I note that if solidarity's ends are neutral, this does not mean that it has no non-instrumental value (we do not multiply by 0); rather, we say that the solidarity *does* have non-instrumental value – value that is neither amplified nor reduced by the further goodness of its ends. This may be the case, for example, in many team sports, where we assume, for the sake of argument, that there are no further positive or negative ends promoted by play of the game, but where players on a team exhibit all the characteristic features of solidarity.
219 As will be evident in a moment, my view of the distinction between justice and solidarity is different than Klaus Rippe's, for example, who writes: 'A look at the modern classics of liberalism (such as Ronald Dworkin or John Rawls) appears to confirm [that solidarity is not a part of liberalism]. Justice, and not solidarity, individual rights and not social ties or mutual obligations are the central themes of such theories' (Rippe 1998, p. 355). I do not believe it is accurate to say that liberalism is not concerned with social ties or mutual obligations. See, e.g., Part III of Rawls 1999 and Dworkin 1986 and Dworkin 2000 on 'liberal community'. That said, it is true that liberals have not had much to say about solidarity as a value, other than to note its role in providing a motivation to abide by principles of justice. As I have argued throughout, solidarity is a value that is not only important in understanding the motivational bases of egalitarianism or the welfare state, but also as a central aspect of non-state associations, such as social movements. On this point, see also Laitinen and Pessi 2015, p. 19.
220 Scanlon 1998, p. 6.
221 See, e.g., Ripstein 2009.

not obligations. Think, for example, of the way calls for solidarity in many social movements – especially where action may be dangerous – entreat one to participate but do not require it as a duty.

Second, there are many cases where solidarity demands more than merely justice. Justice may often allow us to act in ways that solidarity would not. Justice, for example, may permit you to fire someone who has not done their job well. But solidarity may (noncoercively) demand that you do otherwise, especially if the person in question (let us assume they are well-off and have options on the job market) has been a committed and loyal member of the firm and has gone above and beyond the call of duty in times of adversity. Your identification with them on the basis of a project-based role, and your mutual commitment to sharing one another's fate, gives you reason to refrain from firing them, even though it would be fully permissible at the bar of justice to do so. Or, consider Britain's decision to exit the EU. Here we may say that there is no *justice*-based reason for Britain to remain (as long as its divorce from the rest of the EU is concluded on fair terms). But there may be reasons of *solidarity* for Britain to stay in, especially given the string of refugee and financial crises of the past few years, and given the trust, commitment, and willingness to share Britain's fate that the rest of Europe has displayed since its accession to the EU.[222]

Third, solidarity and justice may pull in opposite directions.[223] Solidarity, for example, might demand that, as a judge, we give special consideration to members of one's own (say, oppressed) group, whereas the impartial demands of our office may prohibit it. In cases like this, it seems plausible to argue that justice should take priority, and so the demands of solidarity are not morally binding. But there are other cases where we may be more torn. Solidarity may, for example, demand that we stand by our solidaries in self-defense, even if they are in the wrong. Here it may be unclear

---

222 Of course, as we have seen in section 3, to make the case that the UK has solidarity-based reasons to remain would also require showing that they have reasons to *identify* with the EU on the basis of, say, a shared project (recall that they may have such reasons, as a normative matter, though they fail to recognize them).
223 Van Parijs forthcoming makes a similar point.

what is the right thing to do; there may be no way to act that leaves us without moral loss.[224]

Fourth, there are cases where solidarity may aid in making the application of justice more *determinate*. Here solidarity expresses what we might call (in a Kantian vein) the *internal* aspect of justice – the attitudes, relations, commitments, and structure of deliberation that ought to lie behind and support a sincere affirmation and realization of principles of social justice.[225] Focusing on the internal, attitudinal dimension of justice might, for example, allow us to describe a societal ethos in ways that mere attention to higher-level institutional principles would not. Illustrations are not hard to find. As a matter of justice, it may be unclear, for example, how much we may demand to do work that we would willingly do at lower rates of pay. Considerations of solidarity may make it evident in such cases that the leeway we are allowed is much narrower than mere attention to the principles themselves might have led us to believe.[226] Our identification with one another as members of an organization, and our recognition of the support our organization has been willing to give us in the past, may, that is, gives us additional project-based reasons not to get as much as we can when at the bargaining table. Another example is the following. It may be the case that it is indeterminate, according to justice, whether we, as Northern Europeans, ought to send monetary compensation to receiving states in Southern Europe in the midst of a refugee crisis, or whether we ought, instead, to open our borders to relieve the pressure. Considerations of solidarity – of what sharing another's fate requires in the midst of crisis and suffering, especially in light of our identification with one another as participants in a worthy supranational project – may make it clear that justice, rightly understood, requires us to do the latter and not the former.

---

224 See, e.g., Williams 1965.
225 In Habermas 1990, p. 244, Habermas argues that solidarity is the 'reverse-side' of justice, by which he means that the deliberatively designed moral point of view cannot give determinate results, or be sustainable, without an 'intersubjectively shared form of life' that underlies it. See also Pensky 2009.
226 Cf., e.g., Cohen's incentives critique in G. A. Cohen 2008, and see in particular responses by Shiffrin 2010; J. Cohen 2001.

Fifth, solidarity can be seen as a crucial *motivating* factor in realizing principles of justice. One might say, for example, that identification with others on one or more of the bases we have discussed gives people reasons to engage in justice-promoting collective actions that are independent of justice. In such cases, reasons flowing from identification with others can reinforce reasons of justice.[227] (Of course, this is not to deny, as we have seen, that the two can also run in opposition to one another.) If we identify with one another on the basis of shared roles, conditions, experiences, causes, or ways of life, we will then be more likely to set aside self-interest in securing what justice requires for each one of us. Returning to our discussion of role-based identification among citizens, identification secures the resilience, robustness, and determination of a political community even when there is profound disagreement regarding what justice requires as well as broad and deep ethnic and cultural diversity. Where and when we identify as authors of common institutions, we are less likely to feel alienated from political life, or to feel that politics does not affirm and include our good.

Seen in this light, solidarity need not be as exclusionary as it is sometimes claimed to be.[228] We have already seen how, even within a single political community, solidarity can be grounded in what we together *do* rather than in who we *are*.[229] In the discussion of sisterhood, we have also seen how the danger of exclusion has been confronted from *within* an ethic of solidarity among women as women. We must also remember that solidarity, while it does require special concern among those with whom one identifies, does *not* require an 'us' and a 'them'. Solidarity requires *adversity*, not *opposition*. For example, a truly cosmopolitan solidarity could be grounded in our mutual exposure to climate change, where mutual exposure counts as a condition that we all share, and on the basis

---

227 See also Rawls 1999, pp. 90–3, who argues that the reverse of what I have suggested is also true: organizing a society according to principles of justice will likely promote solidarity, since people will be see that no one in the society gains at the expense of others. Solidarity and justice, on this picture, are mutually reinforcing.
228 Cf. Levy 2005.
229 See also the powerful account of plantation politics in Gooding-Williams 2009, pp. 186ff.

of which we can identify with one another.[230] A wider and more encompassing cosmopolitan solidarity could, furthermore, be based on our role as authors of international institutions or as contributors to an international division of labor that reinforces rather than alleviates inequality. Solidarities at different levels, finally, can be mutually reinforcing rather than mutually exclusive: our narrower solidarities can be marshalled in support of our broader ones, and our broader ones can contribute to the flourishing of our narrower.

Solidarity is, however, also narrower than justice. There are two ways in which it is narrower. First, duties of justice may arise between individuals who share no identification with one another (and no reason to identify) and create no further demands to join in collective action. Negative duties of justice provide an example. I have argued that demands of solidarity, on the other hand, only ever arise in the presence of identification. Reasons to act in solidarity, that is, must be grounded in identification with others on the basis of a cause, role, condition, set of experiences, or way of life. But, as we have seen in section 3, if one does not *already* identify with others on one or more of these bases, there is very little non-prudential normative pressure that we can put on another to identify. This should not be surprising: the normative, epistemic, and affective degree of

---

230 See, for example, Straehle 2010; Gould 2007, defending cosmopolitan and transnational forms of solidarity, and for a response Lenard 2010. Cf. Rorty 1989, p. 192. See also Munoz-Dardé forthcoming, defending the idea that solidarity essentially involves an 'us' against a 'them'. Wiggins, in an unconventional discussion of solidarity, treats it as the 'root of the ethical' (Wiggins 2006, pp. 244–7). Although he does not define it, he treats solidarity as the disposition to recognize another as a separate, embodied, feeling subjectivity against whom one feels it is impossible, without much resistance, to do certain things (for example, 'wilful killing'). This 'ethic of solidarity' is used by Wiggins to undermine simple forms of maximizing consequentialism. As a disposition oriented to others as human, solidarity, on this view, has a scope that extends to all human beings (if not animals that display similar sorts of subjectivity). In our terms, it is closest, perhaps, to the idea of identification with others on the basis of a condition. But because his discussion is not trying to capture the descriptive, normative, historical, or evaluative dimensions of the social and political practices in which the term has predominantly figured, I don't think it competes with any of the views discussed in this essay.

commitment required by solidarity far outstrips what is required
– *by way of our attitudes rather than our actions* – to meet the
demands of justice. The nature of our identifications is intimate and
personal, precisely because such identifications in large part define
who we are (and how others see us).[231] In principle, it is possible,
as Kant noted, for us to comply with the demands of justice whatever
our internal attitudes toward that compliance are. Not so with
respect to solidarity, where the attitudes are essential. This makes
solidarity a rare, but also precious, public good.

Second, solidarity has much more descriptive content than justice.
Justice most often refers to a set of *principles* that applies to institutional settings. Solidarity refers to a set of *practices* with normative
and evaluative significance. If the account that I have offered is
correct, it refers to a distinctive way of *acting together*. As we have
seen, on some views, the concept of solidarity is treated as *thick*,
as combining both evaluative/normative and descriptive elements.[232]
This is the case, for example, if one believes that for two or more
individuals to act in solidarity, the actions and attitudes involved
must either be morally permissible, morally required, or good in
some other way. On the view I have defended, by contrast, the
concept of solidarity can be deployed in normatively and evaluatively
neutral ways. Recall, for example, that though we can rightly say
that the Mafiosi act in solidarity, their solidarity lacks value. Whether
something is or is not solidarity, and whether it is good, are, on my
view, two separate questions. But on either view, the concept's
descriptive content goes far beyond the content of justice as a concept,
which is, indeed, usually treated as *thin*.

As I mentioned in the introduction, solidarity therefore lies within
the wider class of what we might call *associational* ethics – the
ethics of life in associations and within social relationships that
extend beyond relations among intimates.[233] Other members of the
class of associational ethics include the ethics of larger social and

---

231 This is an important theme in Viehoff forthcoming.
232 On thick and thin concepts, see, more recently, Väyrynen 2013.
233 On the need for such an intermediate category, see also Fraser 1985 and
Honneth 1996, pp. 129–30, who situates solidarity as a form of symmetrical
recognition present within (modern) societal groups that are no longer
bound together by corporative, honor-based ties.

economic collectivities, such as corporations and social movements. This area has been much less studied than the ethics of family and friendship, on one hand, and the classical concerns of political justice such as the state, human rights, and international relations, on the other. By bringing solidarity to the fore, I have tried to suggest that it is a value that is worth studying more carefully in its own right and for its own sake.

4.2 Silent and passive solidarity

I now turn to an important objection that will allow me to clarify the overall account, and especially the role of the evaluative considerations that have been central to this section. Michael Zhao starts an article on solidarity with the following examples:

> A prisoner-of-war is secretly offered release by his captors, who know that his father is an important figure in the military. He decides to remain in captivity in solidarity with his platoon mates.
>
> A young girl is undergoing chemotherapy for leukaemia, which has caused her hair to fall out. Her parents and older siblings shave their own heads in solidarity with her. ...
>
> Marie is a young woman living in East Germany in the late 1980s. On the night of November 9, 1989, the Berlin Wall opens, reuniting East and West Germany after 44 years of separation. A group of young people from both countries have climbed atop the wall and spontaneously begin singing the *Deutschlandlied*, a song of German unity. Marie, watching from her own home, sings in solidarity with them.[234]

These kinds of examples may seem to pose a challenge to my account. In each of them, there is an action by an agent, but the agent is not acting together with others. There is no sense, it seems, in which the prisoner-of-war [POW], the young girl, or Marie are doing their part in some joint activity. But they are (except for Marie) symbolically sharing one another's fate. While not sharing anyone's fate, Marie signals her support for the cause, with which she identifies. If I am

---

234 Zhao 2019. See also Bommarito 2016, pp. 447–8, who argues that entirely private acts of self-sacrifice – in which someone symbolically shares another's fate by voluntarily giving up benefits that another cannot enjoy – can be acts of solidarity.

right about solidarity being a form of joint action, then what is there to say about such cases?

Let us take the POW first. I think there is an evident way in which his action does in fact count as a form of acting together. When he forgoes being freed, he is now in a position to stand with his fellow soldiers. He is now available for coordinating, overcoming resistance, and so on. He is doing his part in the joint activity of resisting the captors. He is also giving them strength by showing his willingness, and by strengthening their collective resolve. Indeed, from this perspective, maintaining resolve and fortitude in the midst of suffering is itself a joint action, in which they all participate and play their respective roles. Similar things can be said with respect to the young girl's family. Their symbolic action strengthens their collective resolve to fight, together, the cancer.

But now suppose that we bring the example closer in line to Marie. Imagine that the soldier's refusal to be freed will not be communicated to his platoon mates, that it will not affect the probability of the platoon's being freed, and this is known by the refusing soldier. His refusal will have no effect on the other soldiers, who all believe he has been freed. On this description, there really is no joint action. Like Marie's singing, there is no cooperation and no mutual aid.

These are, I believe, limit cases. On one hand, they do not fit well with the history of solidarity (none of the predominant traditions in which solidarity has figured takes such cases as significant). But, on the other, they do share some important features with the central cases we have been discussing throughout. There are two ways in which such cases are relevantly similar. First, they only make sense to us as instances of solidarity, I want to claim, *in the shadow* of nearby forms of possible joint action. The soldier's actions, *in the normal course of events*, would have formed part of a joint action; in the normal course of events, people like Marie are there to participate in the joint action. It is also germane here that the relevant action *takes the form that it would have taken* had the action been joint. For example, had Marie merely raised a glass to the supporters, or yelled out 'hurrah', the action would have been an instance of showing support, not of solidarity. Similarly, had the family merely commiserated with one another regarding the young child's condition, this commiseration would not have been solidarity. Without the shadow cast by a nearby joint action, such shows of support and self-sacrifice might be laudable but they do not count as solidarity. Solidarity requires us to stand *together*.

The second way in which the cases are similar is that they are instances of the same *expressive* value discussed in this section. In Marie's case, they express commitment to a worthy cause that is shared by others with whom she identifies. When she sings the song she acts for the sake of the cause and for the sake of others who act together to promote it, even if her own action does not promote it, and does not help anyone. In the soldier's case, the action expresses his commitment to his fellow soldiers, and his willingness to suffer alongside them. He acts for their sake and for the sake of the cause, even if his actions are futile. In this sense, they therefore share an important feature with paradigmatic forms of solidarity. What they lack, however, is the other feature of solidarity that makes its value distinctive, namely the non-instrumental value of investing our agency in forms of cooperation that aim at overcoming, in ways that no individual could do alone, weighty forms of adversity. Both actions do not play a role in a wider, collective action, they are not instances of overcoming adversity together, and there is no mutual aid. This is what makes them limit, or borderline, cases. The conclusion I think we should draw is that they are the exceptions that prove the rule: while we can classify them as instances of solidarity, if we want, we should not classify them as central, but as peripheral or incomplete, and as parasitic on the paradigmatic forms that we have discussed throughout.

Conclusion

In this essay, I have argued for an account of the nature, grounds, and value of solidarity. I end with a list of the main claims I have defended.

1. Solidarity is the name of a practice that has evolved since the early nineteenth century. My aim has been to introduce a concept that can capture the distinctiveness of the practice, and that can be used to develop normative and empirical conceptions of solidarity across different contexts. The account should be assessed, therefore, according to whether it (a) is useful in elucidating the practice and its development over the past

two centuries, (b) captures what is distinctive about solidarity compared to related phenomena, and (c) makes sense of what we find valuable and normatively compelling in solidarity. It should not be assessed by asking whether it tracks our linguistic intuitions.

2 Solidarity is a complex and distinctive form of joint action in which participants take themselves to have reasons to act together in virtue of identifying with one another on the basis of a way of life, role, condition, set of experiences, or cause.

3 Both *de re* and *de dicto* identification have three constitutive components: epistemic, affective, and normative.

4 Solidarity can be grounded in merely *de dicto* identification, and hence can extend beyond one's circle of intimates and friends.

5 Joint action of the relevant kind requires (1) an intention to overcome, together, significant adversity; (2a) a willingness to set aside narrow self-interest; (2b) a commitment not to bypass other participants' wills; (3) a disposition to share one another's fate; and (4) mutual trust.

6 One can understand the general concept of solidarity as a formula whose values can be fixed according to context. Depending on one's theoretical and/or practical interests, this allows for the development of both empirical/descriptive and normative/moral conceptions of solidarity.

7 The general concept of solidarity can be used to make sense of solidarity's history, and, in particular, to capture both the diversity and unity among five dominant traditions of thought and practice: solidarism, socialism, liberal nationalism, Christianity, and twentieth-century social movements.

8 Unlike fellow-feeling, solidarity, although grounded in forms of identification that have an affective component, is not itself an emotion, sentiment, or feeling.

9 Unlike mere support for a worthy cause, solidarity requires acting together to achieve ends that no one could achieve alone and a willingness to share other participants' fate in that pursuit.

10 Unlike charity or altruism, solidarity is symmetrical and omnilateral, rather than asymmetrical and unilateral. The account of solidarity defended here therefore departs from common usage, which is more permissive.

11 Unlike special responsibilities grounded in a sense of preexisting community, solidarity must involve acting together against significant adversity. Picking up my brother from the airport is not an instance of solidarity, even though I am discharging a special responsibility grounded in preexisting community, viz. the family.
12 While there are limit cases of solidarity that involve individual action that is not coordinated with others (recall: the prisoners, the POW), these only make sense *in the shadow* of nearby forms of joint action (e.g., where joint action would have been preferred but was not possible). They are therefore the exceptions that prove the rule.
13 My identification with you on the basis of a way of life, role, condition, set of experiences, or cause gives me both prudential and moral reasons to act in solidarity with you when adversity threatens. My identification reflects the fact that I value the relationship (grounded in way of life, etc.) between us. This gives me *prudential* reasons to join the struggle. But I also have *moral* reasons of fairness to join, flowing from what is required to maintain what is of value to each one of us.
14 Does someone who is a member of a group, but alienated from the way of life, cause, etc., that grounds the identification among members have reasons to identify? Of course, there can be prudential reasons, if such identification would make our lives better. There is also normative pressure to identify when our alienation is based on mistakes regarding the reasons we take ourselves to have. Given that identification involves affective elements that are not under our direct voluntary control, we might also be in a position where we see that we have reason to identify but fail to do so.
15 Solidarity has both instrumental and non-instrumental value. The non-instrumental value of solidarity has three components. (i) Solidarity instantiates the non-instrumental value of, *inter alia*, mutual commitment, where what is valued is not just my standing by you, or your standing by me, but the conjunction of the two. The value of this kind of mutual commitment is evident in thinking through cases in which we prefer struggling together against adversity than surrendering, even if we know we will be overwhelmed. (ii) Solidarity instantiates a form of

non-instrumentally valuable cooperation in which we each participate in the complementary excellences of all, and take pleasure in the collective realization of ends that none of us could achieve alone. (iii) When we act in solidarity, we also rightly take pleasure in the fact that we can see our collective agency reflected in our joint, coordinated, and beneficial activity; we can say, for example, not only that justice was done, but that *we* did it.

16 The non-instrumental value of solidarity is, however, conditional on the promotion of good ends. This is true of many activities that we value for their own sake. As Hume notes, we value, for example, the working-through of a difficult mathematical problem for its own sake, but we only value it on condition that the solutions we reach are worth reaching. If the solutions were trivial or boring, the activity would lack non-instrumental value. And so it is with solidarity: we value the activity in the ways specified in 15, but only if they promote good ends. This is as it should be: Mafia and terrorist groups may act in solidarity, but we are not thereby forced to say that their solidarity has non-instrumental (or instrumental) value.

17 Solidarity is both broader and narrower than justice. It is broader in the following five senses: solidarity (i) can involve reasons that are neither enforceable nor institutional; (ii) can require of us things that principles of justice alone would leave open; (iii) solidarity can pull in the opposite direction to justice; (iv) can sometimes be invoked to make justice more determinate; (v) can play a motivating role in complying with the demands of justice. However, solidarity is also narrower than justice in two senses. First, duties of justice may apply to individuals who do not identify with one another (and have no reason to identify with one another), and have no reason to join together in collective action. Negative duties of justice provide an example. Second, justice most often refers to sets of *principles* that apply in institutional settings. Solidarity, by contrast, refers to a set of *practices*. The concept of solidarity has, therefore, much more descriptive content than the concept of justice.

Solidarity is not just a fuzzy stand-in for diffuse feelings of togetherness, sympathy, or community. It is also not synonymous with a disposition to give to others in need. It is a distinctive social practice for an age anxious about its increasingly fragmented, unequal, and divisive politics, and hungry for forms of collective resistance that can right the balance.

References

Alcoff, L. M. (2005), *Visible Identities: Race, Gender, and the Self* (Oxford: Oxford University Press).
Alonso, F. (2009), 'Shared Intention, Reliance, and Interpersonal Obligations', *Ethics* 119: 444–75.
Arendt, H. (1990 [1963]), *On Revolution* (London: Penguin Books).
Arneson, R. (1982), 'The Principle of Fairness and Free-Rider Problems', *Ethics* 92: 616–33.
Ash, T. G. (2002), *The Polish Revolution: Solidarity* (New Haven: Yale University Press).
Banks, D. and R. Erdoes (2005), *Ojibwa Warrior: Dennis Banks and the Rise of the American Indian Movement* (Norman: University of Oklahoma Press).
Banting, K. and W. Kymlicka (2017), *The Strains of Commitment: The Political Sources of Solidarity in Diverse Societies* (Oxford: Oxford University Press).
Bartky, S. L. (2002), *'Sympathy and Solidarity' and Other Essays* (Lanham: Rowman & Littlefield Publishers).
Bauböck, R. (2017), 'Citizenship and Collective Identities as Political Sources of Solidarity in the European Union', in *The Strains of Commitment: The Political Sources of Solidarity in Diverse Societies*, eds. Keith Banting and Will Kymlicka (Oxford: Oxford University Press), pp. 80–107.
Bayertz, K. (1999a), 'Four Uses of "Solidarity"', in *Solidarity*, ed. Kurt Bayertz (London: Springer), pp. 3–28.
Bayertz, K., ed. (1999b), *Solidarity* (London: Springer).
Beyer, G. (2014), 'The Meaning of Solidarity in Catholic Social Teaching', *Political Theology* 15: 7–25.
Blais, M.-C. (2007), *La Solidarité: Histoire d'une Idée* (Paris: Gallimard).
Blum, L. (2007), 'Three Kinds of Race-Related Solidarity', *Journal of Social Philosophy* 38: 53–72.
Bommarito, N. (2016), 'Private Solidarity', *Ethical Theory and Moral Practice* 19: 445–55.
Bourgeois, L. (1902), 'Rapport de M. Léon Bourgeois au Congrès d'Éducation Sociale en 1900', in *Solidarité* (Paris: Armand Colin), pp. 159–88.

Boyd, R. (1991), 'Realism, Anti-Foundationalism and the Enthusiasm for Natural Kinds', *Philosophical Studies* 61: 127–48.

Bradley, M., J. Milner, B. Peruniak, and F. Crépeau, eds. (2019), *Refugees' Roles in Resolving Displacement and Building Peace* (Washington, DC: Georgetown University Press).

Brandes, T. H. (2021), 'Solidarity as a Constitutional Value', *Buffalo Human Rights Law Review* 27: 59–89.

Bratman, M. (2014), *Shared Agency: A Planning Theory of Acting Together* (Oxford: Oxford University Press).

Brewer, M. (2003), *Intergroup Relations*, 2nd edn. (Buckingham: Open University Press).

Brownmiller, S. (1999), *In Our Time: Memoir of a Revolution* (New York: Dial Press).

Brunkhorst, H. (2005), *Solidarity: From Civic Friendship to a Global Legal Community* (Cambridge, MA: MIT Press).

Calhoun, C. (2009), 'What Good Is Commitment?', *Ethics* 119: 613–41.

Cappelen, H. (2018), *Fixing Language: An Essay on Conceptual Engineering* (Oxford: Oxford University Press).

Cappelen, H. and D. Plunkett, eds. (2020), *Conceptual Engineering and Conceptual Ethics* (Oxford: Oxford University Press).

Carastathis, A. (2014), 'The Concept of Intersectionality in Feminist Theory', *Philosophy Compass* 9: 304–14.

Carter, I. (1999), *A Measure of Freedom* (New York: Oxford University Press).

Clark, M. (forthcoming), 'Transforming Interdependence into Social Virtue: Solidarity in Catholic Social Thought', in *The Virtue of Solidarity*, eds. Andrea Sangiovanni and Juri Viehoff (Oxford: Oxford University Press).

Cohen, G. A. (2008), *Rescuing Justice and Equality* (Cambridge, MA: Harvard University Press).

Cohen, G. A. (2009), *Why Not Socialism?* (Princeton: Princeton University Press).

Cohen, J. (2001), 'Taking People as They Are?', *Philosophy & Public Affairs* 30: 363–86.

Collins, P. H. (2019), *Intersectionality as Critical Social Theory* (Durham, NC: Duke University Press).

Combahee River Collective (1983 [1977]), 'A Black Feminist Statement', in *Home Girls: A Black Feminist Anthology*, ed. Barbara Smith (Kitchen Table, Women of Color Press), pp. 272–92.

Coulthard, G. (2014), *Red Skin, White Masks: Rejecting the Colonial Politics of Recognition* (Minneapolis: University of Minnesota Press).

Coulthard, G. and L. B. Simpson (2016), 'Grounded Normativity/Place-Based Solidarity', *American Quarterly* 68: 249–55.

Crenshaw, K. (1990), 'Mapping the Margins: Intersectionality, Identity Politics, and Violence against Women of Color', *Stanford Law Review* 43: 1241–300.
Crenshaw, K. (2017), *On Intersectionality: Essential Writings* (New York: The New Press).
Cruse, H. (1967), *The Crisis of the Negro Intellectual: A Historical Analysis of the Failure of Black Leadership* (New York: William Morrow).
Cullity, G. (1995), 'Moral Free Riding', *Philosophy & Public Affairs* 24: 3–34.
Dawson, M. C. (2003), *Black Visions: The Roots of Contemporary African-American Political Ideologies* (Chicago: University of Chicago Press).
Dean, J. (1995), 'Reflective Solidarity', *Constellations* 2: 114–40.
de Beauvoir, S. (2012 [1949]), *The Second Sex* (New York: Vintage).
Della Porta, D. and M. Diani (2020), *Social Movements: An Introduction* (London: Wiley-Blackwell).
Derpmann, S. (2015), 'Solidarity, Mutual Recognition, and Communality', in *Solidarity: Theory and Practice*, eds. Arto Laitinen and Anne Birgitta Pessi (London: Lexington Books), pp. 83–97.
Deveaux, M. (2021), *Poverty, Solidarity, and Poor-Led Social Movements* (Oxford: Oxford University Press).
Doran, K. (1996), *Solidarity: A Synthesis of Personalism and Communalism in the Thought of Karol Wojtyla/Pope John Paul II* (New York: Lang).
Durkheim, É. (1984 [1893]), *The Division of Labor in Society*, ed. Steven Lukes (London: Palgrave Macmillan).
Dworkin, R. (1986), *Law's Empire* (Cambridge, MA: Harvard University Press).
Dworkin, R. (2000), *Sovereign Virtue* (Cambridge, MA: Harvard University Press).
Faucci, R. and A. Rancan (2009), 'Transforming the Economy: Saint-Simon and His Influence on Mazzini', *History of Economic Ideas* 9: 79–105.
Feinberg, J. (1973), *Social Philosophy* (Englewood Cliffs, NJ: Prentice-Hall).
Feinberg, J. (1974), *Doing and Deserving: Essays in the Theory of Responsibility* (Princeton, NJ: Princeton University Press).
Foot, P. (2001), *Natural Goodness* (Oxford: Clarendon Press).
Forst, R. (forthcoming), 'Solidarity: Concept, Conceptions, and Contexts', in *The Virtue of Solidarity*, eds. Andrea Sangiovanni and Juri Viehoff (Oxford: Oxford University Press).
Frankfurt, H. (1999), *Necessity, Volition, and Love* (Cambridge: Cambridge University Press).
Fraser, N. (1985), 'Toward a Discourse Ethics of Solidarity', *Praxis International* 5: 425–9.
Freire, P. (1993 [1970]), *Pedagogy of the Oppressed* (New York: Continuum).

Fricker, M. (2007), *Epistemic Injustice: Power and the Ethics of Knowing* (Oxford: Oxford University Press).
Gardner, J. (2002), 'Reasons for Teamwork', *Legal Theory* 8: 495–509.
Gilbert, M. (1996), *Living Together: Rationality, Sociality, and Obligation* (Lanham, MD: Rowman & Littlefield).
Gilbert, M. (2000), *Sociality and Responsibility: New Essays in Plural Subject Theory* (Lanham, MD: Rowman & Littlefield).
Godman, M. (2020), *The Epistemology and Morality of Human Kinds* (London: Routledge).
Gooding-Williams, R. (2009), *In the Shadow of Du Bois: Afro-Modern Political Thought in America* (Cambridge, MA: Harvard University Press).
Gould, C. (2007), 'Transnational Solidarities', *Journal of Social Philosophy* 38: 148–64.
Gould, C. (2020), 'Motivating Solidarity with Distant Others', in *The Oxford Handbook of Global Justice*, ed. Thom Brooks (Oxford: Oxford University Press).
Gould, C. (forthcoming), 'Rethinking Solidarity through the Lens of Critical Social Ontology', in *The Virtue of Solidarity*, eds. Andrea Sangiovanni and Juri Viehoff (Oxford: Oxford University Press).
Gutiérrez, G. (1973), *A Theology of Liberation: History, Politics, and Salvation*, trans. Inda Caridad and John Eagleson (Maryknoll, NY: Orbis Books).
Haakonssen, L. (1997), *Medicine and Morals in the Enlightenment: John Gregory, Thomas Percival and Benjamin Rush* (Amsterdam: Rodopi).
Habermas, J. (1990), 'Justice and Solidarity: On the Discussion Concerning Stage 6', in *The Moral Domain: Essays in the Ongoing Discussion between Philosophy and the Social Sciences*, eds. Thomas Wren, Wolfgang Edelstein, and Gertrud Nunner-Winkler (Cambridge, MA: MIT Press), pp. 224–54.
Habermas, J. (2001), 'The Postnational Constellation and the Future of Democracy', in *The Postnational Constellation: Political Essays* (Oxford: Polity Press), pp. 80–134.
Hacking, I. (1999), *The Social Construction of What?* (Cambridge, MA: Harvard University Press).
Hall, K. (2009), 'Queer Breasted Experience', in *'You've Changed': Sex Reassignment and Personal Identity*, ed. Laurie Shrage (Oxford: Oxford University Press), pp. 121–35.
Harris, F. (2015), 'The Next Civil Rights Movement?', *Dissent* 62: 34–40.
Haslanger, S. (2012), *Resisting Reality: Social Construction and Social Critique* (Oxford: Oxford University Press).
Hayward, J. E. S. (1959), 'Solidarity: The Social History of an Idea in Nineteenth Century France', *International Review of Social History* 4: 261–84.

Hayward, J. E. S. (1961), 'The Official Social Philosophy of the French Third Republic: Léon Bourgeois and Solidarism', *International Review of Social History* 6: 19–48.

Hogg, M. and S. Hains (1996), 'Intergroup Relations and Group Solidarity: Effects of Group Identification and Social Beliefs on Depersonalized Attraction', *Journal of Personality and Social Psychology* 70: 295–309.

Holton, R. (1994), 'Deciding to Trust, Coming to Believe', *Australasian Journal of Philosophy* 72: 63–76.

Honey, M. (2018), *To the Promised Land: Martin Luther King and the Fight for Economic Justice* (New York: Norton).

Honneth, A. (1996), *The Struggle for Recognition: The Moral Grammar of Social Conflicts* (Cambridge, MA: MIT Press).

hooks, b. (2015a), *Feminism Is for Everybody: Passionate Politics* (London: Routledge).

hooks, b. (2015b), *Feminist Theory: From Margin to Center* (London: Routledge).

Hume, D. (1978 [1739]), *A Treatise of Human Nature*, ed. Lewis Amherst Selby-Bigge (Oxford: Oxford University Press).

Hurka, T. (1998), 'Two Kinds of Organic Unity', *The Journal of Ethics* 2: 299–320.

Ingram, A. (1996), 'Constitutional Patriotism', *Philosophy and Social Criticism* 22: 1–18.

Kautsky, K. (1910 [1892]), *The Class Struggle: Erfurt Program*, trans. William Bohn (New York: Kerr & Co.).

King, D. (1995), 'Multiple Jeopardy, Multiple Consciousness: The Context for Black Feminist Ideology', in *Words of Fire: An Anthology of African-American Feminist Thought*, ed. Beverly Guy-Sheftall (New York: New Press), pp. 294–317.

Kohn, M. (2018), 'Solidarity and Social Rights', *Critical Review of International Social and Political Philosophy* 21: 616–30.

Kolers, A. (2016), *A Moral Theory of Solidarity* (Oxford: Oxford University Press).

Korsgaard, C. (1996), 'Two Distinctions in Goodness', in *Creating the Kingdom of Ends* (Cambridge: Cambridge University Press), pp. 249–75.

Koslowski, P. (2000), 'Solidarism, Capitalism, and Economic Ethics in Heinrich Pesch', in *The Theory of Capitalism in the German Economic Tradition: Historism, Ordo-Liberalism, Critical Theory, Solidarism*, ed. Peter Koslowski (Berlin: Springer), pp. 371–96.

Kramer, R. M. and M. B. Brewer (1984), 'Effects of Group Identity on Resource Use in a Simulated Commons Dilemma', *Journal of Personality and Social Psychology* 46: 1044–57.

Kraut, R. (2007), *What Is Good and Why* (Cambridge, MA: Harvard University Press).
Kraut, R. (2011), *Against Absolute Goodness* (Oxford: Oxford University Press).
Kutz, C. (2000a), 'Acting Together', *Philosophical and Phenomenological Research* 61: 1–31.
Kutz, C. (2000b), *Complicity* (Cambridge: Cambridge University Press).
Laitinen, A. and A. B. Pessi, eds. (2015), *Solidarity: Theory and Practice* (London: Lexington Books).
Land, C. (2015), *Decolonizing Solidarity: Dilemmas and Directions for Supporters of Indigenous Struggles* (London: Bloomsbury Publishing).
Laplanche, J. and J.-B. Pontalis (2018 [1973]), *The Language of Psychoanalysis*, trans. Donald Nicholson-Smith (New York: Routledge).
Lenard, P. T. (2010), 'What Is Solidaristic about Global Solidarity?', *Contemporary Political Theory* 9: 100–10.
Leroux, P. (1845), *De L'humanité* (Paris: Perrotin).
Levy, N. (2005), 'The Good, the Bad and the Blameworthy', *Journal of Ethics and Social Philosophy* 1: 1–16.
Lorde, A. (1984), *Sister Outsider* (Trumansburg, NY: Crossing).
Lorde, A. (2009), *I Am Your Sister: Collected and Unpublished Works of Audre Lorde*, eds. Rudolph Byrd, Johnnetta Betsch-Cole, and Beverly Guy-Sheftall (Oxford: Oxford University Press).
Lu, C. (2000), 'The One and Many Faces of Cosmopolitanism', *Journal of Political Philosophy* 8: 244–67.
Lu, C. (2017), *Justice and Reconciliation in World Politics* (Cambridge: Cambridge University Press).
Lugones, M. (1987), 'Playfulness, 'World'-Travelling, and Loving Perception', *Hypatia* 2: 3–19.
MacCallum, G. C., Jr. (1967), 'Negative and Positive Freedom', *The Philosophical Review* 76: 312–34.
Mallon, R. (2016), *The Construction of Human Kinds* (Oxford: Oxford University Press).
Marin, M. (2018), 'Racial Structural Solidarity', *Critical Review of International Social and Political Philosophy* 21: 586–600.
Marx, K. (1978), 'The Possibility of Non-Violent Revolution', in *The Marx-Engels Reader*, ed. R. C. Tucker (London: Norton), pp. 522–4.
Mason, A. (2000), *Community, Solidarity, and Belonging* (Cambridge: Cambridge University Press).
May, L. (1996), *The Socially Responsive Self: Social Theory and Professional Ethics* (Chicago: University of Chicago Press).
Mazzini, G. (2009), *A Cosmopolitanism of Nations*, ed. Nadia Urbinati, trans. Stefano Recchia (Princeton: Princeton University Press).

Michnik, A. (1985), 'Letter from the Gdansk Prison', *New York Review of Books*, July 18.
Mikkola, M. (2007), 'Gender Sceptics and Feminist Politics', *Res Publica* 13: 361–80.
Miller, D. (1995), *On Nationality* (Oxford: Oxford University Press).
Miller, D. (2017), 'Solidarity and Its Sources', in *The Strains of Commitment: The Political Sources of Solidarity in Diverse Societies*, eds. Keith Banting and Will Kymlicka (Oxford: Oxford University Press), pp. 61–80.
Millikan, R. G. (2000), *On Clear and Confused Ideas: An Essay About Substance Concepts* (Cambridge: Cambridge University Press).
Mohanty, C. (2003), *Feminism without Borders* (Durham, NC: Duke University Press).
Moore, G. E. (1993 [1903]), *Principia Ethica*, ed. Thomas Baldwin (Cambridge: Cambridge University Press).
Moses, W. J. (1988), *The Golden Age of Black Nationalism, 1850–1925* (Oxford: Oxford University Press).
Müller, J.-W. (2007), *Constitutional Patriotism* (Princeton: Princeton University Press,).
Munoz-Dardé, V. (forthcoming), 'The Cost of Belonging: Universalism vs the Political Ideal of Solidarity', in *The Virtue of Solidarity*, eds. Andrea Sangiovanni and Juri Viehoff (Oxford: Oxford University Press).
Nozick, R. (1983), *Philosophical Explanations* (Cambridge, MA: Harvard University Press).
O'Neill, O. (1996), *Towards Justice and Virtue* (Cambridge: Cambridge University Press).
Owen, D. (2021), 'Solidarity with Refugees', ms.
Owens, D. (forthcoming), *Bound by Convention*.
Parfit, D. (1984), *Reasons and Persons* (Oxford: Oxford University Press).
Pensky, M. (2009), *The Ends of Solidarity: Discourse Theory in Ethics and Politics* (Albany: SUNY Press).
Pesch, H. (2004 [1918]), *Ethics and the National Economy*, trans. Rupert Ederer (Norfolk, VA: IHS Press).
Plunkett, D. (2016), 'Conceptual History, Conceptual Ethics, and the Aims of Inquiry: A Framework for Thinking About the Relevance of the History/Genealogy of Concepts to Normative Inquiry', *Ergo* 3: 27–64.
Plunkett, D. and T. Sundell (2013a), 'Disagreement and the Semantics of Normative and Evaluative Terms', *Philosopher's Imprint* 13: 1–37.
Plunkett, D. and T. Sundell (2013b), 'Dworkin's Interpretivism and the Pragmatics of Legal Disputes', *Legal Theory* 19: 242–81.
Potter, M. (2009), 'Solidarity as Spiritual Exercise: A Contribution to the Development of Solidarity in the Catholic Social Tradition', PhD dissertation, Department of Theology, Boston College.

Prainsack, B. and A. Buyx (2012), 'Solidarity in Contemporary Bioethics – Towards a New Approach', *Bioethics* 26: 343–50.

Rawls, J. (1999), *A Theory of Justice* (Cambridge, MA: Harvard University Press).

Renan, E. (1882), *Qu'est Que C'est Qu'une Nation?* (Paris: Calmann-Lévy).

Riley, D. (1988), *'Am I That Name?': Feminism and the Category of 'Women'in History* (Basingstoke: Macmillan Press).

Rippe, K. (1998), 'Diminishing Solidarity', *Ethical Theory and Moral Practice* 1: 355–73.

Ripstein, A. (2009), *Force and Freedom: Kant's Legal and Political Philosophy* (Cambridge, MA: Harvard University Press).

Rivers, E. (1995), 'Beyond the Nationalism of Fools: Toward an Agenda for Black Intellectuals', *Boston Review* 20: 16–18.

Robinson, D. (2001), *Black Nationalism in American Politics and Thought* (Cambridge: Cambridge University Press).

Rorty, R. (1989), *Contingency, Irony, and Solidarity* (Cambridge: Cambridge University Press).

Ross, M. and Y. Borgmann-Prebil, eds. (2010), *Promoting Solidarity in the European Union* (Oxford: Oxford University Press).

Sangiovanni, A. (2007), 'Global Justice, Reciprocity, and the State', *Philosophy & Public Affairs* 35: 2–39.

Sangiovanni, A. (2013), 'Solidarity in the European Union', *Oxford Journal of Legal Studies* 33: 213–41.

Sangiovanni, A. (2015), 'Solidarity as Joint Action', *Journal of Applied Philosophy* 32: 340–59.

Sangiovanni, A. (forthcoming), 'Challenges to Solidarity', in *The Virtue of Solidarity*, eds. Andrea Sangiovanni and Juri Viehoff (Oxford: Oxford University Press).

Sangiovanni, A. 'A Defense of Fair Play', ms. (a).

Sangiovanni, A. 'Solidarity as a Social Kind', ms. (b).

Scanlon, T. (1998), *What We Owe to Each Other* (Cambridge, MA: Harvard University Press).

Scheffler, S. (1997), 'Relationships and Responsibilities', *Philosophy & Public Affairs* 26: 189–209.

Scheffler, S. (2010), 'Valuing', in *Equality and Tradition: Questions of Value in Moral and Political Theory* (Oxford: Oxford University Press), pp. 15–40.

Scheler, M. (2017 [1923]), *The Nature of Sympathy* (London: Routledge).

Scholz, S. (2010), *Political Solidarity* (Philadelphia: Penn State Press).

Schor, N. (1994), 'This Essentialism which Is not One: Coming to Grips with Irigaray', in *Engaging with Irigaray: Feminist Philosophy and Modern European Thought*, eds. Carolyn Burke, Naomi Schor, and M. Whitford (New York: Columbia University Press), pp. 57–79.

Searle, J. R. (1990), 'Collective Intentions and Actions', in *Intentions in Communication*, eds. Philip R. Cohen, Jerry Morgan, and Martha E. Pollack (Cambridge: MIT Press).
Sewell, W. (1980), *Work and Revolution in France: The Language of Labor from the Old Regime to 1848* (Cambridge: Cambridge University Press).
Shapiro, S. (2014), 'Massively Shared Agency', in *Rational and Social Agency: The Philosophy of Michael Bratman*, eds. Manuel Vargas and Gideon Yaffe (Oxford: Oxford University Press), pp. 257–93.
Shelby, T. (2009), *We Who Are Dark: The Philosophical Foundations of Black Solidarity* (Cambridge, MA: Harvard University Press).
Shelby, T. and B. Terry, eds. (2018), *To Shape a New World: Essays on the Political Philosophy of Martin Luther King, Jr.* (Cambridge, MA: Harvard University Press).
Shiffrin, S. V. (2010), 'Incentives, Motives, and Talents', *Philosophy & Public Affairs* 38: 111–42.
Simmons, A. J. (1979), 'The Principle of Fair Play', *Philosophy & Public Affairs* 8: 307–37.
Simmons, A. J. (1996), 'Associative Political Obligations', *Ethics* 106: 247–73.
Simmons, A. J. (2001), 'Fair Play and Political Obligation: Twenty Years Later', in *Justification and Legitimacy: Essays on Rights and Obligations* (Cambridge: Cambridge University Press), pp. 27–43.
Sobrino, J. (1994), *Principle of Mercy: Taking the Crucified People from the Cross* (Maryknoll, NY: Orbis Books).
Somek, A. (forthcoming), 'Transnational Solidarity: A Durkheimian View', in *Solidarity*, eds. Andrea Sangiovanni and Juri Viehoff (Oxford: Oxford University Press).
Spelman, E. (1988), *Inessential Woman: Problems of Exclusion in Feminist Thought* (Boston, MA: Beacon Press).
Stevens, D. (1920), *Jailed for Freedom* (New York: Boni and Liveright).
Stilz, A. (2016), 'The Value of Self-Determination', in *Oxford Studies in Political Philosophy, Vol 2*, eds. David Sobel, Peter Vallentyne, and Steven Wall (Oxford: Oxford University Press), pp. 98–127.
Stjernø, S. (2005), *Solidarity in Europe: The History of an Idea* (Cambridge: Cambridge University Press).
Stoljar, N. (1995), 'Essence, Identity, and the Concept of Woman', *Philosophical Topics* 23: 261–93.
Stone, A. (2004), 'Essentialism and Anti-Essentialism in Feminist Philosophy', *Journal of Moral Philosophy* 1: 135–53.
Stone, A. (2007), *An Introduction to Feminist Philosophy* (Cambridge: Polity).
Straehle, C. (2010), 'National and Cosmopolitan Solidarity', *Contemporary Political Theory* 9: 110–20.
Sugden, R. (2000), 'Team Preferences', *Economics and Philosophy* 16: 175–204.

Sugden, R. (2003), 'The Logic of Team Reasoning', *Philosophical Explorations* 6: 165–81.
Taylor, A. E. (2015), 'Solidarity: Obligations and Expressions', *Journal of Political Philosophy* 23: 128–45.
Taylor, C. (1989), 'Cross-Purposes: The Liberal-Communitarian Debate', in *Liberalism and the Moral Life*, ed. Nancy Rosenblum (Cambridge, MA: Harvard University Press), pp. 159–82.
Thompson, M. (2008), *Life and Action* (Cambridge, MA: Harvard University Press).
Tillery, A. B. (2019), 'What Kind of Movement Is Black Lives Matter? The View from Twitter', *Journal of Race, Ethnicity and Politics* 4: 297–323.
Tischner, J. (1984 [1982]), *The Ethics of Solidarity*, trans. Marek Zaleski and Benjamin Fiore (San Francisco: Harper & Row).
Tönnies, F. (1980), *Community and Society*, ed. Charles Loomis (New York: Basic Books).
Tuomela, R. (2013), *Social Ontology: Collective Intentionality and Group Agents* (Oxford: Oxford University Press).
Van Kersbergen, K. (2003), *Social Capitalism: A Study of Christian Democracy and the Welfare State* (London: Routledge).
Van Parijs, P. (forthcoming), 'Solidarity and the Just Society', in *The Virtue of Solidarity*, eds. Andrea Sangiovanni and Juri Viehoff (Oxford: Oxford University Press).
Vasak, K. (1979), 'For the Third Generation of Human Rights: The Rights of Solidarity', *Inaugural Lecture, Tenth Study Session, International Institute of Human Rights*.
Väyrynen, P. (2013), *The Lewd, the Rude and the Nasty: A Study of Thick Concepts in Ethics* (Oxford: Oxford University Press).
Velleman, D. (1997), 'How to Share an Intention', *Philosophy and Phenomenological Research* 57: 28–49.
Velleman, D. (1999), 'Love as a Moral Emotion', *Ethics* 109: 338–74.
Viehoff, J. (forthcoming), 'Personal Sacrifice, Commitment, and the Function of Solidarity', in *The Virtue of Solidarity*, eds. Andrea Sangiovanni and Juri Viehoff (Oxford: Oxford University Press).
Wellman, C. (2000), 'Solidarity, the Individual and Human Rights', *Human Rights Quarterly* 22: 639–57.
Wenar, L. (2023), 'The Value of Unity', *Philosophy & Public Affairs*, Online Early.
West-Oram, P., A. Buyx, and B. Prainsack (2016), 'Solidarity in Bioethics', in *Encyclopedia of Life Sciences* (Chichester: Wiley & Sons), pp. 1–5.
Wiggins, D. (2006), *Ethics: Twelve Lectures on the Philosophy of Morality* (Cambridge, MA: Harvard University Press).
Wildt, A. (1999), 'Solidarity: Its History and Contemporary Definition', in *Solidarity*, ed. Kurt Bayertz (London: Springer), pp. 209–23.

Williams, B. (1965), 'Ethical Consistency', *Proceedings of the Aristotelian Society (Supplement)* 39: 103–24.

Wollheim, R. (1974), 'Identification and Imagination', in *Freud: A Collection of Critical Essays*, ed. Richard Wollheim (New York: Anchor Books), pp. 172–96.

X, Malcolm (1992), *By Any Means Necessary* (New York: Pathfinder).

Young, I. M. (1994), 'Gender as Seriality: Thinking about Women as a Social Collective', *Signs* 19: 713–38.

Zack, N. (2005), *Inclusive Feminism: A Third Wave Theory of Women's Commonality* (Lanham: Rowman & Littlefield).

Zakaria, R. (2021), *Against White Feminism* (New York: Norton).

Zhao, M. (2019), 'Solidarity, Fate-Sharing, and Community', *Philosopher's Imprint* 19: 1–13.

Part II

Responses

2

Solidarity is not joint action

Avery Kolers

Andrea Sangiovanni's ambitious and attractive account of the 'nature, grounds, and value' of solidarity contributes a great deal to theorizing this elusive concept. My objections to his account come down to the following claim. Sangiovanni has richly and accurately described *something people might do* in solidarity, and given some reasons they might do it, but he has not isolated the nature of the concept or, consequently, its grounds or value. Solidarity often involves joint action but it is not definitionally a form of joint action; it is better thought of as a kind of team membership through which we are able to engage in a distinctive kind of teamwork. It is most needed not only when traditional bonds weaken but when we lack the capacity to integrate individuals into a corporate agent. Moreover, solidarity often involves identification in important ways, but it is not grounded in identification, and we should be glad it is not. And consequently, solidarity is *asymmetric* in that the 'joiners' do not have the agenda-setting and leadership role that the core members do. And although there are typically pathways through which joiners can become core members, the existence or availability of such pathways is not a necessary condition of solidarity.

Sangiovanni's account fits together as a whole with mutually reinforcing parts. Hence there is a risk that, in making my case, what seem to me to be fundamental challenges will come across as tinkering around the edges. So I begin with an illustration of a real case, then make my argument, and then conclude by laying out what I think an account of solidarity must do, if it is to capture the nature, grounds, and value of the concept.

Maple or Shannon?

In his enigmatic memoir and social history of cricket, *Beyond a Boundary*, C. L. R. James reflects on the consequences of his choice of which club team to play for. Because colonial Trinidad was riven by class, caste, and racial cleavages,[1] this 'apparently simple' decision 'plunged [him] into a social and moral crisis which had a profound effect on [his] whole future life' (James 1993, p. 49). The elite Queen's Park club and the White Catholic Shamrock were inaccessible to him due to the facts of his birth; those same facts placed the 'plebeian' all-Black Stingo club beneath him. 'Queen's Park and Shamrock were too high and Stingo was too low. I accepted this as easily in the one case as in the other' (James 1993, p. 50).

That left him two options: 'Maple, the club of the brown-skinned middle class', founded 'on the principle that they didn't want any dark people in their club', and Shannon, 'the club of the black lower-middle class' (James 1993, p. 50). Hence, although 'none of these lines was absolute', James had to choose one or the other of the two social groupings between which there was 'a continual rivalry, distrust and ill-feeling, which, skilfully played upon by the European peoples, poisons the life of the community' (James 1993, p. 51).[2] This division was not, however, a rivalry of equals: 'in a West Indian colony the surest sign of a man having arrived is the fact that he keeps company with people lighter in complexion than himself' (James 1993, p. 52).[3]

Though James himself was dark-skinned, his social and familial links with members of the lighter-skinned team gave him options; he opted for Maple.

> Faced with the fundamental divisions in the island, I had gone to the right and, by cutting myself off from the popular side, delayed my political development for years. But no one could see that then, least of all me. (James 1993, p. 53)

Though it seems doubtful that *no one* could see it at the time, what James failed to appreciate was that his choice was about whom to

---

1 As well as level-of-play cleavages, which he leaves aside; that he would play for a 'first class' club 'was clear'. See James 1993, p. 49.
2 Quoting James 1933, p. 8.
3 Quoting James 1933, p. 8.

identify and associate with, whose cause to make his own. He chose to climb. This is a completely understandable choice; few of us do otherwise even in the face of consequences far less momentous than those engendered by colonial social engineering. Even so, it seems – James clearly sees it retrospectively as – a striking failure to do *what one ought to do*, namely, to choose 'the popular side' (by which he means the side of the people).

When James chose to join Maple instead of Shannon or Stingo, he threw in his lot with a higher caste and implicitly – but manifestly – declared that he could not be trusted to side with or still less share the fate of those who were darker skinned. He violated Eugene Debs's admonition that one should not 'seek to rise *from* the ranks, but *with* the ranks' (Salvatore 1982, p. 292). His error could be criticized on epistemic grounds, since he failed to be aware, at the time, of what was at stake: that 'the cricket field was a stage on which selected individuals played representative roles which were charged with social significance' (James 1993, p. 66). He was arguably also open to ethical criticism insofar as those who were lower down the unjust caste system could object to his failure to stand with them. I want to put aside these evaluative issues and consider the conceptual aspects. For it seems clear that, whatever exactly solidarity is, by choosing Maple, James failed to act in solidarity.

Choosing – or refusing – Maple

Reading *Beyond a Boundary*, it is intriguing to reflect on what James does and does not make of the choice. He presents the choice in the part of the book that is a memoir of his own cricketing life. The choice confronted him when he left school and had to choose a club team to join. He leaves it there, never really interrogating the ways in which the choice cut him off from 'the popular side' and 'delayed [his] political development'. But the issue returns later, when James is profiling some of the leading players of his era. There one comes across the contrasting case of Wilton St. Hill, who was also offered a place with Maple:

> A member of my cricket clique once ... said to St. Hill, 'Maple would be glad to have a man like you.' The reply was instantaneous. 'Yes, but they wouldn't want my brothers.' (James 1993, p. 90)

Unlike St. Hill, James in his youthful ignorance focused on his own preferences and aspirations rather than those of a broader group. He preferred to 'keep[] company with people lighter in complexion than himself', even if he didn't think of it politically that way. Instead of choosing 'the popular side', he went 'to the right'. It was a failure of solidarity with the people.

If, like St. Hill, James had refused to play for Maple, he could thereby have identified with a lower caste of Trinidadians. The choice so to identify would have been an act of solidarity. That is, such identification might have been what he did in solidarity; by choosing Shannon or Stingo he could have *thereby* identified with the dark-skinned working class or lower middle class, making their cause – whatever form it takes, however they pursue it – his own. The choice did not involve discerning his *antecedent* identification and acting on the basis of it. Rather, in this kind of case, the identification *is* the solidarity. It might be politically significant to identify that way precisely because the agent in fact, or as a matter of social recognition, does not or need not share that identity. For instance, we might embody a privileged identity but publicly identify with or as a less privileged group. Hence Wilton St. Hill's own skin was light enough for Maple, but since light skin was the criterion, he refused.

To emphasize this point: identification need not be the impetus toward solidarity, it might constitute solidarity. And it's a good thing, too, because *antecedent* identification is normatively suspect. Accounts of solidarity grounded in antecedent identification standardly face the problem that identification stratifies us vertically and Balkanizes us horizontally.[4] When the status or power of a tenured professor or a surgeon is challenged from below, they find it easiest to kick downward while making common cause with others of their status. When competing social groups confront a shrinking pool of resources, individuals find those who are most saliently like themselves – those for whom the ascent to trustworthiness is least demanding, and who are most likely to share fates whether they want to or not. Such salience, such empirical identification and fate-sharing, is typically heteronomous or 'given': we find ourselves 'thrown' into groupings along with our coethnics, conationals, professional associations, or those who share our racial and class identities.

---

4 This issue is most powerfully confronted in Dean 1996.

One might think this is what we see in St. Hill's case; James indicates that in objecting to Maple, St. Hill was invoking not some wide 'brotherhood' of darker-skinned Trinidadians but his own family (James 1993, p. 90). So this might seem to be straightforward identification-based solidarity. But St. Hill did not refuse participation on the national (all-West Indian intercolonial) team just because his brothers were not chosen. He refused to join a color-coded higher-status team because it was color-coded. The (heteronomous) identification gave him a shorthand that would explain his choice to the Maple representative, but the political identification was the act of solidarity.

Though James did not know it at the time, these acts of self-identification were manifest political choices with socially salient consequences. But they were not *collective* actions. Although solidarity is importantly about *us*, about how we make it the case that *we're in this together* and express that unity to others, such expression is fundamentally the action of individual agents. Solidarity is what we accomplish or manifest by taking action, it is not the action we take.

To say that James failed to be in solidarity may seem harsh; if he didn't know the salience of the choice he was making, how can we blame him? Indeed, given what we know about who he was and what he became, lack of awareness is the only plausible explanation for such a failure. But that's just it; that James could fail to be in solidarity without understanding the situation he is in reflects a crucial feature of the phenomenon, namely, that what solidarity demands of him *isn't up to him*. It isn't about him. It isn't about what he intends. The terms of solidarity are set not by the individuals of whom solidarity is demanded, those for whom the question of whether to act in solidarity is at issue, but by the social groups or affected parties whose life chances are most directly at stake – whose adversity needs to be overcome. Often, of course, we play both roles: in later writing for independence from Britain, James was, at one and the same time, acting in solidarity with the independence movement *and* one of the people who would thereby gain independence as a result of it. Insofar as he participated in the organizing, he was both a subject of solidarity and part of the core or target group. This duality of positions in the context of solidarity often confuses us into thinking that subject *is* object: that the fundamental agent of solidarity is the *we*, and that, since identity is a symmetric relationship (x=y iff y=x), then solidarity must be symmetric in the same way (I am with you iff you are with me). But the subject and object positions are analytically distinct. By being in solidarity I may earn the capacity to speak and act as 'we'. But I am not the arbiter of whether I have earned this capacity. This asymmetry means that attempts at solidarity can fail, for instance if I try to stand with you but you repudiate or shun me.

The choice of which cricket club to join became salient because it mattered to the lower-status people of Trinidad. By being in solidarity with them, St. Hill expressed and manifested his commitment to their cause. He made their cause his. James failed to do the same. His political development was delayed for years because choosing Maple sent him back to square one in being able to earn the right to say 'we' and mean we *the people* of Trinidad.

To summarize these first two sections: solidarity is not grounded in antecedent identification, and it's a good thing, too. In a given case, however, solidarity might *consist in* the act of identification. This is because the act of identification can be a manifest political choice, an expression of whose lot I'm throwing in with, whose fate I am making my own. Fundamentally, solidarity lies in this act of throwing in my lot with others, and so fundamentally solidarity is an individual act. It is the act through which I can become – and remain, but also become – part of the we. That this is the choice I face is not up to me. The meaning of the choice I make, and the context in which I am required to make it, is not determined by my intentions. By choosing solidarity I do not thereby choose that anyone else is in solidarity with me, and hence, solidarity is not logically symmetric; but by manifesting solidarity I may earn their solidarity in return. This account diverges from Sangiovanni's in each of the respects I have emphasized.

Sangiovanni on solidarity: a definition and a credo

Sangiovanni approaches solidarity as joint intention and mutual commitment, grounded in antecedent identification. By way of definition, he proposes that solidarity is essentially a form of *joint action* aimed at overcoming a significant adversity that clouds the participants' shared fate.

Hence for Sangiovanni,[5]

a acts in solidarity with $b_1, b_2, \ldots b_n$ iff, on grounds of each agent's identification with one another on some basis or other,

i a and each b_i intend to do their part in overcoming significant adversity X by pursuing together some more proximate shared goal Y;
ii a and each b_i are individually committed to overcoming X by doing Y, and to not bypassing one another's wills in doing so;
iii a and each b_i are committed to sharing one another's fates in ways relevant to X and Y; and
iv a and each b_i trust one another to follow through on their intention in (i) and to uphold their commitments in (ii) and (iii).

Because of the densely interactive or meshed character of conditions (ii) through (iv), this account of shared agency amounts not just to joint action but to joint *intention*, *mutual trust*, and 'something close to common knowledge' (p. 63 n. 134). These additional aspects are crucial. Mere joint *action* includes cases such as that where passengers line up to board a bus, or an electorate chooses a new government. For Sangiovanni, solidarity also entails joint *intention*, such as cases where two movers haul a couch up a flight of stairs or a duet harmonizes. Joint intention requires a high level of mutual responsiveness and mutual reliance on the other to do their part, a meshing of plans. And solidarity doesn't stop there; the goals and the shared intentions must additionally be the objects of *commitments* that participants are right to *trust*; hence if one breaks faith they have not just gone their separate ways but abandoned or betrayed the other.

This strong thesis has important implications on each side. Suppose Sam and Janet are, to take a familiar example, planning to move a couch up a flight of stairs. Abruptly, Janet announces that she doesn't actually feel like helping out, leaving Sam to find a new partner. In the absence of a promise or commitment, and assuming that she does not thereby cause or risk harm to others, Janet would not have wronged anyone by quitting. But solidarity, for Sangiovanni, is not like that precisely because if one agent threw up their hands and

---

5 What follows is my gloss on his formula. I am grateful to Andrea Sangiovanni (in personal communication) for endorsing this restatement.

said they didn't care about X or Y and would no longer do their part, they would thereby violate their own commitment as well as betray the trust of their comrades, breaking the solidarity relation. This much seems obvious: to wash one's hands of the work is to break solidarity. Crucially, however, the strong thesis also works at the other end. Sam and Janet might haul couches all day without complaint or conflict, responding to one another's cues, safely and reliably furnishing walk-up apartments all over town. But if they did not commit to one another to remain engaged, and hence did not come to trust one another and be trustworthy to remain engaged, then no matter how long they worked together they would not be in solidarity. It would be 'like Cato's coming into the theatre, only to go out again' (Locke 1988, II.98). For Sangiovanni, solidarity requires the added glue of commitment, trust, and trustworthiness.

This high degree of mutuality brings with it additional features that Sangiovanni takes to be either essential or noncontingently accidental to solidarity, including a logical symmetry to the solidarity relation – I act in solidarity with you iff you act in solidarity with me – as well as its moral analogue, equality among participants. These features draw a stark contrast between solidarity and charity, which risks demeaning recipients by treating them as mere patients, and servility (where the giver is deferential to the recipient) (p. 57). Neither of these latter relations is either logically or morally symmetric.

All of this mutuality is, though, a lot to ask, and hence, says Sangiovanni, we are likely to be *trustworthy* in such commitments only when they are spurred by *identification*: only if I identify with you on some salient basis can I be expected to be committed, trusting, and trustworthy in these ways; only then would I be right to feel *betrayed* rather than just disappointed or frustrated if you dropped the ball. Identification propels each of us into the *we*, the plural subject that takes action and advances the cause. If commitment, trust, and trustworthiness are the glue, then identification is the force that brings the glued objects together and holds them until they set.

One analytically attractive feature of Sangiovanni's definition is its multiple realizability, which he underscores by applying the analysis to cases ranging from welfare state solidarism to the transnational BLM to Catholic social teaching. By taking solidarity as a form of joint action and the elements of *identification*, *adversity*, *action*, and *shared fate* as variables, he provides participants with a portable credo:[6]

> S On the basis of our shared identification as [G], we seek to overcome [A] by doing [Y], and in committing to this course of action we also commit to share our fate of being [F].

Hence those who play their club cricket with Shannon instead of Maple – or Stingo instead of Shannon – might say:

> C On the basis of our shared *colonized and caste-subordinated status*, we seek to overcome *our debasement at the hands of a colonial elite* by *making their game ours and beating them at it*, and in committing to this course of action we also commit to share our fate by *publicly affirming our membership of a lower-status group, and forswearing opportunities to 'arrive'*.

Whereas a member of a union on strike might say:

> U On the basis of our shared *condition of being exploited*, we seek to overcome *our intolerable working conditions* by *striking for a better contract*, and in committing to do so we also commit to share our fate by *enduring together a work-stoppage, temporary hardship, and a risk of longer-term or serious physical and economic harms*.

Who are we?

One thing these credos lay bare is that the subject of the sentence elides two senses of 'we' – an aggregate sense and a distributive sense. It is *we in the aggregate* who share a condition and are working to overcome adversity. The analysis of joint action explains how this collective work is realized. But it is not we in the aggregate who commit to share our fates despite having an opportunity to 'arrive' or to cross the picket line, and thus avoid the shared fate; it is we in the sense of *each of us*. G. A. Cohen famously illustrates this distinction with the analogy of ten people locked in a room such that one and only one could escape, but if anyone did, the means of escape would no longer be available to the rest (Cohen 1983, p. 9). In Cohen's case, we in the aggregate are stuck in the

---

6 This is my gloss on Sangiovanni (p. 66). I am again grateful to Andrea Sangiovanni for endorsing this restatement, in personal communication.

room, even though we in the distributive sense – each of us – are free to leave. Solidarity lies in each of us eschewing this option. Hence Sangiovanni has not quite escaped the idea that the agent of solidarity is fundamentally *I* rather than *we*.

Put otherwise: if we win our struggle, then we will share our fate in virtue of *all* being out of Cohen's locked room, all having abolished caste domination, etc. But this – *collective success* – is not the fate we have to pledge to share.[7] The fates we have to pledge to share are, for as long as the struggle continues, the adversity we're trying to overcome and the burdens of the struggle itself, and, if we lose, the costs of having rebelled. It would make no sense for we in the aggregate to pledge to share fates.

Sangiovanni could reply that, although the 'we' is grammatically ambiguous in this way, *identification* glues us together and makes it possible for each to affirm that the 'we' is also 'I'. By making the cause my own I eliminate the distinction between each and all. After all, x=y iff y=x.

The cases of C. L. R. James and Wilton St. Hill showed that identification is both morally risky and conceptually inapt for serving this purpose. But Sangiovanni might reply that I did not appreciate the pluralistic character of identification. For him, identification is not heteronomously imposed from without, it is autonomous or freely affirmed. We are not doomed to be whomever we get lumped in with by the sum on our paychecks or the check-boxes for 'race' on census forms. To the contrary; the movement gives us an opportunity to find our people, and our own place among them.

The key to this reply is that Sangiovanni does not think that every member needs to identify on the same basis; instead, identifications can function as an 'overlapping consensus'. I identify with some of my comrades as suffering exploitation, with others as sharing a role, with still others by a shared identification with the cause, and so on, but solidarity remains possible as long as all of these

7 To be more precise, *on Sangiovanni's view* success can't be the fate we have to pledge to share. On my own view it might be, in the sense that, since I might join up deferentially, I can thereby commit to share the fate of living in a world that goes worse for me, prudentially, than the current one. This is what (antecedently advantaged) class traitors and (White) race traitors presumably do when they join poor people's social movements and movements for racial emancipation and equality.

modes of identification converge on a single 'we', whatever each person's grounds might be with respect to every other participant. For example, consider my union – the United Campus Workers (UCW) of Kentucky.[8] Though it lacks collective bargaining rights and so is more like an affinity organization than a traditional labor union, the UCW stands for and offers to represent anyone who is employed in a postsecondary educational institution or teaching hospital in the Commonwealth of Kentucky. On its face, identification could go either of two ways. It could take a *collective* object, or a *web of individual objects*.

Because his account is methodologically individualistic in the sense that there is nothing *to* the 'we' except the shared agency created through joint intention, Sangiovanni must mean that we identify with one another as individuals. Hence, for him, identification-with is a web of individual relations between I and you, I and him, I and her, you and him, you and her, she and him, and so on. Then Sangiovanni could explain my solidarity with the UCW as follows. With fellow faculty members I identify by role; with other employees at my campus I identify on the basis of workplace. Many nonacademic staff and adjunct faculty are deeply exploited, and hence may mutually identify on the basis of that condition, but I am not (or do not identify as) deeply exploited, so this cannot ground my identification with them. Yet I can identify with them, and they with me, on the basis of the cause we share, namely, justice for campus workers, or advancing the enterprise of higher education. Some of my faculty colleagues *feel* deeply exploited but the nonacademic staff and adjunct faculty do not believe they are; hence these faculty identify with the nonacademic staff on the basis of condition (as exploited) while the latter identify with these faculty members on the basis of a shared cause. Each person needs to have some basis or other for identifying with each of the other members, but not everyone need have the same basis, and each may have multiple bases for identifying with various others, and their bilateral link may be impelled by different identifications for each. This is key: because my identification with you might be different from yours with me, successful identification generates a crisscrossing system

---

[8] www.ucwkentucky.org (accessed 12 January 2022).

of *unilateral* relations each of which is reciprocated by the same or a different identification but *not symmetric*.

Unfortunately, this crisscrossing plurality of bases for identification causes problems of its own. In the first place, it implies that a group may be 'gappy' if it is made up of some who are not genuinely in solidarity, since one or more others do not identify with them on any basis. This failure of mutuality would taint the collective action that constitutes solidarity because, since you don't buy the basis of my identification, you don't trust my commitment and you don't commit not to bypass my will; that relative mistrust may or may not be a matter of common knowledge. I might mistakenly think I am fully accepted as one of the proletariat because I identify as such, but you look at me as petit bourgeois and suspect that I will be bought off when the going gets tough. Solidarity is then not achieved, or perhaps it characterizes only a subset of the group.[9]

Sangiovanni could reply that this poisonous gappiness is an unfortunate fact of life. And this is plausibly true: solidarity is hard to achieve and harder to maintain. But this generates two further problems. First, it throws into question one of the signature aspects of his account, namely, its generality. For can we really then say that solidarism could characterize the welfare state, or that Catholic solidarity is anything more than a pipe dream? The relations between BLM supporters worldwide are also in some question due to anonymity and weak ties. Much apparent solidarity has to be recast as quasi-solidarity or pseudo-solidarity: successful collective

---

9 Sangiovanni might reply that we can identify on the basis of cause, and these problems fall away. (At p. 91 n. 189 he ascribes such an account to me in order to draw my view under the umbrella of identification.) I think this is a nonstarter. Identification was supposed to be the basis of commitment, trust, and trustworthiness: a relation directly between persons. I see myself in you and you in me. Identification on the basis of cause redirects identification away from the particular others and toward an abstraction or the goal of the action. This makes such identification an altogether different beast. Further, Sangiovanni defines 'identification with a cause' in terms of *commitment* to the cause (pp. 14–15). But identification was required in order to spur commitment. Moreover, two people who are both committed to a cause may be quite bitterly opposed in how to pursue it, and may diverge in their politics even as they recognize one another as worthy adversaries based on their shared passion for, say, health justice or an improved social safety net or whatever.

actions that were coordinated efforts to overcome adversity but lacked one or more of the requisite mutual trust, mutual commitment, mutual identification, or common knowledge of these. Put otherwise, Sangiovanni's formula may indicate an ideal type, at most, but not a definition.

The second problematic implication is more fundamental. Recall that Sangiovanni treats *symmetry* as both a logical and a moral feature of the solidarity relation. If movements can be gappy then there will be a core group of *genuine* solidaries – those who are unquestionably identifiable as the most affected, the ones whose lives are literally on the line; and they will be surrounded or backed by those with weaker or unilateral ties of identification, commitment, and trust. The former group's status relative to the struggle is most central, their say-so is the crucial condition of moving forward with an action, and so on; the relationship between the former and the latter is essentially and importantly asymmetric.

A situation like this became explicit in the US in the summer of 2020, when support actions such as the doctors' 'White Coats for Black Lives', the teachers' 'Educators for Black lives', and so on, were all instances of solidarity efforts that required, and were explicitly called upon to affirm, coordination with and approval by Black leadership. In Louisville, where I live, marching to (what came to be called) Injustice Square – a downtown plaza formally named for a slaveholder who was the third president of the US – was a standard mode of expressing solidarity with BLM, yet the square was *movement property*, such that if you planned to march there you needed an accountability partner from within the core group. Sangiovanni would have to say that the 'White Coats' and the Educators and all the other solidarity marches were not in fact instances of solidarity because there was a very clear system of deference to those most affected. On his view this is a violation of the equality that is essential to solidarity. But that is a category mistake. Solidarity is attractive when it *affirms* equality, and those who are in solidarity affirm equality *by* deferring to the judgment of those whose lives are most directly on the line, *by* affirming their leadership and agency in the struggle. It is the solidaries who refuse to bypass the will of the most-affected, typically not the other way around. This deference is specifically what distinguishes solidarity from free-floating support and sympathy or more standard coalition building.

Sangiovanni rejects deference on grounds that it makes the relationship subservient and anti-egalitarian. This is a false dichotomy. Consider the Educators for Black Lives I mentioned a moment ago. In the summer of 2020, the Educators' role was deferential with respect to Black leadership in Injustice Square. But a few years earlier, when the right-wing then-governor was making war on public education, roles were reversed; it was the teachers' struggle that brought 'Red for Ed' marches to the State House. Deferring to BLM about 'Red for Ed' would have been odd and inappropriate. This says nothing at all about whether each group is the other's moral equal; it says something about which struggle is being joined, and who is on the 'front lines' of that struggle. To put it in terms of (my gloss on) Sangiovanni's definition, if adversity X is experienced directly by a, and the b_i join in solidarity with a, then *while engaged in a's struggle*, the b_i ought to *defer* to a's judgment about whether a given contract offer is fair or acceptable, or whether a particular police reform is to be supported, and about tactics to be adopted in the struggle. If a asks the b_i to boycott, then they should boycott; if a asks them to rally, then they should rally; to post on social media, they should do that; and so on. The accountability simply does not run in the other direction in the same way. It's not that a is *unaccountable* to the b_i, but a's accountability is more restricted since what's on the table right now is a's struggle. Now suppose one of the b_i, call her Betty, becomes deeply and extensively engaged, going out of her way to participate in organizing and deliberation. Betty may then emerge as a core member in developing plans and so on; she can become an honorary part of a through continuous solidarity, earning the right to speak as part of the 'we'. Even then, however, insofar as her exit potential is greater, for instance if she is White or not a teacher, Betty must remain cognizant of the primacy of Black leadership or the organized teachers, respectively, in shaping the movement and determining what risks to take and costs to bear. Here, a has priority in determining which adversity to try to overcome, what strategy to adopt in trying to overcome it, and what tactics to choose in implementing that strategy. This does not mean that the b_i are subservient but it does mean that they should defer on these questions. When the shoe is on the other foot, then the roles will be reversed.

To be sure, if the b_i *try* to give *a* their solidarity but *a* rejects it, then solidarity does not occur despite the b_is' best intentions. In that sense solidarity needs *requital*. But it doesn't follow that solidarity is a symmetric relationship because the fact that the b_i are in solidarity with *a* – pushing to overcome *a*'s adversity – does not imply that *a* is symmetrically in solidarity with them. The b_i can be in solidarity with *a* even if it would be strained, at best, for *a* to claim to be in solidarity with the b_i. For example, BLM went out of their way to acknowledge, embrace, and include participants from a wide variety of organizations and walks of life, giving people opportunities to get involved and thanking them for their solidarity. But does it follow that the members of BLM were *in that instance and in the same respects* symmetrically in solidarity with the White Coats and the Educators? I suppose Sangiovanni could stand on this point. But I think this mistakes how solidarity works and feels. Solidarity does require uptake and recognition; if BLM had shunned the Educators or responded to them with Strawsonian 'objective attitudes', the Educators' solidarity would have failed. Uptake is a necessary condition. But symmetry is not.

So what *is* solidarity, then?

As I understand it, the core idea of solidarity is *manifest, consequential, autonomous unification*. To unpack:

Manifest: The unification is *realized* somehow, not just in the aspirations or sympathies of an agent. I might manifest solidarity by participating in collective action, but I might also manifest it through what I wear or eat, where I go, how I wear my hair, whom I associate with, or which identities I affirm.

Consequential: How one's life goes afterward is, in some way, affected by what one chose in this instance: you threw your lot in with someone, and now you share their fate in some way. Failure to be in solidarity, by contrast, can amount to a *betrayal* in part because one extricates oneself from the previously shared fate, like a ship's captain leaping into the lifeboat and leaving the passengers stranded.

Autonomous: Solidarity is unification that could have been otherwise: those who act in solidarity are (empirically) free to do otherwise than join up. This is why solidarity is, as Sangiovanni says, an issue in the *ethics* of association.

Unification: Adhesion or teamwork: many becoming as one, for purposes of identification or action. Team reasoning replaces individualized reasoning; each chooses a course of action by asking, 'what does the movement need me to do right now?'[10] This may but need not be, and most often is not, full-on joint intention. Formal corporate agents do not require solidarity.[11] It is needed precisely because we are *not* that integrated.

For C. L. R. James, the question of solidarity was whether to choose 'the popular side' or go 'to the right': with whom should he throw in his lot? His (retrospectively self-ascribed) error lay in choosing the latter, and thereby manifesting an intention to avoid the fate of the dark-skinned lower middle class in hopes of eventually 'arriving' by associating with the lighter-skinned caste. By choosing Shannon or Stingo he would have autonomously manifested his adhesion with the outgroup, in ways that would have had significant consequences for his future. But he would not thereby have been jointly intending to overcome significant adversity on the basis of antecedent identification.[12]

References

Cohen, G. A. (1983), 'The Structure of Proletarian Unfreedom', *Philosophy & Public Affairs* 12: 3–33.
Dean, J. (1996), *Solidarity of Strangers* (Berkeley and Los Angeles: University of California Press).
Gold, N. and R. Sugden (2007), 'Collective Intentions and Team Agency', *Journal of Philosophy* 104: 109–37.
James, C. L. R. (1933), *The Case for West-Indian Self-government*.

10 On team reasoning see Gold and Sugden 2007.
11 I have in mind the kind of agent described in List and Pettit 2011.
12 I am grateful to Andrea Sangiovanni for clarification of some aspects of his view, to Adam Kolers for helping me think through the response, and to John Gibson for his comments on a previous draft.

James, C. L. R. (1993), *Beyond a Boundary*, 50th Anniversary Edition (Durham, NC: Duke University Press).
List, C. and P. Pettit (2011), *Group Agency: The Possibility, Design, and Status of Corporate Agents* (New York: Oxford University Press).
Locke, J. (1988), *Two Treatises of Government*, ed. Peter Laslett (Cambridge: Cambridge University Press).
Salvatore, N. (1982), *Eugene V. Debs: Citizen and Socialist* (Urbana: University of Illinois Press).

3

The (anti)colonial limits of solidarity: history, theory, practice

Jared Holley

Introduction

Andrea Sangiovanni's lead essay is perhaps the most perspicuous and certainly the most ambitious theoretical account of solidarity to date. Its perspicacity derives both from Sangiovanni's facility with the methods and language of analytic philosophy, and from his willingness to clarify that language via engagement with neighboring discussions in critical social theory, social psychology, and the history of political thought. The pluralist spirit that guides his inquiry also signals its ambition. The account is designed to apply trans-contextually – that is, to be capable of clarifying practices and theories of solidarity that emerge from any given geographical space at any given time in (modern) history.

My aim in this response is to test the limits of Sangiovanni's account by placing it in dialogue with the history and present of anticolonial solidarity. I raise two main points. First, Sangiovanni's conceptual history of solidarity is limited by a neglect of the colonial context in which the concept of solidarity first emerged. I suggest that recontextualizing nineteenth-century solidarism in relation to French imperialism reveals some colonial limits to Léon Bourgeois's theory of solidarity. I then ask how contemporary theorists can avoid these limits. Second, Sangiovanni's normative account of solidarity is limited by a neglect of anticolonial solidarity. Surveying the history of anticolonial (inter)nationalism and contemporary anticolonial movements reveals a range of ways of seeing solidarity somewhat differently. Concepts like *contestation* and *critique*, and distinctions like *hegemonic-subaltern* and *inclusive-exclusive*, are central to the theory and practice of anticolonial solidarity. But they play almost no role in Sangiovanni's account. I therefore ask if these historical and practical limits suggest a possible theoretical one: namely, a difficulty in tracking the diverse kinds of practices that may be seen as central to anticolonial solidarity today. I call this a 'possible' limit because I hope that raising these points will provide an opportunity for Sangiovanni to correct any of my misinterpretations and to clarify his account by continuing the dialogue he so generously initiated.

Which history? Whose solidarity?

We lack a definitive history or even a robust historiographical discussion of solidarity.[1] In this context, Sangiovanni's reconstruction of solidarity's conceptual history is a valuable contribution. This is the case, I emphasize, independent of the relationship between that history and Sangiovanni's more elaborate normative theory. But how should we see that relationship? After introducing his novel concept of solidarity, Sangiovanni suggests that 'tracing the history of solidarity … is so important' because

> The history both provides a testing ground for the usefulness of the concept introduced and is important for understanding the political uses and possibilities of solidarity, including what makes it relevant to social and political life today. Understanding how and when the concept of solidarity emerged – including especially what solidarity emerged as a response *to* – will help us appreciate the centrality and distinctiveness of certain aspects of solidarity that we might not have appreciated before. (p. 8)

1 Especially for Anglophone readers, the touchstone remains J. Hayward's PhD thesis 'The Idea of Solidarity in French Social and Political Thought in the Nineteenth and Early Twentieth Centuries' (Hayward 1958). Its story has recently been updated for French readers by historian of philosophy M.-C. Blais in *La solidarité: Histoire d'une idée* (Blais 2007). We also know more about the 'conceptual transfer' from French *solidarité* to German *Solidarität* thanks to German historians A. Wildt (see Wildt 1995) and Thomas Fiegle (see Fiegle 2003). This relatively fallow field is rounded out by sporadic studies like S. Stjernø's *Solidarity in Europe* (Stjernø 2005) and Peter Baldwin's *The Politics of Social Solidarity* (Baldwin 1990).

This is a welcome defense of a close relationship between historical understanding and political judgment. Its importance can be clarified by stating it negatively: if we were to *mis*understand (i) 'how and when' solidarity emerged as a concept, then we would risk *mis*understanding both (ii) the social and political problems the concept was initially designed to address and (iii) its role in our own practical and discursive contexts today. Note that this is more than a call for an intellectual division of labor between historians and theorists. On Sangiovanni's own terms, a normative theory of solidarity requires history to clarify its political relevance, and that history must be built in at the foundations.

The few intellectual histories of solidarity we have usually start with its rise to public prominence in France's Third Republic. The concept dates to the Roman law of obligations and appears in the Napoleonic Civil Code. Throughout the nineteenth century, philosophers, social reformers, and politicians used various understandings of solidarity to debate solutions to the 'social question' stemming from increasing inequality under the industrial division of labor. As the sense and reference of solidarity was expanded from a narrowly legal to a more broadly socio-political idea, it came to be seen as offering a middle position between the extreme poles of laissez-faire economic liberalism and communist collectivism. Thereby, it became integral to the theory and practice of early French liberalism, especially through the Radical Republican Party and the social movement for 'solidarism' (pp. 34–6).

This history is both accurate and limited. Even in such potted form, it meets the internal demands of Sangiovanni's account – it tells us how and when solidarity emerged (Third Republican social theory and practice), what it responded to (inequality), and what it could do for us (help us understand and address inequality). It is thus entirely appropriate for Sangiovanni and other political theorists to ground their normative theories on something like this story. But while 'solidarism' was indeed something like the 'official philosophy for the Third Republic' (p. 35 n. 66), historians of French imperialism have long emphasized that the idea of 'the civilizing mission' functioned concurrently as 'the official ideology of the Third Republic's vast new empire' (Conklin 1997, p. 11). The literature on civilization and the civilizing mission is immense, especially as compared to the nascent literature on solidarity.[2] But despite the centrality of both 'solidarity' and 'civilization' to nineteenth-century French political thought, these literatures have never been brought together. What happens to our usual way of seeing 'solidarity' if we see it as emerging alongside 'civilization' in the practical and discursive context of France's Third Republic? Would this angle of vision allow us to appreciate certain aspects of solidarity that we might not have appreciated before?

The connection is clear in Durkheim's *Division of Labour in Society* (1893). We are familiar with his famous distinction between 'mechanical solidarity', which derives from similarities and subsumes the individual personality within the group; and 'organic solidarity', which links individuals to society through differential and specialized functions in the division of labor. Less familiar is how that distinction is connected to a hierarchical contrast between 'higher' civilized and 'lower' uncivilized peoples. Durkheim's concluding discussion of international politics clarifies his view: by 'backward' societies characterized by mechanical solidarity, he means to identify not just remnants of Europe's feudal past but contemporary non-European societies. The 'uncivilized-mechanical'/'civilized-organic' contrast provides a schema for Durkheim to claim that uncivilized non-Europeans are incapable of both freedom and justice. That is, they can achieve only an 'apparent' liberty and their morality is less 'rational' and less 'human'. The colonial implications of this schema are equally clear: industrial nations should pursue the goal of 'universal brotherhood' by organizing a 'society of European peoples' and continuing their colonial policies, or what Durkheim calls 'the absorption or elimination of less advanced societies'.[3] Durkheim's view of empire is of course contested.[4] My point here is simply that

---

2 For instance, Bowden 2009; Koskenniemi 2001.
3 See Durkheim 1984, esp. 333–4, 335–8, 341 fn. 6. While Durkheim holds that mechanical and organic solidarity are 'no different in nature' and that the need to realize the collective and to specialize are 'both moral', the societies in which one or the other predominates are hierarchically ranked.
4 For conflicting interpretations of colonialism in Durkheim, compare Fields 2002, Kurasawa 2013, and Bhambra and Holmwood 2021, esp. pp. 141–75. For the claim that Durkheim's mechanical/organic solidarity adopts the conventional 'racial mapping of the global space', see da Silva 2007, p. 137.

the close internal relationship of 'solidarity' and 'civilization' in his text allowed them to function together in a language that, at a minimum, legitimated the Third Republic's colonial policies. We can see a similar connection in Durkheim's contemporary Léon Bourgeois, a French statesman who briefly served as prime minister and was one of the initial architects of the League of Nations. Bourgeois's pamphlet *Solidarité* (1895) was the intellectual foundation of the solidarist movement. Sangiovanni rightly draws our attention to his influence and helpfully clarifies his account of solidarity (pp. 35–9). To briefly reiterate, two aspects are fundamental. The first is Bourgeois's view of contemporary inequalities as the accumulated product of joint social production in the division of labor over time. The second follows from this extended temporal perspective: we are born into society owing a 'social debt' to both past generations and our contemporaries. Bourgeois's real innovation was to devise a thought experiment to specify the content of this debt at a given moment. What he called the 'quasi-contract' comes rather close to Rawls' 'original position': like Rawls, Bourgeois suggested that we should imagine what distribution of the benefits and burdens of social interdependence we would agree to if we were free and equal members of a contract prior to our association. This thought experiment then provides a normative standard against which to evaluate social institutions and which guides policies for their reform (Bourgeois 1902, pp. 136–40).[5] Also like Rawls, Bourgeois saw this theory as supporting a social democratic vision of distributive justice and increasing social solidarity. This is obviously an appealing view for many political philosophers today.

While this reconstruction is accurate, it neglects the extent to which Bourgeois's political career was marked from beginning to end by France's colonial entanglements. The central plank of his Radical Republican platform was an income tax reform bill that he hoped would address France's roiling political, fiscal, and colonial crises. The Long Depression of 1873–95 had put the social question back on the map, and the 1884 law permitting trade unions signaled the growing strength of the socialist movement. But the immediate context of his brief stint as prime minister was a deeply controversial

---

5 As Sangiovanni notes (p. 37 n. 70), Rawls identifies the difference principle with 'fraternity.' See Rawls 1999, pp. 90–1.

colonial policy. He entered office in November 1895, just after French troops occupied Madagascar in an operation that was widely recognized as an expense of both funds and human life wildly disproportionate to its presumed difficulty and potential benefit (Blais 2007, pp. 22ff). He left office in April 1896, after losing a vote on the credits necessary to repatriate the imperial forces from Madagascar. While parts of *Solidarité* had appeared in serialized form, it was this political failure that led him to publish it, unchanged, as his hugely successful pamphlet. In short, Bourgeois's brief stint in France's highest political office was decisively shaped by his involvement in French colonial policy.

It is of course not wrong to see solidarity as emerging in response to the social question. Bourgeois argued that the great strength of solidarity was its orientation to overcoming economic and social inequality. It was a 'materialist' concept, devoid of the 'metaphysical' trappings of the older idea of fraternity, which it ought therefore to replace in an updated Radical Republican triad (Comte 1883, pp. 100–1). But solidarity was also in some sense a new master concept – rather than merely sit alongside the principles of liberty and equality, it presupposed and expressed their existence and unity. Following Alfred Fouillée's theory of modern society as a 'contractual regime', it was also intended to replace prevailing Christian notions of charity, seen as unable to address the stark inequalities of industrial society. Instead, modern citizens needed to recognize the duty of what Fouillée called 'reparative justice'. Where charity was an asymmetrical duty of the rich to relieve the suffering of the poor, reparative justice was symmetrical, a duty of each to repair the historically rooted contemporary injustices felt by all (Fouillée 1880, pp. 420–1, 325ff., 357–62). Bourgeois saw his idea of the social debt as developing Fouillée's reparative justice in a more practical direction. He rejected the language of 'duty' as overly abstract, repeatedly defending his choice of 'debt' precisely because of its concrete grounding in real inequalities (Bourgeois 1902, pp. 106ff).[6] With the idea of social debt at its core, then, Bourgeois's view of solidarity is distinguished from charity because it is material and historical. The ground of our obligation to redress contemporary

---

6 Cf. Stock-Morton 1988, pp. 109ff.

inequality is not merely an abstract ideal of justice or moral equality. Rather, the obligation to repair injustice is in the first instance an obligation to repay a debt, as material inequalities are the legacy of joint social production through history.

But Bourgeois and his contemporaries were perfectly aware that the social question could not neatly be separated from the colonial question. When his pamphlet was published, colonization was widely coming to be considered what the political economist Paul Leroy-Beaulieu called 'a matter of life and death for France'. The most important ideologist of French imperialism, Leroy-Beaulieu's reference text *Modern Colonization* was even more influential than Bourgeois's pamphlet. As he explained to his many readers, the relationship between metropole and colonies was rightly understood as one of 'a permanent exchange of influences, a reciprocity of services, a continuity of relations – in a word, mutual dependence' (Leroy-Beaulieu 1877).[7] As a monarchist and laissez-faire economist, it should come as no surprise that Leroy-Beaulieu objected to the solidarists' view of solidarity. For him, solidarity should be seen as more like charity, a duty of conscience felt by the well-off to elevate the downtrodden. The problem with the language of a social debt was that it left the 'so-called creditors' in the position to determine the actual legal terms of repayment. If the rich came to see themselves as legally obligated to repay a debt, they would be entirely at the discretion of the poor to fix the terms – and moreover to do so endlessly.[8] The same would be true, by analogy, if an imperial power that recognized its mutual dependence on its colonial subjects came to conceive of that relationship as establishing a legal debt.

Some of his early readers attacked Bourgeois for failing to address the French Empire or colonialism in his pamphlet on solidarity. Edmond Demolins was a monarchist critic of the Third Republic who opposed solidarism from the antidemocratic right. He was best known as a supporter of 'Anglo-Saxon' models of public education,

---

7 The text was published in six new editions between 1874 and 1908. Cf. Hayward, p. 33.
8 La solidarité sociale, ses nouvelles formules/par M. Eugène d'Eichthal. La solidarité sociale comme principe des lois/par M. Charles Brunot. Observations/ par Frédéric Passy, Paul Leroy-Beaulieu, Levasseur, ... [et al.] pp. 89–97 (my translation).

which he explained as following from and enforcing an individualist spirit of 'particularism'. On his view, the 'recent fashion' for 'solidarity in French thought' was an attempt by Bourgeois and his followers to subject the individual to the community, which would ultimately destroy the individualism that drove historical progress (Demolins 1897, p. 322).[9] In a mostly laborious critique, Demolins intriguingly accused Bourgeois of having been insufficiently attentive to and unrealistic about contemporary French imperialism. Colonial rule is despotic from top to bottom; a feudal system of property, arbitrary justice, and servitude in which the 'soldier sets an example for the civilian' in their attempt to 'master' native servants. It enforces the moral degeneration of the colonizer, leading even the 'most civilized' to revert to 'barbaric' treatment of the colonized as lower than domestic animals. Demolins criticized Bourgeois for failing to consider such 'examples from our colonization processes'. If he had, he would have seen that human beings were naturally less inclined to support than to exploit and dominate others. And this, in turn, proved that the solidarists' faith in modern Europeans to recognize a legal debt and moral obligation to their fellow citizens was an unrealistic fantasy.

Bourgeois did not respond to Demolins. But he did eventually clarify his agreement with Leroy-Beaulieu that solidarity could not be extended to the colonies. Well before he was named first president of the League of Nations, he put the language of solidarity to sporadic but revealing use in his international thought. As early as 1899, he argued that a growing recognition of the 'ever-closer economic solidarity of nations' had made 'world peace' a real possibility. All that was needed was for a 'society of nations' to actualize this latent unity by organizing and defining the common material, economic, intellectual, and moral interests of civilized states. The 'civilized-uncivilized' opposition grounds his view of international legislation, which he saw as creating a domain of equality 'open to all civilized states', which it would 'envelop' in a 'network of peace'. He celebrated the 1907 International Convention of Arbitration in the same terms, as affirming what, in this context, he was willing to call the 'duty of solidarity' that applied 'between civilized peoples'. By the time he discussed the Balkan Crisis of 1913, it was clear that

9 My translation.

his real concern was with 'the great powers' acting on 'the solidarity of *their* permanent interests' (Bourgeois 1913, pp. 22, 40, 62–3, 228–9, 239–40).[10] And while he saw Japan's proposed racial equality bill at the Paris Peace Conference as grounded in an 'indisputable principle of justice', he refused to apply it universally, restricting it to 'civilized' members of the League (Shimazu 2002, pp. 29, 119).[11] In this way, he reduced the universal principle of 'human solidarity' to a parochial one, the 'solidarity of European interests' (Bourgeois 1913, p. 239).

This brief recontextualization of Bourgeois's account of solidarity provides a slightly different answer to Sangiovanni's historical questions. On this view, solidarity *emerged* in the metropole of a rapidly expanding empire as a *response to* intertwined social, fiscal, and colonial crises. This allows us better to understand its contested *political uses* as (i) a normative standard of welfare policies, (ii) an index of European social and civilizational superiority, and (iii) a core feature of legitimating discourses of colonialism. A charitable interpretation would see Bourgeois's colonial limits as surprising. Like Leroy-Beaulieu, he knew that the Third Republic and its colonies were mutually dependent. If nothing else, his political failure to pass tax reform clearly demonstrated that any attempt to redress contemporary inequalities through welfare policy at home was inseparable from colonial policy abroad. The emphasis on material interdependence and gestures to a sort of historical injustice in his theory of solidarity gave him resources to extend it to the colonies. But for him, solidarity is a feature only of European societies that have reached that state of civilizational development at which the fair distribution of the benefits and burdens of the social division of labor has become the central political problem. The quasi-contract thought experiment responds to the contemporary inequalities it purports to address by abstracting away from their real historical roots. It thereby disavows what we know that he knew – namely, that the very possibility of relations of solidarity among citizens of the metropole is itself dependent upon extractive relations with the colonies. In this way, it shields from view the colonial origins of the benefits to be redistributed and generates a

10 My translation, my emphasis. Cf. 80, 122, 127, 135–6, 187.
11 Citing Conférence de paix de Paris 1919–20, pp. 175–6.

*mis*understanding of the European societies to which it was designed to apply.

The contemporary implications of returning to Bourgeois are thus at least ambiguous. For Sangiovanni, the point of doing so is primarily to introduce two sets of analytical distinctions that play a prominent role throughout his essay. It provides an account of 'social solidarity' understood as both material interdependence and moral identification with others in the division of labor, and generates a distinction between the *grounds*, *object*, and *scope* of solidarity (pp. 38–9). But it also serves as an 'analogue' for the original normative argument about the grounds of 'civic solidarity': for Sangiovanni, citizens identify with one another as joint participants not simply in the division of labor but 'in reproducing, reforming, and authoring common institutions', a 'more fundamental contribution to the basic structure that makes our contribution through work to the joint social product possible in the first place' (p. 77). A recontextualized Bourgeois reminds us of his and his contemporaries' understanding that colonization makes citizens' contributions to the basic structure possible in the first place. For the metropolitan division of labor is part of the political economy of empire, which supports national civic institutions and generates whatever wealth might be redistributed through them. To root an account of solidarity in a genealogy starting with Bourgeois does not commit us to a developmentalist philosophy of history or hierarchical schema of civilization. But insofar as the lineages of empire persist through mechanisms of both formal and informal imperialism today, we must avoid reproducing accounts of solidarity that obscure the history and present of neocolonialism. For if we fail to do so, we misrepresent our own societies to ourselves, and misunderstand the political uses to which our theories of solidarity might be put in them.

Sangiovanni's account of civic solidarity has promising resources to avoid these kinds of misrepresentations. Seeing citizenship as something like joint authorship is intended to ground an account of civic solidarity as a 'commitment to overcoming, together, the adversity created by ... legacies of racism, sexism, colonialism, and other forms of arbitrary exclusion and oppression' (p. 78). The language of basic structures and arbitrary exclusions comes from Rawls: I have already noted the points of contact between Rawls and Bourgeois's ideas, and there is a sense in which the foregoing provides a sort of genealogical analogue of certain philosophical critiques of Rawls' liberalism. One of these, most familiar from the late Charles Mills, emphasizes that the 'exclusions' of racism and colonialism are more than merely morally arbitrary: they are both *materially* constitutive of the political-economic basic structure of modern Western societies, and *normatively* constitutive of the very distinction between reasonableness and arbitrariness. Sangiovanni's account is not an instance of what Mills called 'ideal theory as ideology', for it seems consistent with what Sangiovanni elsewhere calls his 'practice-dependent institutionalism' (Sangiovanni 2016, pp. 3–23). Nor does it evade the history of colonization. Its commitment to (conceptual) history distances it from the attempt to transcend history shared by Rawls' veil of ignorance and Bourgeois's quasi-contract. But there is an opening here to ask how, exactly, an account of civic solidarity grounded in Bourgeois and gesturing to Rawls, avoids what Mills called the 'coloniality of Rawls' sociopolitical and normative assumptions'. Sangiovanni notes that these assumptions are in a sense prefigured in Bourgeois. I have suggested that what Mills called their 'coloniality' is, too. What difference, if any, does this deeper sense of 'how and when the concept of solidarity emerged' make to our understanding of its 'political uses and possibilities' today? Should this history be incorporated into Sangiovanni's account, or can it be safely disregarded? If the former, how; if the latter, why?

What is 'anticolonial' 'solidarity'?

On November 18–21, 2021, Canada's paramilitary Royal Canadian Mounted Police invaded unceded Gidimt'en Clan territories of the Wet'suwet'en First Nation in the north-western central interior of British Columbia (BC). They forcibly removed Wet'suwet'en land defenders under an injunction granted to Coastal GasLink, a company constructing a 670-kilometer fracked-gas pipeline as part of the single largest private investment in Canadian history. Each clan within the Wet'suwet'en Nation have full jurisdiction under their law to control access to their territory. Peaceful women and elders were faced with heavy assault rifles and the full colonial violence of a state invasion on unceded territories. Approximately twenty land defenders and accredited media were arrested. This was the third such invasion of Wet'suwet'en territories since 2019.[12]

Wet'suwet'en Hereditary Chiefs and land defenders engage in a range of solidarity practices as part of their ongoing resistance to settler colonialism. These include reconnecting to traditional territories through the kinds of local exercises of individual and collective self-determination known as indigenous 'resurgence', such as at the Unist'ot'en reoccupation Camp.[13] They extend to solidarity with other Indigenous nations, such as the historic meeting with the Mohawk Nations that helped to coordinate the Shut Down Canada blockade, which halted the entire eastern network of the Canadian National Railway.[14] Or the issuing of 'invitations' to engage in place-based solidarity on Indigenous territory, such as the Tiny House Warrior Project in which settler activists construct small structures (tiny houses), which they transport and place on the proposed pipeline route to block construction.[15] Or yet wider 'calls' to 'international solidarity' issued by the Wet'suwet'en Hereditary Chiefs, to which thousands of anticolonial and environmental activists have responded in a global wave of demonstrations, direct actions, and traffic, rail, and port blockades.[16]

These practices 'of and for freedom' have long and complicated histories.[17] Any attempt to think of them *together* as practices of solidarity raises challenging theoretical and practical questions. What does it mean for settlers to act in solidarity with local practitioners of Indigenous resurgence?[18] How is the nation-to-nation solidarity of Indigenous peoples similar to the solidarity between Indigenous

---

12 For discussion, see e.g., Craig-Sparrow, Zoe et al. 2021.
13 See the collection of materials at https://unistoten.camp/ (accessed December 14, 2020).
14 On the Shut Down Canada protests, and their relevance for political theories of 'populism', see Cherry 2021, p. 422. For a discussion of Indigenous internationalism, see Simpson, 2017, pp. 55–70.
15 See www.tinyhousewarriors.com (accessed April 27, 2023). For discussion, and what could be considered an attempt to theorize the possibilities for Indigenous–settler solidarity, see Swain 2022.
16 Hereditary Chiefs of the Wet'suwet'en 2020: International Call to Solidarity, https://unistoten.camp/ (accessed December 14, 2020).
17 See Tully 2008, pp. 257–88 and Asch 2002.
18 On 'settler', see Lowman and Barker 2015.

peoples and settlers? What are the relevant differences between an 'invitation' to place-based solidarity *on* Indigenous territory, and an international 'call' to solidarity *with* Indigenous peoples? Perhaps most important in this context, should we expect a concept of solidarity to account for all these practices?

In approaching these questions, I find it helpful to think of 'anticolonial solidarity' as an uncertain combination of two contested family-resemblance concepts. They are (i) *contested* in that their meanings are fought over in the practical struggles in which they are deployed to (re)describe and (re)evaluate the practices and relationships being contested.[19] They are (ii) *family-resemblance* concepts in that their criteria necessarily vary between the actors who deploy them and across contexts of struggle. To identify a given practice as one of 'anticolonial solidarity' is simply to say that the practices and attitudes of the actors share sufficient criteria of 'solidarity' and 'anticolonialism' to bear the name 'anticolonial solidarity'.[20] In this way of proceeding, the above questions are answered by surveying the contemporary and historical practices or families of 'anticolonial solidarity'. What follows is one such (partial and defeasible) survey.[21] The point of the survey is not to excavate a concept with a set of (universally valid) conditions against which to evaluate political practices, thereby settling the contest of meanings. Rather, my aim is to approach the history of 'anticolonial' political thought in a way that illuminates both the contested nature

---

19 Both 'anticolonial' and 'solidarity' are what in German one would call 'Kampfbegriffe', i.e., concepts deployed as weapons in a struggle. See Koselleck 1995, p. 111.
20 I associate this approach with Tully 2003, pp. 17–42. For one view of the relationship between the family-resemblance approach and the contestability of concepts, see Janik 2003, esp. 108–11.
21 The following survey focuses primarily on twentieth-century anticolonial thinkers and contemporary practices of anticolonial solidarity. But it is important to emphasize that anticolonial critiques of European discourses of solidarity, on the one hand, and theories and practices of specifically anticolonial solidarity, on the other, have always been there in solidarity's conceptual history. One of the most interesting appeared in 1885 – i.e., 10 years before Bourgeois's pamphlet – from Haitian statesman and early anthropologist Anténor Firmin (see Firmin 2002, esp. 379–91). For discussion, see Holley 2023.

of 'solidarity' and the vibrant field of practices of 'anticolonial solidarity' today.

Sangiovanni does not discuss (Indigenous) anticolonialism in any detail. But there are hints that its framework can help to make sense of such practices. Section 3 explores four 'grounds' or 'right reasons' for acting in solidarity: way of life, role, condition and experience, or cause (pp. 67–91). This framework is helpful because it allows us clearly to distinguish between different types of solidarity. The ground of socialist solidarity is either the workers' *role* as producers in the division of labor or their *condition* as oppressed or exploited by capitalism (pp. 45–7). The ground of feminist solidarity is women's *condition* of 'subjection to a subordinating gendered social structure' (p. 85). The ground of nationalist solidarity is identification with others based on a shared *way of life*. The 'Sioux nation' provides an intriguing example (pp. 68–71), and a footnote suggests that this framework can track my examples, by analogy, as instances of 'anticolonial solidarities'. Like Third World anticolonial nationalisms, local Indigenous resurgence could be seen as solidarity grounded in a shared *way of life*; like Pan-African or Red Power anticolonialism, Indigenous internationalism could be seen as solidarity grounded in a common *condition* as 'structurally dominated by settler powers'. Respondents to local 'invitations' or global 'calls' could then be seen as 'allies in these struggles', who 'count as acting in solidarity on the basis of identification with' the *cause* of anticolonialism (p. 68 n. 146).

These analogies are productive but potentially limited. Many Indigenous thinkers and activists have understood their nationalisms in opposition to both First and Third World varieties.[22] Sangiovanni adopts David Miller's account of nationalism as belief in a 'territorially defined public culture that binds together a group of people across generations'. Because this definition includes nationalists that do 'not seek statehood' (p. 68), it seems to account for those Indigenous nationalisms that are specifically 'non-statist' (Alfred 1995, p. 9). But how well it can track the ways that Indigenous nationalists understand their efforts 'to govern and determine themselves' (p. 68) is initially unclear. For Lakota scholar Vine Deloria Jr., 'nationhood' and 'self-government' are not simply two possible goals of

22 See Go and Watson 2019.

Indigenous political movements but, rather, 'two entirely different positions in the world.' For 'self-government' is 'not an Indian idea' but a legacy of European theory and practice. Though 'an exceedingly useful concept' around which Indigenous movements had organized, in the US 'self-government' had come to be understood in terms of 'domestic dependent nation' status.[23] It could therefore 'never supplant the intangible, spiritual, and emotional aspirations of American Indians' captured by their understanding of 'nationhood'. For Deloria, Indigenous nations are 'unique in the world' because, while they understood 'self-government' in more expansive terms, they were constrained to practice it in the context of 'a wholly new and modern civilization that has been transported to their lands' (Deloria and Lytle 1984, pp. 13, 15, 2). As Hawaiian nationalist Huanani-Kay Trask explained, following Deloria, Indigenous nationalists therefore had to 'speak in a different language than Old World nationalism' (Trask 1999, p. 59, cf. p. 62).[24] The understanding of concepts generated from reflection on European nationalism cannot, then, be assumed to apply by analogy to Indigenous anticolonialisms. Testing their ability to track those practices would require a more contextual and comparative approach than Sangiovanni provides.

The same is true of ideas of 'self-determination' in Indigenous and Third World internationalisms.[25] Pan-Africanists like Tanzania's Julius Nyerere coupled the expulsion of colonial rulers through national independence with attempts to secure non-hierarchical forms of international interdependence through institutions like the New International Economic Order (NIEO) (Getachew, 2019).[26] But Indigenous groups contested Third World politics of self-determination from both sides. Members of one of Tanzania's largest Indigenous groups, the Maasai, argued that Nyerere's national development strategies were a continuation of the 'alienation of our land and its resources' initiated by European colonizers (Parkipuny 1989).[27] For

23 See *Cherokee Nation v Georgia* 1831 and Duthu 2013.
24 Trask positions herself in a genealogy with Deloria and Russel Means of the American Indian Movement – which Sangiovanni discusses (p. 68 n. 146) – at p. 54 n. 2.
25 This paragraph is indebted to Acosta 2022.
26 Cf. Manela 2007a; Massad 2018; Manela 2007b.
27 From Center for World Indigenous Studies, Chief George Manuel Memorial Indigenous Library, *Fourth World Documentation Project*, sec. 1, para. 8.

the World Council of Indigenous Peoples (WCIP), the NIEO was an attempt to institutionalize at a global level these very strategies that were 'ravaging tribal areas to which indigenous peoples have been moved'. As such, it was a 'blueprint for the total destruction of indigenous peoples'. In response, they argued for a 'global dialogue' on the NIEO that would include Indigenous peoples and guaranteed their 'right of self-determination'.[28] They also critically distinguished their view of self-determination from familiar Third World understandings: where Nyerere saw national self-determination as grounded in and scaling up from individual 'self-reliance', the WCIP saw self-determination as a right of ethnic 'groups' or 'peoples'; where the NIEO sought the economic interdependence of capitalist and socialist postcolonial nation-states, the WCIP's aim of 'sovereignty' over Indigenous 'land and culture' explicitly rejected understandings of land 'ownership' common to both capitalist and socialist schools of industrial development. From the perspective of these Indigenous 'Fourth World' anticolonialists, Third World uses of self-determination were less a reinvention than a continuation of a truncated and colonial understanding of a purportedly universal value.

I provide these examples not to suggest that any given view of self-government or self-determination is in some sense the 'correct' one. I want rather to emphasize that these and other concepts central to anticolonial political theory and practice have always been deeply contested. For Mohawk scholar Taiaiake Alfred, such contestation is 'the necessary by-product of rejecting the legacy of an unjust history and the struggle to re-integrate traditional values in the community'. For just as 'challenging the laws and structures of a colonial regime' leads to 'reaction by, and confrontation with, the state', so does it lead activists to contest the 'nature and meaning of tradition' itself, generating 'factionalism and conflict' within the movement (Alfred 1995, p. 2).[29]

Sangiovanni's brief discussion of Sioux nationalist solidarity does not register anything like this political-conceptual contestation. It suggests that solidarists can see the grounds of their identification

---

28 Ryser et al., The New International Economic Order, sec. 4, para. 2. Cited in Acosta 2022, p. 62.
29 Alfred's account of 'self-conscious traditionalism' is a key precursor to the contemporary resurgence movement: Alfred 2009.

differently, and even take these 'differences and disagreements' themselves to be partly constitutive of 'what it means to be', say, Sioux (p. 15). Yet it remains unclear the degree to which Sangiovanni takes this mode of identification to be open to revision, how pragmatic (or pragmatist) it is.[30] For while solidarity is said not to 'preclude even profound disagreement' (p. 22), only the account of 'civic solidarity' foregrounds 'profound disagreement about the character and requirements of the values and ideals that underlie common institutions'; also noting citizens' 'readiness to define them through deliberation (and sometimes more open conflict)' (p. 78). This is explicitly contrasted with (Sioux) nationalist solidarity: citizens are attached to modern states because of 'what they *do* together, which defines, in part, who they *are*', whereas 'nationalists have it the other way around: who we *are* should define what we *do* together' (p. 78). Insofar as Indigenous and other anticolonial (inter)nationalists emphasize the centrality of precisely these kinds of contestation to their practices, why should they be restricted to the practices of citizens of modern states? If Sangiovanni's account of nationalist solidarity is to be exemplified by the Sioux and extended by analogy to Indigenous resurgence, it could be strengthened by clarifying its approach to these more agonistic dimensions of anticolonial theory and practice. It would thereby avoid ascribing an implausible degree of pre-political unity, consensus – or worse, mechanical solidarity – to anticolonial (inter)nationalisms, Indigenous or otherwise.[31]

---

30 For a critique of 'foundationalist' accounts of identity and solidarity, see Gooding-Williams 2009, pp. 223–42. Critiquing Shelby 2009, which Sangiovanni cites favourably throughout. For a critical extension of Gooding-Williams, see Marin 2018.

31 One way of doing this might be to say more about what it means to ground solidarity in a way of life. Although not specified in the text, Sangiovanni follows the definition of a way a life in Mason 2000, pp. 22-3: 'a set of rule governed practices, which are at least loosely woven together, and which constitute at least some central areas of social, political and economic activity'. A 'culture', then, is a shared way of life that is 'informed by a set of interconnected traditions of thought and inquiry'. While any way of life, finally, 'necessarily involves cooperative activity', the participants 'need not value cooperation for its own sake' – rather, they must cooperate in abiding by the rules that govern practices which, themselves, permit a high degree non-cooperation with each other'.

This is important because these kinds of contestation are especially prominent in discussions of anticolonial solidarity. In 1977, the WCIP's Workshop on 'Indigenous Ideology and Philosophy' introduced a distinction between different kinds of solidarity (my emphases):

> *Solidarity* with the members of the dominant society is demanded from the indigenous peoples *on the conditions of the dominant majority*. The *kind of solidarity the dominant society expects* from its members towards the indigenous peoples will normally again be *on the conditions of the dominant society*. This demonstrates again that respect for groups also depends upon the expedition of power. Just and unjust principles may be of no interest without power. This way of thinking may have been intelligible in a period when a man might have had a right if he could shoot faster than another. But is it also valid in 1977?

Settler colonialism produces a rift between 'dominant society' and 'dominated' ethnic groups, which may or may not be numerical 'minorities'. The former has 'dominant political and economic influence', 'cultural and linguistic prestige', and 'a tendency to expand its norm system beyond the borders of its ethnic area'. As 'solidarity' is central to the colonial system of norms, members of the dominant society set the terms and 'conditions' of what it means for both settlers and Indigenous peoples to act in 'solidarity'. Its 'representatives' consolidate these conditions through 'legislation' and, especially, by demanding 'respect' for a 'legal system' that systematically 'disregards the ethnic and cultural plurality of citizens'.[32] The rift in settler society is thus simultaneously discursive and practical: political power attempts to settle the meaning of the concepts through which it is exercised.

The history of anticolonial political thought is replete with such critiques and the distinction (implicit here) between 'hegemonic'

---

32 Robert Petersen, *Indigenous Ideology and Philosophy Workshop II*. Statement by World Council of Indigenous Peoples to workshop participants, 1981. From Center for World Indigenous Studies, Chief George Manuel Memorial Indigenous Library, *Fourth World Documentation Project* www.cwis.org/wp-content/uploads/documents/grouprt.txt (accessed April 26, 2023). For discussion, though not about solidarity, see Acosta 2022, pp. 49–50.

and 'counter-hegemonic' or 'subaltern' solidarities.[33] Each of Deloria Jr., Trask, Alfred, and the WCIP, in different contexts, argued that hegemonic understandings of normative concepts were integral to the ongoing colonization of Indigenous peoples. In response, they engaged in alternative practices of self-government, self-determination, and solidarity, and articulated counter-hegemonic understandings of those concepts to track those practices. This critical framework is hardly unique to Indigenous anticolonialisms. W. E. B. Du Bois famously argued that solidarity among European peoples and states facilitated an imperial project rooted in the false 'idea of an exclusive White Man's World'. As he put it in 1924, Western imperialism had created a world system in which 'blacks and browns and yellows, subdued, cajoled and governed by white men, form a laboring proletariat subject to European white democracy which industry controls'. As such, including the world's majority of dominated 'darker races' in a truly democratic global system would constitute a 'tremendous revolt against the solidarity of the West'. Crucially, imperial solidarity also dominated White Europeans. The 'myth' of White supremacy 'misled' the 'dimly thinking' working classes, rendering them mere 'blind executives' of their industrial-imperialist masters (Du Bois 1925, pp. 431, 442).[34] The hegemonic understanding of solidarity was therefore ideological in the fullest sense: grounded in a false belief that, in legitimating practices of colonization, brings those who hold it into unwitting contradiction with the democratic values they otherwise purport to hold and, thereby, into a condition of unfreedom.[35]

Sangiovanni's account addresses neither the critique of hegemonic solidarity nor the distinction with counter-hegemonic or subaltern

---

33 My use here of '(counter-)hegemonic' does not invoke a specific theory of hegemony. Rather, with James Tully, 'it just disposes us to look for the hegemonic and subaltern traditions of political thought at play, the hegemonic and subaltern relationships of power in the practices, systems and global networks in which these regimes of knowledge are employed, the modes of relational subjectification and self-awareness of the unequal and interdependent participants, the ongoing practices of contestation and counter-contestation of the participants, and our own places within them'. See Tully forthcoming.
34 For discussion, see Valdez forthcoming.
35 On ideology, see Geuss 1981, pp. 4–26. For more recent discussions of race, racism, and racial inferiority as ideology, see Fields and Fields 2014 and Haslanger 2017.

solidarity common to anticolonial political thought. It does, however, suggest that 'solidarity always aims ... to change the order of things'; that it is 'transformative and critical' (p. 34). And yet, as we have seen, many anticolonial thinkers emphasize the multiple ways that appeals to 'solidarity' are frequently used to consolidate rather than transform the (neo)colonial order. They agree with Sangiovanni's gloss that solidarity among and between colonized peoples can be grounded in their common *condition* of 'structural[] dominat[ion] by settler powers' (p. 68 n. 146). They insist that precisely this condition generates ideological and practical conflict. They also insist, further, that it necessitates an approach to 'solidarity' grounded in explicit critique of the political-ideological structures and everyday practices constituting the given injustice or practice of domination to which counter-hegemonic practices of solidarity respond and seek to transform. The mode of 'critique' of course varies across thinkers and contexts. In 1924, Du Bois urged a global historical perspective to reorient political thinking 'to the periphery of the vast circle and to the unseen and inarticulate workers within the World Shadow'.[36] The WCIP projected Indigenous voices to break the 'conspiracy of silence regarding the condition of indigenous nations' and illuminated practices that, in 1981, remained 'in the shadows of nation-state exploitation'.[37] In each case, critique is seen as inseparable from, and a necessary starting point, of anticolonial solidarity, for it both unmasks hegemonic understandings of solidarity as ideological and alerts us to those subaltern theories and practices of solidarity we might otherwise miss. Sangiovanni has elsewhere suggested a 'dialectic' between 'constructive' and 'demystifying' approaches to political philosophy.[38] If his account is an instance of the former, then perhaps pursuing that suggestion would enable it more closely to track theories and practices of anticolonial solidarity, in which the latter is so prominent.

This emphasis on contestation and critique allows us to return to the contemporary practices of anticolonial solidarity among and

---

36 Du Bois 1925, p. 423.
37 Rudolph C. Ryser, *Remarks before the Sub-Committee on Petitions, Information and Assistance of the World Council of Indigenous Peoples*. Speech by Special Assistant Rudolph C. Ryser. From Center for World Indigenous Studies, Chief George Manuel Memorial Indigenous Library, *Fourth World Documentation Project*, sec. 2, para. 2.
38 Sangiovanni 2008, pp. 137–64 (esp. 163).

with the Wet'suwet'en people with which I began. In academic and activist contexts across Canada, there are two main ways of describing efforts to establish new forms of Indigenous–settler relations: 'reconciliation' and 'resurgence'. These are deeply contested concepts utilized by both Indigenous and settler people. For some, reconciliation is a new form of (state-sponsored) recolonization, from which resurgence necessarily 'turns away' or 'refuses' (Simpson 2014).[39] Others see reconciliation as a transformative practice, alongside which resurgence might operate in a more nuanced 'double decolonization strategy'.[40] Both approaches start from critique of, and opposition to, settler colonialism. They share an analysis of colonial violence towards Indigenous persons and peoples. However, as Nishnaabeg legal theorist Aaron Mills explains, they diverge in their analyses of (i) the 'structural violence' of settler society and (ii) how power organizes 'the field of possible movement' for anticolonial practice more broadly (Mills 2018, pp. 136–7).[41] Resurgence generally sees structural violence as '*subjection to* settler life ways' enforced by the constitutional order; anticolonial practice must therefore be organized 'outside of the formal mechanisms' of dissent. Reconciliation generally sees structural violence as '*exclusion from*' the constitutional order; anticolonial practice should therefore pragmatically demand reform and eventual transformation of that order, especially by including Indigenous legal orders and resurgent modes of relationality within or alongside it (Mills 2018, esp. 139–40; 144–5).[42]

As this (contestable) sketch suggests, the divergence between resurgence and reconciliation arguably extends to how practitioners

---

39 The idea of 'the turn away' was formulated by Taiaiake Alfred but 'has since become a kind of short-hand for the resurgent orientation': Mills 2018, p. 138. Cf. Coulthard 2014, pp. 154–9.
40 Tully forthcoming. Cf. Borrows and Tully 2018, pp. 3–28.
41 They also diverge on their understandings of 'the relationship between identity and decolonization' (Mills 2018, p. 138).
42 Mills notes that the 'relationship between reformative means and transformative ends is far from clear. Adherents of this [reconciliation] approach must argue, not assume, that reformation creates more fertile ground for transformation. The counter-assumption is, of course, that reformation (1) further entrenches settler supremacy by providing it a firmer foundation, and, perhaps more significantly (2) as participation within the imposed liberal constitutional order, validates settler supremacy' (Mills 2019, p. 165 n. 33).

see both the form 'solidarity' might take and the possibilities for building it between Indigenous and non-Indigenous people. Both are committed to what Indigenous thinkers Glen Coulthard and Leanne Simpson have called 'grounded normativity' as a kind of 'place-based solidarity'. Coulthard describes grounded normativities as 'modalities of Indigenous land-connected practices and longstanding experiential knowledge that inform and structure our ethical engagements with the world and our relationships with human and non-human others over time' (Coulthard 2014, p. 13). Grounded normativities *ground* expansive relations of solidarity between people, land, and more-than-human nature. But because they generate 'profoundly different conceptualizations of nationhood and governmentality' in local contexts, the ethical or political responsibilities they generate are unique to a given nation (Simpson 2017, p. 22). While resurgence and reconciliation agree that grounded normativity *grounds* Indigenous nationalist solidarity, they disagree about what this entails for solidarity with other humans beyond a given nation.

To track this aspect of the disagreement, it helps to introduce a further distinction between 'inclusive' and 'exclusive' solidarity. While largely absent from Sangiovanni's account, the distinction does appear in the brief account of 'social movement solidarity'. Social movement solidarity is distinct because it is oppositional, like socialism, but differs according to each movement's view of the 'grounds and object of solidaristic action'. While Sangiovanni's essay notes 'the civil rights movement, feminism, disability, and LGBTQ movements' (p. 53), its analysis might well be extended to anticolonialism. On one hand, 'Black nationalist' social movements are like anticolonial nationalism, in that they are grounded in both a shared *condition* of oppression and a *way of life* 'centered on shared history, mores, and folkways'. Moreover, the 'aim' of establishing a Black nation permits the kind of internal contestation we have seen in anticolonial nationalist movements – here, whether Black nationalists should pursue (i) a separate state (Garvey) or (ii) 'self-governing institutions and self-help' (Malcolm X). On the other hand, Martin Luther King's approach to civil rights twinned socialism's oppositional character with a more 'universalist and Christian form of mutualism and interdependence', which allowed for 'coalition between the civil rights and labor movements' (pp. 55–6). King's view of solidarity is thus more 'inclusive' than Black nationalist solidarity, which, because it aims for 'autonomy from White America' (p. 55) is more 'exclusive'.

This distinction is central to the politics of solidarity in anticolonial social movements today. Resurgence sees solidarity in more *exclusive* terms. For Simpson, grounded normativity allows for solidarity with non-Indigenous others *grounded* in resistance to settler colonialism understood as 'dispossession, capitalism, white supremacy, and heteropatriarchy'. Solidarists are 'allies' from 'communities of co-resistance' who see and resist settler colonialism in the same way, radically uncoupled from dominant institutions. As such, resurgence solidarity requires exclusion of adversaries, especially 'liberal white Canadians' who 'uphold' settler colonialism; indeed, 'there is virtually no room for white people in resurgence'. However, Simpson notes, when 'constellations of co-resistance within grounded normativities … refuse to center whiteness, our real white allies show up in solidarity anyway' (Simpson 2017, pp. 228–31).

Conversely (transformative) reconciliation sees solidarity in more *inclusive* terms. For Mills, the *ground* of this wider solidarity is the 'mutual rootedness' through which all humans are 'always already in relationships'. Recognizing and building intentionally on mutual rootedness facilitates 'treaty' relations between communities. Proponents of reconciliation reject the binary oppositions in resurgence (real allies/false opponents) as a mistaken legacy of Third Worldism's 'master–slave dialectics' (colonizer/colonized), which they argue failed to bring about decolonization and is misapplied in Indigenous contexts. They 'strongly reject' visions of reconciliation that would 'perpetuate unjust relationships of dispossession, domination, exploitation, and patriarchy' (Burrows and Tully 2018, pp. 5–6). But Mills insists that relations of solidarity grounded in mutual rootedness can be strengthened 'no matter the degree of difference in our norms'. While achieving a 'good', 'non-violent relationship both within political communities and across them' requires much hard work, it is 'at least, always possible' (Mills 2018, pp. 160, 156).[43] The necessary exclusion of some White settlers in resurgence

---

43 The language of 'solidarity' is less prominent in reconciliation than in resurgence. While it would require further discussion, I think we can at least tentatively see 'treaty' relations in transformative reconciliation as a kind of 'solidarity' in Sangiovanni's capacious sense.

solidarity is seen as undermining the more inclusive solidarity in transformative reconciliation.

What are we to make of this survey of the history and present of anticolonial solidarity? Sangiovanni's essay is introduced by a concern with the widely felt 'need for some form of collective resistance and mobilization that looks beyond electoral politics', a hunger 'for forms of meaningful and transformative joint action' (p. 3). In the contested field of 'solidarity', 'anticolonial' theories and practices offer some of the most compelling such forms of resistance and transformation. I have suggested that approaching solidarity as a contested family-resemblance concept helps to foreground precisely those practices. Sangiovanni's essay explicitly rejects this approach (p. 5). Yet in doing so it neglects the ideas and distinctions central to anticolonial solidarity – like contestation and critique, and hegemonic-subaltern and inclusion-exclusion. Nor do the practices of anticolonial solidarity that flourish today, across diverse local, transnational, and global contexts, appear on its pages. Political theorists should celebrate Sangiovanni's effort to 'guide our reflection' on solidarity as a 'distinctive social practice' tied to 'forms of collective resistance' that might 'right the balance' of a 'fragmented, unequal, and divisive politics' (p. 124). But we must take care not to overlook those practices of solidarity in the first place.

References

Acosta, C. (2022), 'The Rise of the Fourth World: The World Council of Indigenous Peoples, the Third World, and a Challenge of Anticolonialisms' (MA thesis, Freie Universität Berlin).

Alfred, G. R. (1995), *Heeding the Voices of Our Ancestors: Kahnawake Mohawk Politics and the Rise of Native Nationalism*, 0 edition (Toronto and New York: Oxford University Press)

Alfred, T. (2009), *Peace, Power, Righteousness: An Indigenous Manifesto*, 2nd edition (Don Mills, Ont. and New York: Oxford University Press).

Asch, M. (2002), *On Being Here to Stay: Treaties and Aboriginal Rights in Canada* (Toronto: University of Toronto Press).

Baldwin, P. (1990), *The Politics of Social Solidarity: Class Bases of the European Welfare State, 1875–1975* (Cambridge: Cambridge University Press).

Bhambra, G. K. and J. Holmwood (2021), *Colonialism and Modern Social Theory* (Cambridge: Polity Press), pp. 141–75.

Blais, M.-C. (2007), *La solidarité: Histoire d'une idée* (Paris: Gallimard).

Borrows, J. and J. Tully (2018), 'Introduction', in *Resurgence and Reconciliation: Indigenous-Settler Relations and Earth Teachings*, eds. Michael Asch, John Borrows, and James Tully (Toronto: University of Toronto Press), pp. 3–28.

Bourgeois, L. (1902), *Solidarité* (Paris: Gallimard).

Bourgeois, L. (1913), *Pour La Société des Nations* (Paris: G. Crès).

Bowden, B. (2009), *The Empire of Civilization: The Evolution of an Imperial Idea* (Chicago: University of Chicago Press).

Cherry, K. (2021), 'Resurgence, Populism, and Politics "From Below"', *Social Sciences* 10 (November): 422, https://doi.org/10.3390/socsci10110422 (accessed April 26, 2023).

Comte, A. (1883), *Plan des travaux scientifiques necessaires pour opuscules de philosophie sociale* (Paris: Gallimard).

Conklin, A. L. (1997), *A Mission to Civilize: The Republican Idea of Empire in France and West Africa, 1895–1930* (Stanford: Stanford University Press).

Coulthard, G. S. (2014), *Red Skin, White Masks: Rejecting the Colonial Politics of Recognition* (Minneapolis: University of Minnesota Press).

Craig-Sparrow, Z. et al. (2021), Request for Early Warning and Urgent Action, Submitted to United Nations Committee on The Elimination of Racial Discrimination for consideration at its 105th Session (November 15, 2021–December 3, 2021). www.justiceforgirls.org/uploads/2/4/5/0/24509463/urgent_submission_to_un_cerd_nov_2021.pdf (accessed November 24, 2021).

da Silva, D. F. (2007), *Toward a Global Idea of Race* (Minneapolis: University of Minnesota Press), pp. 134–8.

Deloria Jr., V. and R. M. Lytle (1984), *The Nations Within: The Past and Future of American Indian Sovereignty* (Austin: University of Texas Press).

Demolins, E. (1897), *A quoi tient la supériorité des Anglo-Saxons* (Paris: Firmin Didot).

Du Bois, W. E. B. (1925), 'Worlds of Color', *Foreign Affairs*, 3(3): 423–44.

Durkheim, E. (1984), *The Division of Labour in Society*, trans. W. D. Halls (London: Macmillan Press).

Duthu, B. (2013), *Shadow Nations: Tribal Sovereignty and the Limits of Legal Pluralism* (Oxford: Oxford University Press).

Fiegle, T. (2003), *Von der Solidarité zur Solidarität: ein französisch-deutscher Begriffstransfer* (Münster: LIT Verlag).

Fields, K. E. (2002), 'Individuality and the Intellectuals: An Imaginary Conversation between W. E. B. Du Bois and Emile Durkheim', *Theory and Society* 31(4): 435–62.

Firmin, A. (2002), *The Equality of the Human Races*, ed. Carolyn Fluehr-Lobban, trans. Asselin Charles (Chicago: University of Illinois Press).

Fouillée, A. (1880), *La science sociale contemporaine* (Paris: Hachette).

Getachew, A. (2019), *Worldmaking after Empire: The Rise and Fall of Self-Determination* (Princeton: Princeton University Press).

Go, J. and J. Watson (2019), 'Anticolonial Nationalism from Imagined Communities to Colonial Conflict', *European Journal of Sociology/ Archives Européennes de Sociologie* 60(1): 31–68, https://doi.org/10.1017/S000397561900002X (accessed April 26, 2023).

Gooding-Williams, R. (2009), *In the Shadow of Du Bois: Afro-Modern Political Thought in America* (Cambridge, MA: Harvard University Press).

Hayward, J. (1958), 'The Idea of Solidarity in French Social and Political Thought in the Nineteenth and Early Twentieth Centuries' (PhD thesis, University of London).

Holley, J. (2023), 'Racial Equality and Anticolonial Solidarity: Anténor Firmin's Global Haitian Liberalism', *American Political Science Review, First View*, pp. 1–14, DOI https://doi.org/10.1017/S0003055423000126 (accessed April 26, 2023).

Janik, A. (2003), 'Notes on the Natural History of Politics', in *The Grammar of Politics: Wittgenstein and Political Philosophy*, ed. Cressida J. Heyes (Ithaca, NY: Cornell University Press, pp. 99–116.

Koselleck, R. (1995), 'Begriffsgeschichte und Sozialgeschichte', in *Vergangene Zukunft: Zur Semantik geschichtlicher Zeiten* (Frankfurt/M.: Suhrkamp).

Koskenniemi, M. (2001), *The Gentle Civilizer of Nations: The Rise and Fall of International Law 130*, Hersch Lauterpacht Memorial Lectures (Cambridge: Cambridge University Press).

Kurasawa, F. (2013), 'The Durkheimian School and Colonialism Exploring the Constitutive Paradox', in *Sociology and Empire: The Imperial Entanglements of a Discipline*, ed. George Steinmetz (New York: Duke University Press), pp. 188–210.

Leroy-Beaulieu, P. (1877), *De La Colonisation Chez Les Peuples Modernes*, 1st edition (Paris).

Lowman, E. B. and A. J. Barker (2015), *Settler: Identity and Colonialism in 21st Century Canada* (Halifax, NS: Fernwood Publishing).

Manela, E. (2007a), 'Dawn of a New Era: The 'Wilsonian Moment' in Colonial Contexts and the Transformation of World Order, 1917–1920', in *Competing Visions of World Order: Global Moments and Movements, 1880s–1930s*, eds. S. Conrad and D. Sachsenmeier (New York: Palgrave Macmillan), pp. 121–49.

Manela, E. (2007b), *The Wilsonian Moment: Self Determination and the International Origins of Anticolonial Nationalism* (Oxford: Oxford University Press).

Marin, M. (2018), 'Racial Structural Solidarity', *Critical Review of International Social and Political Philosophy*, 21: 586–600.

Mason, A. (2000), *Community, Solidarity, and Belonging* (Cambridge: Cambridge University Press).

Massad, J. (2018), 'Against Self-Determination', *Humanity: An International Journal of Human Rights, Humanitarianism, and Development* 9(2): 161–91.

Mills, A. (2018), 'Rooted Constitutionalism: Growing Political Community', in Michael Asch, John Borrows, and James Tully eds., *Resurgence and Reconciliation: Indigenous-Settler Relations and Earth Teachings*, eds. Michael Asch, John Borrows, and James Tully (Toronto: University of Toronto Press), pp. 134–73.

Parkipuny, M. (1989), *The Indigenous Peoples Rights Question in Africa*. Statement to the Working Group on Indigenous Populations, 1989. From Center for World Indigenous Studies, Chief George Manuel Memorial Indigenous Library, *Fourth World Documentation Project*, section 1, paragraph 8.

Rawls, J. (1999), *A Theory of Justice* (Oxford: Oxford University Press).

Sangiovanni, A. (2008), 'Justice and the Priority of Politics to Morality', *Journal of Political Philosophy* 16(2): 137–64.

Sangiovanni, A. (2016), 'How Practices Matter', *Journal of Political Philosophy* 24(1): 3–23.

Shelby, T. (2009), *We Who Are Dark: The Philosophical Foundations of Black Solidarity* (Cambridge, MA: Harvard University Press).

Shimazu, N. (2002), *Japan, Race and Equality: The Racial Equality Proposal of 1919* (London: Routledge).

Simpson, A. (2014), *Mohawk Interruptus: Political Life across the Borders of Settler States* (Durham, NC: Duke University Press).

Simpson, L. B. (2017), *As We Have always Done: Indigenous Freedom through Radical Resistance* (London: University of Minnesota Press).

Stjernø, S. (2005), *Solidarity in Europe: The History of an Idea* (Cambridge: Cambridge University Press).

Stock-Morton, P. (1988), *Moral Education for a Secular Society: The Development of Moral Laique in Nineteenth Century France* (New York: SUNY Press).

Swain, S. (2022), 'Cracking the Settler Colonial Concrete: Theorizing Engagements with Indigenous Resurgence through the Politics from Below', in *Democratic Multiplicity: Perceiving, Enacting and Integrating Democratic Diversity*, eds. J. Tully, K. Cherry, F. Forman et al. (Cambridge: Cambridge University Press), pp. 234–58.

Trask, H.-K. (1999), *From a Native Daughter: Colonialism and Sovereignty in Hawaii* (Honolulu, HI: Latitude 20 Books).

Tully, J. (2003), 'Wittgenstein and Political Philosophy', in *The Grammar of Politics: Wittgenstein and Political Philosophy*, ed. C. Heyes (Ithaca, NY: Cornell University Press), pp. 17–42.

Tully, J. ed. (2008), 'The Struggles of Indigenous Peoples for and of Freedom', in *Public Philosophy in a New Key: Volume 1: Democracy and Civic Freedom*, Ideas in Context (Cambridge: Cambridge University Press), pp. 257–88.

Tully, J. (forthcoming), *Dialogue and Decolonization* (London: Bloomsbury).

Valdez, I. (forthcoming), *Democracy and Empire: Labor, Migration, and the Reproduction of Western Capitalism* (Cambridge: Cambridge University Press).

Wildt, A. (1995), 'Solidarität', in *Historisches Wörterbuch der Philosophie* 9, eds. J. Ritter and K. Gründer, Wissenschaftliche Buchgesellschaft, pp. 1004–115.

4

Collective transformative hope: on *living* in solidarity

Sally Scholz

At the time of writing, 'solidarity' is used in popular discourse to acknowledge and inspire person-to-person assistance as well as anonymous commitment to global health as the COVID-19 pandemic wears on; it announces the commitment to racial and gender justice; it serves as a reminder that people around the world face adverse effects of climate change and that we have the power to change; it is a political statement for citizens and governments to recognize the needs and contributions of migrants; and it compels creative response from a distance to the victims of a brutally unjust war.

These ordinary language uses of solidarity point to something distinct and elusive. As theorists, we try to pin down relevant criteria to help understand what is and ought to count as solidarity. At times, misguided popular usage of the term will feed off of that distinct and elusive quality, hoping perhaps to persuade through rhetoric that there is something present that is not; these parasitical solidarities risk weakening the importance of solidarity as a social, moral, or political concept (Scholz 2008, pp. 46–8). Most public calls for solidarity, however, are doing something different. Most calls for solidarity are not just unintended signaling or meaningless rhetoric. The communicators conceive of themselves, in the first personal singular, as an 'I' in relation to a we; the first-person plural is also often present, as a 'we' in relation to the world. 'Solidarity' declares an individual's commitment to something and proclaims a hope that others will similarly commit, while also communicating a collective relation that proclaims the hope that others will likewise see themselves as part of the we-collective. Invocations of solidarity assert the value of a particular human relationship, sometimes in order to inspire its reformation or extension, sometimes in an effort to highlight its presence, and sometimes in a plea to create it when it appears lacking or necessary.

Solidarity is not about the *things* that we do, it is about the *way* things are done by 'us' even while our relation is mediated by the *doing*. As a relation, solidarity cannot be reduced merely to actions. Relations or relationships are transformative. In that sense, 'actions in solidarity' can only tell part of the story, actions offer only a glimpse into the outward manifestation of solidarity. *Living* in solidarity, *existing* in solidarity or the lived relation of solidarity, points to the way the relations to self, others, and the world are made different because of solidarity.

Calls for solidarity and ordinary appeals to solidarity reveal something important about the transformative value of solidarity. They distinguish solidarity from society per se and in doing so create what might be called a new social or a new social space, a new form of sociality, or a new social imaginary (Hall 2017). Of course, they also remind us or invite us to renew existing social relations. Solidarity is a lived relation that changes or transforms how we live, how we relate to one another, and how we see the world. Surely there are times when the word is used when 'support' or 'sympathy' would reflect better the project at hand. However, I think there is wisdom to be found in the calls for solidarity. A wisdom that signals the possibility of a collective experience that opens a different future, an inducement to others that, together, we can transform the possibilities in front of us to a new set of possibilities, or we can extend the possibilities we encounter to others who lack them. In this, there is hope.

In this chapter, I explore four facets of solidarity's transformative value. Each contributes to or is drawn from the common understanding of solidarity, and each suggests how the experience of collective transformation opens new possibilities. Part phenomenology and part social philosophy, I argue that there are multiple overlapping transformations at work in relations of solidarity. The social transformation for which the collective is engaged in action in concert is the most obvious and tends to be the focus of accounts of solidarity, but other transformations help to explain the unique and varied aspects of the solidary relation for individuals as well as fellow participants. These facets of transformation or transformative experiences within solidarity point to a distinction between *living* in solidarity and *acting* in solidarity. The transformative lens through which to understand solidarity contributes to the distinctness of it as a social relation. The common understanding of the term, as it has been used in racial justice movements, climate change activism, gender justice campaigns, migrant rights efforts, anti-violence or anti-poverty social justice work, as well as in day-to-day social expectations and civic obligations, relies on the sustenance of transformative and transforming solidaristic relations – on living in solidarity. Collective transformative experience – and transformative hope – recollects relationships in a civic or social whole through foregrounding the social 'we' or social togetherness. Throughout, I suggest that even if relations of solidarity are made manifest through acts, the uniqueness of *living in solidarity* exceeds *acting* collectively. Ordinary invocations of the concept demonstrate an understanding of both the transformative power and the relational endurance of *living in solidarity*.[1]

In the first section, I consider aspects of solidarity's transformative value relevant to individual selves. The second section considers the solidary group and is followed by a discussion of the transformative experience of solidarity itself in section three. In the fourth section, I focus on the facet of transformation pertinent to other social relations. The fifth section concludes.

Transforming selves

There is a sense in which solidarity is grounded in personal transformation: something compels an individual to consider social relations or to seek opportunities to bring about social change. In such contexts, collectivizing – uniting one's actions with the actions of others in solidarity – may be the most promising means to accomplish a transformation of society or, in those societies that already have strong communal ties, to reignite the lived experience of solidarity within the community. In other words, the moral

---

1 In an earlier article, I argued that these personal transformations of solidarity may be understood in a twofold manner: both a person's relation *to* their community and a person's relation *in* their community changes. I build on that here by dissecting the multiple transformative aspects of solidarity further. See Scholz 2010.

transformation of individuals might be one of the factors compelling the formation of relations of solidarity.[2]

In addition to this possible grounding of solidarity in personal transformation, solidarity itself may be personally transformative for each individual participant. The experience of working with others reveals the power and agency individuals contribute to collective action. In addition to this impact on personal empowerment, the personal transformation of solidarity entails a change in how individuals understand the meaningfulness of particular decisions that they enact individually. Actors in solidarity understand social and material relations and enact their moral commitments in different ways when informed by the collective relation of solidarity.

The personally transformative facet of solidarity, in other words, may be understood as part of the grounds or the value of solidarity. In this section, I reflect on the personally transformative facet of solidarity (a) as the basis for conceiving the self as part of the social in a different way, (b) as a power within solidarity activities, and (c) as a valuable source of personal empowerment or agency.

Conceiving the self in the social in a different way

Solidarity is a *relation* unlike any other. However, like other relations, the relation is transformative for the self in response to or alongside other participants. Although it is impossible to be in solidarity with oneself, relations of solidarity affect what it means to *be* as an individual in community with others. Something fundamental about how one exists in the world, with others, and with oneself – opening new possibilities and foreclosing others – is embraced in the solidary relation. Opening oneself up to solidarity, accepting the invitation that is issued in at least some of the ordinary uses of the term, entails opening oneself up to the transformative potential of a unique relationship with others that asks one to consider the good of all

---

2 Some scholars argue that empathy transforms a person's understanding of a situation and compels the commitment to join with others to bring about social change in solidarity. I argue that empathy is neither a necessary motive for, nor a sufficient ground of, solidarity. Empathetic bonds, I argue, might motivate some individuals to act in solidarity, but they fail to account for the wide variety of reasons, emotions, and relationships that motivate different individuals to commit to solidarity (Scholz 2010).

those others prior to (albeit also in addition to) the good for oneself. In turn, those others similarly accept the risk that collective engagement entails, as well as the risk that the relation will similarly have a transformative impact on the self.

In my work on political solidarity, as well as an essay on personal transformation, I posited that the commitment to solidarity – which is sometimes experienced rather than consciously adopted – is inwardly transformative and outwardly manifest in the activity of solidarity (Scholz 2008; 2010). Through commitment to solidarity, individuals conceive of their relation to the social world in a different way. Within political solidarity, for instance, the moral relation that mediates between individuals and a group united for a cause, commitment to a shared end creates a 'unity of peoples on a range of interpersonal to social-political levels with a social justice goal of liberation of the oppressed, cessation of injustice, or protection against social vulnerabilities; it simultaneously fosters individual self-determination, empowerment, cooperative action, collective vision, and social criticism among those in solidarity' (Scholz 2008, p. 58). Given the wide array of reasons that compel individual participants to commit to political solidarity, I argue that 'personal transformation may be as unique as the individuals involved' (Scholz 2010, p. 26).

Other forms of solidarity similarly exhibit the transformative potential for the self in relation to the social. Solidarity is sometimes contrasted with individualism, isolation, selfishness, or autonomy. The self does not disappear in the solidary relation, but it is reconceived through the collective when looked at through that lens. In solidary relations, the question is not 'what can I do?' but rather, 'what can we do together?' and 'what is required of me for us to be together?'

Not every type of solidarity includes sacrifice or harm, but commitment indicates something important that distinguishes solidarity from other forms of collective action: living in solidarity means committing to a sociality that is not always organized to facilitate one's own benefit. In spite of opportunities to choose alternative social arrangements that do function to benefit the self, solidarity transforms the self-interested individual into a socially minded (or collectively oriented) participant. Individuality is not subsumed in the collective, but it is committed to the collective in a meaningful way. In my earlier account of personal transformation of political solidarity, I argued that a 'fundamental change in how a person sees the world must occur in order for that person to make a commitment that will most certainly involve sacrifice and potential harm' (2010, p. 20). Although emphasizing *choice* rather than *commitment*, L. A. Paul makes a similar point in the important book *Transformative Experience*; Paul argues that big decisions 'involve the choice to undergo a dramatically new experience that will change your life in important ways, and an essential part of your deliberation concerns what your future life will be like if you decide to undergo the change. But as it turns out ... many of these big decisions involve choices to have experiences that teach us things we cannot know about from any other source but the experience itself' (Paul 2014, p. 3).

Solidarity is usually a response to some other order or community, or a situation of opposition, or adversity, as seen in Sangiovanni's account. Solidarity's sociality may disrupt the existing order or it may reignite something within the existing order. Coming to solidarity, or living in solidarity, for some participants includes 'new understandings of how their own subjectivities are shaped by those dynamics from which they seek to step away' (Russo 2018, p. 132) as well as new understandings of how their subjectivities are shaped by the dynamics delineated as the solidary relation. In other words, solidarity is transformative for the self.

Some of the calls for solidarity during the coronavirus pandemic (COVID-19), for instance, recollect the centrality of the social for the individual self and announce a hoped-for recommitment to that collective bond. They ask individuals to be socially minded in a way that does not always facilitate the individual's own benefit but that allows for the shaping of a collective future that will reflect the individual's experiences. Not acting in solidarity may, perhaps, open different options that affect the self in alternative ways. Solidarity mediates or filters individual experience through the collective. Donning a mask or obtaining a vaccine in solidarity interprets those actions through the social, even while also potentially benefiting the self. When asked to wear a mask in solidarity with others, individuals are being asked to consider a transformed conception of the self, one that exists in and with others, as part of a social or with renewed sociality. This is not to say that the transformative impact of solidarity is necessarily permanent or even long lasting; but it is a collective relation that impacts the self, mobilized against some other possible future.

Meaningfulness of personal decisions

Another aspect of the orientation of solidarity is simply believing in something bigger than oneself. Like faith, believing in something that is bigger than oneself – the solidarity for which we risk together – allows the participant individual to let go of the desire to secure one's own person or property, to take risks alongside of committed others, and to look for the positive in collective action because one's own preservation is not the central focus. Perhaps even more importantly, belief in something bigger than oneself is what sustains hope in solidarity. Opening oneself up to solidarity has a transformative impact on one's thinking and decision making. With the relationship to others in the forefront of one's mind, other matters cede to the back. Solidarity provokes a transformation in thinking, giving a different perspective to things that in other circumstances would matter differently.

Commitment to solidarity is lived out through decisions that extend beyond the actions that are engaged jointly. During the early days of the COVID-19 pandemic, for instance, people around the world appealed to 'solidarity' in thinking about particular decisions in daily life. Simple decisions, like whether to go to a grocery store or travel outside the home, were reconfigured through the lens of solidarity as decisions with collective import. This sort of reconfiguring or filtering demonstrates the transformative impact of solidarity on the meaningfulness of individual decisions, even seemingly mundane ones.[3]

---

3 A similar example is found in the classic American case of solidarity: the National Farm Workers Association strike and consumer grape boycott in the late 1960s. The farmworkers risked their livelihoods and company-supplied housing in choosing to strike, but they were engaged in a movement for civil rights, not just a labor struggle. At the behest of the farmworkers, consumers and other unions participated in boycotts which helped to equalize the power imbalance between workers and growers, but also made the farmworkers' cause a national campaign lived in daily decisions at the market as well as grand demonstrations at the farms. The movement argued for the rights of farmworkers, including the right to unionize and collectively negotiate, and

Power/empowerment and agency

Relational ethics emphasize the importance of context and social position, especially with regard to social vulnerability or inequality. This is seen in solidarity through the relative assessment of risk within the relation as well as within the action undertaken in concert (Scholz 2014; 2018; 2020). Solidarity creates a new sociality. Every sociality carries risks as part of the relation itself, even beyond what those in relation undertake together. At least part of the draw of social life is that existence together is conceived to lessen overall risk to individual participants. Assuming that solidarity is a social relation, then it too carries risks within the relation itself. Rather than emphasizing equal vulnerability, the sociality of solidarity seeks to foster awareness of the varying risks within larger contexts of social inequality that solidary actors face (Scholz 2014) and the unique power that each contributes. Trust within the solidary relation is built through a continual process of evaluating risks on fellow participants and readjusting the relation to ensure an equitable sharing of the social risks of the relationship itself. Equitable sharing of social risk does not mean that all the risks in solidarity are evenly distributed; rather, it means that the risks of the relations must be adjusted to account for the social vulnerabilities and inequalities that each participant carries entering into the relation. In acknowledging and accounting for the social risks, which affect individuals differently because of their positioning in the external (i.e., outside of the solidaristic relation) social context, relations of solidarity might adjust to create conditions for the flourishing of personal agency and empowerment (Scholz 2014, p. 55).

Acting collectively does not replace individual action or subsume the power of the individual in the collective whole. Rather, the solidary relation affirms individual power and agency, collectivizing the unique contributions of each participant into the solidary relation. Among the many rich insights stemming from Catholic social teaching (CST) on solidarity as a concept is the understanding that individual actions contribute to collective power, even when those actions are private,

---

connected their arguments and strategies directly with the civil rights movement of the era. See 'Workers United: The Delano Grape Strike and Boycott', www.nps.gov/articles/000/workers-united-the-delano-grape-strike-and-boycott.htm (accessed May 9, 2023).

quiet, or seemingly isolated. The reverse is also the case: individual action or inaction might be complicit in social sin or structures of sin (Himes 1986). CST encourages each person to see how action or inaction in everyday life contributes to structures and systems. Inspiring individuals to see their own power within a collective, with the encouragement that their actions ought to be conducted in accordance with justice and the common good, CST offers an account of solidarity that acknowledges the power of individuals to transform unjust structures, to take up as an obligation their role in social relations. CST addresses multiple audience levels – individuals, institutions, communities, states, and the 'one human family' – to affirm a delicate balance between the individual and the collective. Each level is meant to take up their moral obligations, without impinging on the ability of levels lower (or higher) to fulfill their moral roles as well. This brief portrait of solidarity for CST offers a glimpse into two aspects of the transformative value of solidarity for individual selves: it transforms the individual into a powerful agent of change, and it affirms the importance of individual agents within collective relations.

The everyday calls for solidarity may be seen, then, as reminders of individual commitment in the social body, as acknowledgments of the power of individual action within collective action, as resource signals for action that is more effectively done collectively. In other words, solidarity's transformative value is evident in how personal power and agency is reconceived; contrasting with the prioritization of self-interest in one's actions, individuals in solidarity prioritize the commitment with others, a relationship that may yield decisions and actions that do not benefit the individual at all or decrease the potential benefit to the individual in favor of the benefit to the solidary group. On the surface, at least for some participants in solidarity, the decisions and actions may not look any different. However, the commitment to solidarity transforms how the individual understands themselves and their pursuits in relation to the whole.

Transformative value for the solidary group

Solidarity has many possible forms and manifestations. Any single individual could be involved in multiple solidary relations (Shelby

2005). Moreover, each person is embedded in a series of other relations or embodied associations which may impact their involvement in any given solidarity. Rather than functioning as a weakness to the solidary relation or an indication of a lack of complete loyalty to a solidary relation, these multiple connections contribute to the richness of solidarity. Each participant effectively brings to the relation an abundant store of information and further relationships, at least some of which may be put to use toward the given solidarity. In this section, I consider some possible ways that the solidary group experiences transformation. The diversity of participants changes the group, affecting collective power and modeling counter-cultural connection. In the next section, I look at how this diversity contributes to the transformative value of the end and purpose of solidarities.

Diversity and inclusiveness

Speaking of the richness of human diversity marshalled for the cause of climate change mitigation, Pope Francis stirringly articulates the value of individual and cultural uniqueness for global solidarity: 'We require a new and universal solidarity. As the bishops of Southern Africa have stated: "Everyone's talents and involvement are needed to redress the damage caused by human abuse of God's creation". All of us can cooperate as instruments of God for the care of creation, each according to his or her own culture, experience, involvements and talents' (Pope Francis, *Laudato Sí*, §14). His words punctuate the transformative value of solidarity understood through the contributions of diverse and unique participants and cultural practices. The solidary group exists because of the participants, and it alters or adjusts as people come and go (Doran 1996; Shelby 2005, pp. 127–8; Scholz 2008, p. 108; forthcoming). The logic of inclusion, as Doran calls it, counters divisiveness, which often plays a prominent role in other social structures.

Living the solidarity commitment, rather than through fulfilling a set of criteria, means that free-riders – those who benefit from the goals of solidarity – are not subject to punishment but might be subject to social pressure of belonging.[4] Importantly, my point here

---

4 Some forms of solidarity are understood as exclusive solidarities or bounded solidarities – a comment on their ontological status. They are grounded in

is about the processes of solidarity, not a comment about the social ontology of solidarity; a fully inclusive solidarity is likely an aspirational goal rather than a lived experience. Processes of inclusivity refer to the recognition of change with the inclusion of new participants.[5] Social relations of all sorts morph in response to the inclusion of new people. Connecting with others compels recognition of the variety of cultural backgrounds and experiences; failure at recognition creates a situation of indifference that undermines the connection. Processes of communication, collaboration, and coordination used in solidary relations challenge participants to recognize, respond, and readjust to others in the group. The commitment to solidarity entails that negotiation (Scholz 2008, ch. 3). *Living* in solidarity, in other words, involves active work on whatever scale is within one's power, understanding that solidarity has a dynamic nature that responds or reacts to the inclusion of differently situated people. *Living* in solidarity is not about adopting the identity of all those others or even deferring to the proposed actions of these others (Kolers 2016). Sandra Bartky astutely observes that 'to stand in solidarity with others is to *work* actively to eliminate their misery, not to arrange one's life so as to share it' (Bartky 2002, p. 74; emphasis added), and Tommie Shelby articulates the importance of

identity-based membership of some sort. By focusing on the processes and relations of solidarity, I imply that exclusive solidarities insufficiently recognize the diversity of their participants and, in doing so, face some challenges for sustaining the group. That is one reason they turn to security measures, policies or procedures of membership, and institutionalization of the benefits of solidarity. Scholars who study the sources of social and civic solidarity affirm the importance of diversity and renewal through political solidarity for creating, sustaining, and reforming institutions of justice (e.g., Hall 2017; Bauböck 2017; Banting and Kymlicka 2017).

5 In the CST tradition, solidarity is built from the empirical fact of interdependence. Solidarity, as the language of 'one human family' in CST indicates, includes all others, even those who may act in unsolidaristic manners. Of course, the Catholic social tradition also calls for a change of heart (which is called 'conversion', but that ought not to be confused with converting to a faith; the idea is a transformed understanding of oneself in relation to community, not a religious conversion). CST's aspirational goal of a fully inclusive solidarity incorporates the need to be responsive to the needs and contributions of participants. That process suggests the transformative value for the solidary relation.

inclusive leadership and judicious organizational structures to meet the needs of diverse participants (Shelby 2005, p. 128). Working and living in solidarity in this way pushes beyond merely acting in solidarity and suggests that taking the relational aspect of solidarity seriously requires an ongoing evaluative process to assess whether the needs of participants are met and the unique contributions valued. Solidarity is about imagining a new social wherein the risks of social existence do not accrue disproportionately on some people. A disproportionate distribution of risks within solidarity potentially exacerbates other vulnerabilities of social existence. Living in solidarity avoids 'suppressing or excluding difference among political allies' (Lyshaug 2006, p. 91; see also Hooker 2009, pp. 32–3).[6]

Interconnected with the manifest purpose of solidarity, then, is an ancillary transformative impact on the solidary group itself. Christine Straehle defends a value of solidarity as providing a source of relational goods. Using the language of 'associative solidarity', Straehle suggests that it is part of what is owed to moral equals; relational needs are part of basic needs, thereby making solidarity important not merely for its uses but because it is a social relation and social relations are 'form(s) of capital' (Straehle 2020, p. 536). Inclusivity in the processes creates more capital for the solidary group to draw upon in addressing its purpose but it also potentially transforms the solidary group itself. That is at least part of Pope Francis's insight in appealing to the demonstrative need for the unique 'culture, experience, involvements and talents' of all in the solidaristic efforts to mitigate climate change. 'Inclusive solidarity cannot be achieved conclusively, but rather demands an infinite process of solidary practices and inclusive ways of relating to one another' (Schwiertz and Schwenken 2020).

Being in solidarity counters other modes of being that dominate social life. Rather than accept the common or dominant modes of social organization – authoritative/subordinate, rich/poor, citizen/noncitizen, etc. – solidarity's emphasis on the collective posits a sociality structured to avoid relations of division. The lived experience of solidarity requires a continual reassessment to avoid recreating relations of exclusion or domination while fostering the collective

---

6 Lyshaug appeals to 'fluid attachment to identity' (2006, p. 91), which appears to be akin to Sangiovanni's categories of identification.

engagement to transform external social structures and relations. Often, the appeal to solidarity accompanies a recognition that the opposition sets up norms intended to divide. Solidarity counters that division by claiming a connection. This is evident, for instance, when Alicia Garza, one of the founders of the Black Lives Matter (BLM) movement, defines solidarity saying, 'Solidarity means trying to understand the ways our communities experience unique forms of oppression and marginalization. It means showing up for one another to bear witness and then expanding our fight to include the challenges faced by other communities besides our own' (Garza 2020, p. 157). Garza's comments demonstrate the transformative value of solidarity (perhaps even the transformative nature of solidarity), expanding in response to diverse needs of participants while 'showing up' and 'bearing witness' for one another, acknowledging within solidarity how social forces affect people differently. It is also a nod to the effect that encountering others has on one's own experience or the experience of the group. Dominant social practices organize social life in a way that fosters division between ethnic and racial groups. Solidarity in countering racism also counters the cultural norms of division or isolation. In addition, critical reflection and expansive readjustment challenges dominant social practices that concentrate burdens of social existence on certain groups – such burdens are themselves among the adversities that solidarity addresses.

Collective power

Emphasizing relational interconnectedness rather than sameness, the grievances and criticisms, the experiences of adversity, are collectivized and consolidated in solidarity. Solidarity is often experienced as a power: the ability to create change together, especially when individualized attempts appear futile or ineffective. Collecting the vibrant diversity of viewpoints, solidarity functions as a medium through which those viewpoints are asserted in the creation of a new or a different social space, a new social imaginary, or a new or renewed experience of sociality.

Ordinary calls for solidarity challenge the individualism and isolation so prominent in modern daily life. Indeed, the call itself is a plea to connect while the mention of solidarity in news reports, for instance, signals a recognition of relations among and between people, a relation that may have been dormant or missing. As appeals, calls for solidarity offer an opportunity to lend one's own power to a collective or to create a collective where one is missing. As signals of recognition, labeling something solidarity points to a new way to perceive or understand relations among people. The term announces the prospect of collective power, in response to adversity, opposition, or oppression. People who go through a struggle together experience something that was not present prior to the struggle. Survivors of a natural disaster, military personnel in combat, protesters seeking social change, or fellow citizens foregrounding and preserving the collective social bond discover a strength in their connection during the struggle, and the connection might endure once the moment of struggle has passed. The struggle, or the process of collective power, in these cases, is that which unites participants and potentially moves them – or some of them – to sustain a relationship beyond the struggle.

Diverse participation in solidarity, and the commitment to avoid replicating the relations of domination and division found in other social relations, means that the enactments of solidarity and communication within solidary groups are varied and diffuse. Creative enactment of solidarity from participants who would carry too high of a social cost in traditional modes of protest, for instance, might include such things as story-telling, public art, information leaks, hunger strikes or boycotts, and even festivals that disrupt dominant modes of social interaction. Each of these, and so many more subtle as well as bold public displays, illustrates how solidarity is lived across difference and performed in day-to-day events that are transformed or politicized according to the solidary commitment. Individual voices speaking up against injustice have power and may be understood as contributing to the collective power of solidarity. Solidaristic actions do not have to be in grand gestures of coordinated activity; they could be in small, personal experiences. Collective power emerges both in the bold actions performed together and in the small actions done in concert; it appears as relationships are built and sustained.

The importance of small measures done with intent to contribute to a large-scale collective effort is evident in the response to the COVID-19 pandemic. Indeed, the World Health Organization Director-General, Tedros Adhanom Ghebreyesus, emphasized the importance of 'solidarity' in remarks offered in the early days of the pandemic. Ghebreyesus's comments use the term to highlight (1) the actions of partners in 'staying the course' in response to the Ebola pandemic in the Democratic Republic of the Congo – noting the government and the people, (2) the cooperation of governments in implementing policies modeled on successful measures of South Korea to address the COVID-19 pandemic, (3) the coalition of medical researchers studying the pandemic and sharing information globally, and (4) the collective effort to raise funds. 'Solidarity' unites all these disparate efforts in part because it signals collective power. The transformative experience wrought by solidarity in response to the Ebola pandemic is marshalled for a new pandemic, encouraging partners at every level of social organization to participate by lending their unique expertise to the collective project. In other words, individual power is transformed into collective power when applied to or called up by solidarity. This transformative value extends through time in the relationships built and the diverse contributions and directions made possible through inclusive processes. Collective power, then, I would argue, is more than joint action. It is living and being in solidarity, not merely acting in solidarity.

Transformative impact on the ends of solidarity

Given the variety of communities with which a person is involved, and given the daily needs of individuals themselves, it seems probable that individuals will occasionally weaken their involvement in a particular solidary relation. Rather than seeing that as lack of resolve or as failure of solidarity, through the lens of transformative experience, recalibrating involvement while maintaining a commitment may be seen as different ways of living in solidarity (Mohanty 2003, p. 161; Shelby 2005; Scholz 2008; 2010). Sometimes a solidary relation transforms into an organized or institutionalized relation. It may still be meaningful to refer to the relation as solidarity, but other organizational or associational concepts may be better suited to explain the more formalized structure of such relations. This leads to questions about the fluidity of solidarity and of the desirability of sustaining solidarity. What does it mean to sustain solidarity?

Do solidarities change when the nature of the original collective changes? What about when the grounds or ends of solidarity change? In this section I consider the ends of solidarity by turning to questions of how solidarity is sustained, how connections are fostered, and how solidarity itself transforms.

Sustain

As we have seen, sustaining solidarity, living in solidarity and not just acting in solidarity, necessitates a scrutiny of the additional adversities faced by fellow solidary actors. Understanding the social, material, and political conditions with which fellow solidary actors exist reveals the complexity of adversity's effects on individuals. Sustaining the unity of solidarity is a challenge because of the need for dynamic critical awareness of shifting circumstances which impact the ends of solidarity. Moreover, the actions solidary groups pursue change the circumstances that gave rise to the solidarity in the first place. Just as individual decisions are transformative and cannot really be comprehended until they are lived, the solidarity group faces a similar condition: the impact of choices, actions, or pursuits in solidarity on the solidary group will not be fully comprehended until they are lived by the group. They carry the potential of destroying the solidary relation even while addressing the grounds and ends of the solidarity.

If, as I have suggested, solidarity reorients an individual perspective to the perspective of the solidary whole as well as the diverse parts, then part of the challenge of solidarity is maintaining or sustaining the commitments of participants while the orientation of the collective continually transforms in response to changing conditions, circumstances, and the collective itself. Discovering what we create together in solidarity involves the openness to the transformed purpose and relation as well as the realization that the collective of solidarity may cease to exist, or morph such that some participants no longer find their commitment contained in the collective project. At least some ordinary uses of the term may be seen as reminders or invitations to continue to find oneself included in the collective even while acknowledging the collective has changed. Sustaining solidarity must include fostering the relations such that the collective project can perdure.

Paul's account of personal decisions that are transformative suggests that 'we only learn what we need to know after we've done it, and we change ourselves in the process of doing it'. For Paul, this uncertainty is embraced in the process of how one chooses. Paul argues that 'the best response to this situation is to choose based on whether we want to discover who we'll become' (Paul 2014, p. 4). Something similar occurs in the solidary relation. Of course, it isn't just the 'we' that transforms; something happens, too, to the grounds and ends of solidarity. Some of the ordinary uses of the term serve as reminders of the solidary relation when conditions within which it took shape have changed.

Activists and advocates aiding migrants in spite of laws that prohibit such aid invoke this facet of solidarity's transformative value when they call their actions 'crimes of solidarity'. They employ (at least) a double referent: the civic solidarity of that state that declares those actions illegal and the social solidarity in aiding fellow human beings. In both cases, they gesture to the transformative value of solidarity in creating a different future (Fekete 2018; Squire 2020). The activists and advocates are doing more than expressing support or sympathy for a cause, their solidarity creates space to imagine social relations differently. In doing so, they collectively embrace the uncertainty that transformative experience brings.

Fluid connections

Seemingly distinct issues become connected as the collective forms and expands, because individual participants offer their insight into how issues are related. The praxis of solidarity transforms in response to or inspired by the acknowledgment of connections between issues. Consider, for instance, how solidarity is invoked in campaigns to end violence (e.g., Weber 2006; Russo 2018). The conditions that give rise to solidarity require meeting basic needs while also changing the social structures that cause the violence in the first place. But some participants may find their personal situation changed (by the solidarity or by something else). Calls for solidarity, in those situations, are at least partly reminders that the collective action is about more than ameliorating one's own situation – or one's own experience of adversity. Commitment to solidarity commits one to a social relation that is not always organized to facilitate one's own advantage.

Solidarity – as a collective relation with some purpose – is fluid and expanding (see also Shelby 2005). The experience of living in solidarity with others can be recalled, recollected, imagined, acknowledged, and recognized by invoking solidarity in similar contexts. Understanding it as fluid, rather than transient or institutionalized, allows for temporal and context variability in relations of solidarity. The nature of the relation, the purpose, and the individual participants are subject to transformation, and we cannot know how the experience will impact the 'I' or the 'we' until we are in or have gone through the experience (see Scholz 2010; Paul 2014). Moreover, multiple, overlapping solidarities dot the social landscape. Individuals are involved in many and bring their connections to the collective experience. The transformative experience for solidarity itself includes the ways in which the social relation merges with others, changes over time, and overlaps with or engages coalitionally with other solidarities.

Of course, even as the solidary relation itself changes, external attitudes toward it also shift. The purpose of solidarity may bring about change or the relation may expand to such an extent that solidary relations characterize the communal social relations. That points to the fourth facet of solidarity's transformative value, which I discuss in the next section.

Transformative potential beyond solidarity

One of the facets of collective transformative experience of the solidarity relation is found in the contrast with what solidarity is not. Solidarity creates a new social, a new sociality, or a new social imaginary. It is often contrasted with or counters individualism, abandonment, alienation, indifference, isolation, domination, or anarchy (among other things). The assertion of solidarity directs attention toward a collective relations and filters decision making and action through it. Ordinary or everyday calls for solidarity announce and invite a redirection of attention onto the social relations upon which or out of which more organized or institutionalized relations are or may be built. When climate activists mobilize solidarity in efforts to mitigate climate change, they create space for talking about and considering social relations in contrast to the individualism of capitalism or the nationalism of international relations. They resist the abandonment of individuals to isolation and, instead, create alternative social space (or a new social imaginary), such as a global relation or a relation that empowers both individual actors and corporate entities as consociates capable of acting together. In other words, transformative value of solidarity is found both in the transformed sociality among solidary participants in facing adversity or creating change together and in the transformative effects of solidary action on a wider community.

The solidary collective itself often provides a sense of belonging or a recognition of sociality that is sometimes lacking in the broader society. Participants may experience other social relations as unjust or alienating. They invest hope for a different future by engaging in actions with others, enacting sociality or recreating the social connection in an unalienated manner. One commonly heard refrain from people who witness solidarity either from the inside of the relation or from the outside is that it renews faith in humanity. Humans need sociality – the isolation of a pandemic, the divisiveness of racial and gender injustice, the upheaval of conflict, and the stressors of economic life make the appeal to solidarity an attractive alternative. Solidarity – the lived experience of solidarity – transforms the isolation, division, upheaval, and stress into challenges that can be overcome if faced *together*. Calls for solidarity recollect, imagine, acknowledge, or recognize a unique relation that connects individuals to a collective, affirms collective power, and suggests a different possible future. This last is the 'hope' aspect of solidarity's transformative value.

Mustering hope

Reorienting attention to the social, reminding ourselves that we exist with others, and that collective power can open up a different possible future is more than merely an expression, it is a lived experience. The four facets of transformative experience described and discussed here suggest that thinking about solidarity involves not only the power of the collective but also the value of the transformative experience on living in solidarity. Individuals do not always have the power, position, fortitude, or time for joint action in solidarity.

Acknowledging the transformative value of solidarity suggests that one may *be in solidarity* even while taking a break from *acting in solidarity*. Of course, openness to the personal, collective, purposive, communal, and dispositional transformative power of solidarity likely means that one cannot help but act in solidarity through living in solidarity. Highlighting these and other possible facets of transformation for solidarity appears to point to another reason that ordinary uses of the term are meaningful: they indicate hope – hope in something different, hope in collective power, hope in the realization of community, hope in transformative change.

Teasing apart the facets of transformation announced by solidarity suggests that it is a unique relation, not one built on some other relation like family or shared identity, but one that, like them, has transformative value for how one lives in the world, with one another, and all together. Collective transformative experience also points to the creative side of solidarity. Participants create or renew a social imaginary, a sociality, a social or social space. In that sense, solidarity is potentially an active creative relation, one that entails hope that the future could be different than the present if we create and work together.

Theorists of solidarity ought to be cautious about the way the concept is discussed in academic circles so as not to exclude the wisdom emergent from its use on the ground and in order to avoid colonizing the concept in a way that excludes. The effort to decolonize concepts like liberty, equality, and solidarity highlights the way the term solidarity has sometimes been used to police membership in communities and dictate methods of appropriate activity. Lived experiences of solidarity often use the concept creatively or generatively in order to evoke a relation that is absent, challenged, or obscured.

Conclusion

Rather than dismiss ordinary uses of the term, perhaps we can look at what such uses signal. Invoking solidarity may be announcing, inviting, recollecting, compelling, or remembering a lived experience, a relation, with transformative value. Referring to different facets of that collective transformative experience under the same guise of 'solidarity' is not lacking analytical rigour but pointing to the complexity of a lived relation that demands openness.

Sangiovanni frames his account of solidarity as a particularly modern practice that emerges in response to the divisive forces of capitalism and industrialism. His recognition that acting in solidarity evolves into a practice, 'a lived system of norms, rules, and expectations that gives rise to new self-understandings, new concepts, and new possibilities for collective action and social relation within complex, modern societies' (p. 33), suggests that solidarity is a lived experience. Living in solidarity, I have suggested, involves an openness to how the experience will transform one's self or subjectivity, fellow solidary actors, the purpose of solidarity, and the larger society. Although there are many points about which we disagree regarding solidarity's nature, grounds, and value, Sangiovanni, too, implies that solidarity entails a transformation (pp. 33–5).

Certainly, the potential for abuse of the term 'solidarity' is great. Nonetheless, I have defended ordinary uses of the term insofar as they redirect or recollect the social, inviting or announcing the creation of a new social imaginary. These ordinary uses point to the transformative value of solidarity. They state or claim a different possible future that, as participants in solidarity, we create together. As Sangiovanni explains, 'solidarity names a practice of collective agency and transformative mobilization' (p. 65). The challenge is how to live in solidarity, how to move beyond mere expressions or one-off collective actions to foster the relationship that centers the social while never subsuming individuals and their singular contributions. The lens of transformation also suggests some caution in how solidarity is framed. Associative ethics tend to focus on expectations of membership; relational ethics, in contrast, tend to focus on what connects the people involved. In association, members uphold obligations of the association. In solidarity, participants create something together.

The relationship of living in solidarity brings out something that *acting* in solidarity does not: with *living*, it becomes easier to see how solidarity counters the indifference of oppression, the individualism of dominant modes of material and political existence, the abandonment of community ties, the isolation and solitude of solitary existence, the powerlessness of individuals to create social and political change – especially individuals who are positioned in subordinate positions in the social structure, the domination and authority of political power and money, and the anarchy and violence of daily life. In offering these opposites of solidarity, the rich variation of ordinary uses of 'solidarity' is highlighted. Perhaps more importantly, solidarity offers a collective transformative experience that allows participants to hope for, create, and live a different future.

References

Banting, K. and W. Kymlicka (2017), *The Strains of Commitment* (Oxford: Oxford University Press).

Bartky, S. (2002), *Sympathy and Solidarity and Other Essays* (Lanham, MD: Rowman and Littlefield).

Bauböck, R. (2017), 'Citizenship and Collective Identities as Political Sources of Solidarity in the European Union', in *The Strains of Commitment*, eds. Keith Banting and Will Kymlicka (Oxford: Oxford University Press) pp. 80–106.

Doran, K. (1996), *Solidarity: A Synthesis of Personalism and Communalism in the Thought of Karol Wojtyla* (New York: Peter Lang).

Fekete, L. (2018), 'Migrants, Borders, and the Criminalisation of Solidarity in the EU', *Race & Class* 59(4): 65–83.

Garza, A. (2020), *The Purpose of Power: How We Come Together when We Fall Apart* (New York: One World).

Ghebreyesus, T. A. (2020), 'WHO Director-General's Opening Remarks at the Media Briefing on COVID-19' (March 18) www.who.int/director-general/speeches/detail/who-director-general-s-opening-remarks-at-the-media-briefing-on-covid-19—18-march-2020 (accessed May 9, 2023).

Hall, P. A. 'The Political Sources of Social Solidarity', in *The Strains of Commitment: The Political Sources of Solidarity in Diverse Societies*, eds. Keith Banting and Will Kymlicka (New York: Oxford University Press, 2017), pp. 201–32.

Himes, K. R. (1986), 'Social Sin and the Role of the Individual', *Annual of the Society of Christian Ethics* 6: 183–218.

Hooker, J. (2009), *Race and the Politics of Solidarity* (Oxford: Oxford University Press).

Kolers, A. (2016), *A Moral Theory of Solidarity* (Oxford: Oxford University Press).

Lyshaug, B. (2006), Solidarity without 'Sisterhood'? Feminism and the Ethics of Coalition Building, *Politics and Gender* 2: 77–100.

Mohanty, C. (2003), *Feminism without Borders: Decolonizing Theory, Practicing Solidarity* (Durham, NC: Duke University Press).
Paul, L. A. (2014), *Transformative Experience* (Oxford: Oxford University Press).
Russo, C. (2018), *Solidarity in Practice: Moral Protest and the US Security State* (Cambridge: Cambridge University Press).
Scholz, S. (2008), *Political Solidarity* (University Park, PA: Penn State University Press).
Scholz, S. (2010), 'Persons Transformed by Political Solidarity', *Appraisal* 8(2): 19–27.
Scholz, S. (2014), 'Solidarity as a Human Right', *Archiv des Völkerrechts* 52(1): 49–67.
Scholz, S. (2018), 'Solidarity and Social Risk', Symposium Paper, World Congress of Philosophy XXIV. Beijing (August 13) International Federation of Philosophical Societies.
Scholz, S. (2020), 'Solidarity, Social Risk, and Community Engagement', *American Journal of Bioethics*, 20(5): 75–7.
Scholz, S. (forthcoming), 'Solidarity's Reach', in *Rethinking Solidarity in the U.S. and Beyond*. Bavarian American Academy.
Schwiertz, H. and H. Schwenken (2020), 'Introduction: Inclusive Solidarity and Citizenship along Migratory Routes in Europe and the Americas', *Citizenship Studies* 24(4): 405–23.
Shelby, T. (2005), *We Who Are Dark: The Philosophical Foundations of Black Solidarity*. (Cambridge, MA: Belknap Press of Harvard University Press).
Squire, V. (2020), *Europe's Migration Crisis: Border Deaths and Human Dignity* (New York: Cambridge University Press).
Straehle, C. (2020), 'Associative Solidarity, Relational Goods, and Autonomy for Refugees: What Does It Mean to Stand in Solidarity with Refugees?' *Journal of Social Philosophy* 51(4): 526–42.
Weber, C. (2006), *Visions of Solidarity: U.S. Peace Activists in Nicaragua from War to Women's Activism and Globalization* (Lanham, MD: Rowman and Littlefield).

5

The meaning(s) of solidarity

Rainer Forst

Andrea Sangiovanni's essay 'Solidarity' is a groundbreaking contribution to the by now large literature on solidarity that brings much-needed clarity to the debate. The way he lays out the nature, history, grounds, and value of solidarity entails far too many essential insights to enumerate here and comment on, but let it be said that this text will undoubtedly be a cornerstone for all future discussions of solidarity.

Still, as is the task for a solidary commentator, the business of thinking about solidarity we both are engaged in urges me to ask a few questions about the sections that Sangiovanni usefully lays out for us.

Concept and conceptions

I begin with commenting on a major agreement between the two of us – or at least what I think is an agreement. In my work on toleration (Forst 2013, ch. 1) and other concepts such as liberty or autonomy (Forst 2012, ch. 5) and, recently, on solidarity (Forst forthcoming), I use the distinction between a *concept* (singular) and various *conceptions* (plural) in a way that is inspired by Rawls, yet differs from his use of the distinction. In particular, when it comes to what I call 'normatively dependent' concepts (toleration, solidarity, legitimacy, trust are examples[1]), I think it is important to recognize that the general core concept is *value-free*, while different *normative* conceptions of it can be formed by relying on other normative

1 On legitimacy, see Forst 2017, ch. 8. On trust, see Forst 2022.

sources that have a more independent status. That is why I agree with Sangiovanni that solidarity as such is *not a value* (p. 29) and that it is *other* justifying grounds that give it normative substance (sometimes with good, sometimes with less good reasons), and that such an approach to the term is useful for purposes of both empirical analysis (of the different conceptions of toleration that have been and are used) and normative assessment (of the justifications for solidarity).

This, however, leads to a possible disagreement between us. I take it that a concept of solidarity appears in the *singular* only and denotes the core content of any meaningful usage of the term, while conceptions provide thicker interpretations of the central concept components. Sangiovanni's stated aim of developing 'a unified concept of solidarity' (p. 5) as a 'more abstract concept' (p. 6) as compared to more particular conceptions seems to suggest that much, as does his general definition of solidarity as 'a particular form of *joint action*' based on an 'identification with others' (p. 5). The features he lists (p. 17) are components of the general concept of solidarity. This is also what he says in the summary, claim 6 (p. 121, see also p. 117). Hence, I am not sure why he calls the result of different interpretations of certain concept components different 'concepts of solidarity' (p. 29) and not 'conceptions' of solidarity (as I would prefer to do).

At times, it looks as if Sangiovanni actually distinguishes *three* and not just two conceptual levels. The first corresponds to what Sangiovanni calls the 'overarching concept of solidarity' (p. 30), while the second level harbours the different 'concepts' that are used when researchers follow different aims, such as 'testing an empirical hypothesis about the relationship between solidarity and levels of support for the welfare state', or exploring historically 'the changing character of French national solidarity' (p. 31). I would here rather speak of different *uses* that such researchers make of the concept of solidarity and I would suggest, more precisely still, that their contrasting scholarly projects are implications of them espousing different particular *conceptions* of *political* solidarity. The same holds for the normative case that Sangiovanni discusses, where he says that those who look for EU solidarity in external policy and those who look for it in the area of economic life work with 'two different, non-competing (normative) *concepts* of solidarity' (p. 32). I would rather say that they use the same concept asking different questions, not that they use different concepts (they may, however, use different conceptions of EU solidarity, but that remains to be seen). Sangiovanni, however, seems to reserve the use of the term 'conceptions' only for a third conceptual level, which comprises cases where different notions of solidarity are employed with regard to one and the same context, as when people think differently about 'solidarity in refugee and asylum policy' (p. 32). But that seems overly restrictive. We can identify different *political conceptions* of solidarity, nationalist or based on constitutional patriotism, if you like, and they may (quite likely) have different *implications* for asylum politics; and we need to compare different *normative conceptions* of solidarity with regard to their different grounds, such as moral, ethical, political, religious, etc. But the aspects of analysis that Sangiovanni mentions (as in the example of internal or external EU solidarity) create neither different concepts nor different conceptions. Otherwise, a tripartite distinction between a meta-concept, aspect-relevant concepts, and particular conceptions would ensue, which is a baroque structure Sangiovanni might not want to adopt.

Being or acting in solidarity?

A second point I want to raise concerns one of the core elements of solidarity, that of 'joint action'. Why is '*action*', as an actual event, required for solidarity? As Sangiovanni's analysis makes convincingly clear, different kinds of justifications provide persons with different '*reason[s]* to act in solidarity' (p. 10) with others. So solidarity implies an identification-based recognized *reason* to act in solidarity and the *willingness* to do so if necessary and if one is in a position to do so. But that practical attitude and willingness seems to be sufficient to *be solidary*, and the actual acting not required, as it depends on contingent circumstances. Contrary to what Sangiovanni says ('To *be* in solidarity is [...] to *act* in solidarity', p. 16), to be in solidarity is to possess a particular practical state of mind. To actually act accordingly merely follows (if circumstances allow for it) and need not be part of the definition of what solidarity is. One can see this also from Sangiovanni's own list of features of solidarity, where he speaks of the 'intention' (p. 17) to do one's part, the 'commitment' to certain shared aims and to sharing 'one's fate', or the attitude of 'trust' in others assuming that they are similarly motivated. All of these denote a *practical attitude* and *willingness* to act in a solidary way based on a common cause or identity (see my definition in Forst forthcoming), not the actual action. Solidarity is, I conclude (at this point), not 'joint action' but the readiness to engage in such action for the right reasons. If you have that attitude but for some reason lose the ability to act according to it, you still *are* solidary, though you cannot act in a solidary way.

Sangiovanni himself mentions, at the end of his text, an example: Marie who sings the *Deutschlandlied* on November 9, 1989, when the Berlin Wall falls, along with people there whom she watches (on television, I assume). Marie feels solidary with the people on site, and I think she thus *is* solidary, identifying with their cause and joy (and I hope, by the way, they only sang the third verse, for otherwise she is a nationalist solidarist, a point I will come back to). Sangiovanni concedes that much but metaphorically adds that this makes sense only '*in the shadow* of nearby forms of possible joint action' (p. 119). This is a beautiful metaphor, but essentially it means that joint action is no necessary requirement of solidarity – rather, a certain state of mind is. He suggests to regard this example as an exception to the rule, but it might be an example that questions the rule as Sangiovanni identifies it (p. 122).

Joint action?

But how about the second part of the 'joint-action' formulation – does solidary action need to be *joint* in the way Sangiovanni explains? I have doubts about that. Sangiovanni follows a rather strong notion of joint action, based on certain accounts of collective agency (such as Tuomela's). Required for solidarity is, as Sangiovanni argues, a 'we-perspective' with shared aims and a shared plan of action ('coordination based on shared intentions', p. 20). He modifies this substantively, though, when he allows for 'different ideas about what the final ends of our action are' (p. 19); and giving the BLM example, he even goes so far as to say that solidary unity at least implies that different groups 'are not actively and intentionally undermining' (p. 22) the activist general aims. At such a level of disagreement between factions of a movement, the definition of 'joint action' becomes strained, I fear.

But that is not my main point. Rather, as much as I think that strong forms of joint action are characteristic of many forms of solidary action, I wonder whether Sangiovanni overlooks some important forms of solidarity in generalizing the criterion of joint action. Think of the workers' movement in a socialist version or of the women's movement. Solidary agents for the common cause of such kinds were always aware that one of the major obstacles or 'significant adversity' (p. 23), as Sangiovanni says, was not just the opposition from the ruling classes and groups, but also the inertia and pluralism of attitudes – ranging from ignorance to outright rejection – among those they actually fought for, workers or women. In his historical argument, Sangiovanni himself points to such a case with reference to liberation theology, which tries to raise the 'awareness among the poor that their situation is a result of social organization, rather than [...] a result of the natural order of things' (p. 53). Thus 'the most dangerous obstacles in the way of liberation are ignorance and silence' (p. 53). This is what I mean. One of the main obstacles in such situations is the very fact that no joint action for the right cause is possible, and not even a common discourse, and whether that is explained by theorems of 'false consciousness' or others, such movements felt and feel that one of the tasks of solidary action is to struggle *for and on behalf of those who were blindfolded by ideology*. So their solidarity included those whose 'real interests' they (thought they) knew better. In (post-)Marxist as well as feminist discourse, the problems of such approaches, especially of an orthodox kind, have been much discussed,[2] and there is no reason to reproduce such versions here. But the point remains that solidarity can include fighting or working for others with whom you identify for a common cause (based on a 'shared condition' in Sangiovanni's sense), which you see as normatively binding but they don't. Think also of struggles against racism and for ecological change – they often contain instances of being solidary with those who feel no solidarity with those who struggle even though the latter think the former (lacking a sense of solidarity) should, while

---

2 The literature on this is abundant. On the discussions within Marxism, see Kallscheuer 1986, ch. 10, as well as Jay 1986. Habermas 1971 provides an account of the philosophical debates until the 1960s. On the debates within feminist theory, see Alcoff and Potter 1993.

they themselves act *in solidarity with and for them*, though *not together with them*. Here, solidarity is not unilateral as in a case of humanitarian solidarity,[3] but it is also not omnilateral; rather, it is an anticipation of the 'true' realization of a common cause (which includes, as I would add, a duty not to paternalize those whom one identifies with and regards as unsolidary). 'We also fight for you' is a slogan often heard across picket lines. So the 'we-perspective' of solidarity can be one which is imaginary, greater than the one of actual solidary action, and based on an identification that is not (yet) fully shared, and you may work with others in joint action (with the 'enlightened') to *make* it shared (among all affected) – as Sangiovanni says with reference to liberation theologians like Gutiérrez. But while you do this, you already act in a solidary way including, in your action, those who are blinded by ideology, yet joint action with *them* is *not* available to you.

There are also cases, I think, in which you act solidary on behalf of others who, for example, struggle for justice in parts of the world you have no contact to – and so you identify with them and their cause of justice, but to call your support (donations, for example) a form of joint action in the sense explained by Sangiovanni seems unjustified. I may not have lots of possibilities to communicate with these groups about their aims and strategies; but what I know is good enough (for me) to act in a solidary way. Solidarity is the willingness to act for the sake of others based on a common cause or identity which motivates you, but it need not be jointly coordinated action. The general concept of solidarity is more capacious than Sangiovanni allows for.[4]

In the historical section, Sangiovanni addresses some such cases. In defending not just the thesis of joint action but also that of symmetrical relations of equality when it comes to solidarity (a point I will come back to below), he argues that a solidarity on behalf of others without actually acting together with them is mere 'support', not 'acting in solidarity *with them*' (p. 63). At this point, the ambivalence of the 'with them' comes to the fore: I may well act

---

3 See O'Neill 1996, p. 201, on solidarity with and solidarity among.
4 I shall only note here in passing that Sangiovanni, in counting ecological movements as solidary movements, seems also to include the notion of solidarity with persons not yet born, and that also excludes joint action.

in solidarity *with* prisoners (as his example says) whose protest I identify with (without them knowing it), but I have no possibility to actually act in a coordinated way *with* them. So I fear that Sangiovanni identifies actual forms of acting with others with solidarity generally, which I consider to be a practical attitude of the willingness to act with and/or for others based on a common cause. To be sure, he allows for '*latent*' (p. 63) solidarity in cases where our protest is in line with theirs, even though we do not and cannot act in concert. But we *could*, given our shared aims. Such a case I would call one of solidarity proper, just not one where we can fully act together. Still, we are motivated by the same cause and act accordingly. The 'acting in concert' condition, if I may call it that (using a phrase by Arendt), is not necessary for solidarity to exist, not even for it to materialize in action. It would cease to be solidarity, however, if the notion to stand in for the others based on a common concern was merely illusionary; there must be grounds for assuming that the cause is actually shared. But a shared intention is too strong as a condition for that; some reflection and reasonable judgment is called for and suffices.

Solidarity and equality

This raises an important conceptual point. In defending the joint action and intention requirement as well as the claim that solidarity 'is understood to embody a commitment *among equals*' (p. 56) and thus conceptually excludes asymmetrical or one-sided relations such as charity or humanitarian aid, Sangiovanni rightly asks why we should use the term solidarity for cases that are close to, or identical with, charity (p. 61) and humanitarian actions (pp. 64–5.): 'What does calling them instances of solidarity add?' (p. 65). Such questions are crucial for analyzing the concept of solidarity. But since Sangiovanni himself tends to only count instances of jointly coordinated action based on an egalitarian normative identification as instances of solidarity – 'Solidarity requires joint action, and joint action requires, at the very least, coordination based on shared intentions' (p. 20) – we might ask him as well what is added by calling such phenomena instances of solidarity rather than instances of morally grounded egalitarian cooperation. This is close to the way Sangiovanni reads

Bourgeois and Durkheim on solidary cooperation, and I think it is very close to his own work on justice and reciprocity (Sangiovanni 2007). But be that as it may, the question here is twofold – what does the term solidarity add to other words describing similar or the same social phenomena, and should it add anything?

We should avoid a common mistake in answering this question. That is the mistake of an exaggerated fear of conceptual overlap, as if solidarity were a phenomenon that could not be connected to practical attitudes such as fighting for justice or identifying with the victims of some distant catastrophe. As Sangiovanni's own argument makes clear, the notion of solidarity needs *additional* normative resources to make sense and gain practical import, so we need to be careful in analyzing the connections and differences to other normative concepts. Occasionally, interpreters[5] think that solidarity must be a completely separate normative mode of action and thus sever its connections to justice and other concepts and practical motives – and thus have trouble giving it content and also linking it to the history of social struggles (against injustice especially).

Yet, that does not mean that solidarity is *reducible* to any such terms. It is a practical attitude of the willingness to act with and/or for others on the basis of a *common bond* grounded in a common cause and/or identity, and the point of solidarity is that it is *that very bond* that motivates action. So when I fight against concrete injustice, my solidary struggle concretely materializes in this particular engagement for this very cause (say, BLM), as it is this project that I am devoted to, that I am willing to take risks for, and may accept certain extra costs for. Or I fight for this particular nation because I am part of it and value it – or I am not a member but admire it nevertheless and support it. Or I support victims of this natural disaster because of some bond that connects me with them, maybe on the basis of religious considerations or because the disaster was so terrible. Solidarity in such ways combines *general* normative considerations of, for example, justice, but places them in a *concrete* setting with particular aims and motivations – and a *particular bond*. Or it is based on a particular community from the start, such as 'my nation', but then those who are solidary in this way can normally give additional reasons for that bond other than mere membership (such as the 'greatness' of their nation).

5 E.g. Derpmann 2013 and Jaeggi 2001.

What solidarity, in all its forms, ethical, legal, political, or moral, adds is the motive of furthering a cause which has *general* value in a *particular* way, as part of a special enterprise or community.[6] It is a motivational force for something particular, yet often as part of general considerations. Solidarity *focuses* such normative commitments in a particular way.

So humanitarian aid can be a case of solidarity, I think, if it focuses a general moral commitment (of respecting others as having equal dignity) on a particular instance of helping others in need, be they refugees as victims of injustice or of a natural disaster (or both). If they are victims of injustice, the aid should not merely be of a humanitarian kind, as one should also be solidary in overcoming the cause of the misery such people are in and help to fight the injustice, especially if the society one lives in is implicated in it. But humanitarian solidarity is not a contradiction in terms. It also need not be identical with charity if the latter is understood as a top-down, condescending attitude.

So why does Sangiovanni defend the joint-action and equal-relations view so vehemently? My impression is that in the course of section 2, Sangiovanni changes his methodological path. Rather than analyzing the *general concept* of solidarity, which he does not regard as a value per se since the Mafia (not the most egalitarian of organizations) can also be solidary (p. 29), Sangiovanni here starts to argue for a *particular normative conception* of solidarity, stressing the '*value* of solidarity for us, which is deeply bound up with the history of egalitarianism as a collective struggle' (p. 62). This is the point of his genealogy (which I will address in the next section), and it is the reason for his defense of the egalitarian nature of coordinated solidary action. For example, in arguing that the Christian 'elision between charity and solidarity' (p. 65) should be abandoned, Sangiovanni says that doing so 'would help to keep in clear view the distinctive value of solidarity – recall its essentially cooperative and egalitarian character – and maintain a connection to its history' (p. 65). But the history, as he just showed, does not have such a clear message, and apart from that, the argument here is straightforwardly normative in character, no longer a conceptual analysis. Which brings me to Sangiovanni's short history of solidarity.

6 See the analysis of contexts of solidarity in Forst forthcoming.

The history of solidarity

In his fascinating historical reconstruction of the discourse on solidarity, Sangiovanni places it in a modern sociological perspective, according to which 'solidarity names an egalitarian, mutualistic, and cooperative practice among strangers [...] in an era when traditional social ties [...] have weakened' (p. 34). Such forms of solidarity, he goes on to argue, are 'omnilateral and symmetrical as well as transformative and critical' (p. 34). He points to five important traditions of that discourse, namely French solidarism (Bourgeois, Durkheim), socialism, liberal nationalism (Renan, Mazzini), Christianity and more recent social movements (p. 53). His presentation is short but highly illuminating of the rich history of solidarity.

But two questions seem in order. First, given Sangiovanni's own account, does this history clearly show that the concept ought to be understood in the egalitarian transformative way he suggests? And second, is this history adequate, or, more precisely, does it neglect the 'dark side' of solidarity, especially in its nationalist forms?

As for the first question, it seems obvious that, from a socialist perspective, the liberal democratic 'solidarism' version of solidarity, which stresses the social division of labor and regards class struggle as a major threat to social cohesion and solidarity (pp. 39; 45), is seen as conservative, non-egalitarian, and as inimical to true (socialist) solidarity. Just think of the difference between Durkheim's notion of 'corporations' and unions in a socialist sense (p. 44). For socialists, the tradition of solidarism moralized and naturalized capitalist social relations as forms of 'organic' (Durkheim) solidarity. The opposition is even starker between socialist and nationalist discourses, even if we restricted (and why should we?) nationalist discourse to 'liberal nationalism' (p. 47). In any case, I conclude that Sangiovanni's own reconstruction of the history of solidarity already sheds doubt on the egalitarian transformative reading, as the five traditions did not all include, or aim at, egalitarian forms of social relations. The socialists, a major tradition in solidarity discourse, regarded liberal, nationalist, and a number of religious notions of solidarity as enemies of equality and solidarity.

As far as the second question is concerned, especially the rivalry between socialist and nationalist notions of solidarity points us to the great catastrophes of recent European history which Sangiovanni does not mention. The conflict between socialist and nationalist solidarities characterized social struggles throughout most of the nineteenth century and culminated in the context of World War One, where socialists and social democrats especially faced the decision of which form of solidarity to give priority to. The fear of being called *Vaterlandsverräter* (traitors to the nation) led to a number of nationalistic choices which would haunt the history of social democracy – and European societies generally (Mommsen 1979; Kruse 1997). Germany is a particular case in point, as the rhetoric of solidarity became closely tied to nationalism, linked to the *Gemeinschaft* of the *Volk* rather than modern *Gesellschaft* (Tönnies 1957). National socialism used this when, for example, it inaugurated a 'day of national solidarity' (*Tag der nationalen Solidarität*) in 1934, a day on which money was collected all over the country for the social organization *Winterhilfswerk des deutschen Volkes* (winter aid organization of the German people) to benefit the poor and jobless (as the Nazis saw fit). As national socialist rule consolidated after the Nuremberg Laws, Jews were placed under 'house arrest' during that day, as they were excluded from that kind of *Volkssolidarität*. The term 'national solidarity' was coined by Goebbels and famously used by Hitler in 1933 to replace any notion of 'international solidarity' – not without success (Schmitz-Berning 2007, pp. 602–3). In the time after World War Two, trying to redefine the term, *Volkssolidarität* was founded in 1945 as a social(ist) organization in East Germany (the GDR) and became a political mass organization (especially caring for the elderly); it still exists today as a major welfare organization.

This is not to say, of course, that in Germany the term solidarity has been captured by nationalist discourse exclusively. But it is to highlight that the very term harbors the great struggles and political tragedies of recent history, and that we should be aware of that history and these ambivalences, to put it mildly, when we reflect on the meaning of the concept. Solidarity can be a term used in emancipatory egalitarian struggles, but also a term used by those who are the deadly enemies of such struggles.

Motivational and normative grounds

The section on the 'grounds' of solidarity fully fleshes out the normative conception of solidarity Sangiovanni wants to defend. The way he discusses reasons of identification with regard to sharing a way of life, a certain role, condition, experience, or a cause seen as valuable and binding is highly illuminating. But I fear the section presents a somewhat misleading way to determine the grounds of solidarity. To be precise, the discussion of identification highlights an essential aspect of the *motivational* grounds of solidarity, but it is underdetermined with regard to the *normative* grounds that justify such identifications. The analysis shows, at least to me, that solidarity is a 'normatively dependent' concept and in need of additional normative substance in order to motivate persons to feel and act solidary. In order to explain this motivation, the *value* of a common way of life that solidary persons defend or want to uphold is relevant (p. 69), and solidarity depends on the importance of that value in the eyes of persons (and their interest in furthering it). Similarly, certain roles lead to solidary identification only if there is a particular value attached to them by the solidary persons, and that can be the social importance of the role (as teacher or doctor) or a sense of its political importance and obligations, such as citizenship as democratic co-authorship (p. 77). The same is true for social conditions seen as relevant for grounding solidarity, which may lie in a common predicament with respect to suffering from structural injustice – and the corresponding affirmation of the imperative of justice (p. 85). Hence there are no reasons of solidary identification 'as such'; rather, the relevant normative reasons for solidarity are based on certain general values or principles together with a sense of obligation to a particular group, often referred to by Sangiovanni as reasons of fairness (pp. 71; 76), of doing one's share. Hence the identification that motivates solidarity is itself *grounded*, it is *not* the ground of solidarity, as the argument in section 3 assumes. The identification arises from *valued* ways of life, roles, and conditions, hence it is a necessary *motivational* component, but it is not *normatively* sufficient to ground solidarity. Identification is not 'giving us grounds for acting in solidarity with others' (p. 67); rather, it rests on certain normative grounds of a substantive nature and thus motivates solidarity.

Given Sangiovanni's discussion, but counter to his explicit argument, it seems that we need to identify the *basic normative grounds* of solidarity in certain contexts (the value attached to a way of life, certain roles, or a project that is pursued, such as structural justice with regard to a particular group) and analyze how that ground leads to particular solidary identifications and motivations. I think this is what Sangiovanni substantively argues, *contre cœur*, but then the different grounds need to be categorized differently, namely with regard to the values or principles animating the sense of importance of the solidary project. This also means, I think, that Sangiovanni is correct to argue that 'shared interests or values' (p. 102) on their own are not sufficient as grounds for solidarity without the component of identification. Yet, this view neglects the important insight that without shared values (or principles) and the interest in actively furthering or defending them, there are no normative grounds for concrete solidary identification. Solidarity has a point, and that point is what grounds solidarity.

In addition, the notion of rationality used to distinguish rational from irrational solidary motivations (such as on p. 88, where Sangiovanni requires 'more than an irrational bias toward those who are "like us"' for justified solidarity) ought to be spelled out. What are the terms of rational justification in the different contexts discussed, what is *rational solidarity*?

Reasons of solidarity

The discussion of the reasons motivating identification – which argues for the fundamentally 'private' (p. 99) character of identification – also raises highly important points using well-chosen examples (pp. 92–4). But it seems that the discussion is richer than the distinction between 'operative' reasons and 'reasons as such' (p. 94) allows for. In particular, we may distinguish more fine-grainedly between (a) the subjective reasons that motivate persons to feel and act solidary with a particular group (and its cause); (b) the reasons of obligation one feels toward the group in determining what one thinks one ought to do to be solidary (often reasons of fairness or reciprocity); (c) the 'objective' reasons of why it is appropriate to identify with the group, given who and what one is; and (d) the general reasons one relies upon to evaluate whether the cause or aims in question are well justified in moral terms. All of these reasons are relevant to understand and evaluate contexts of solidary identification (or the lack of it).

Aristotelian Rawlsianism

Finally, Sangiovanni's discussion of the non-instrumental value of solidarity is highly illuminating, not just because it confirms my impression that solidarity for him basically is a form of egalitarian social cooperation. When he stresses the value of solidaristic reciprocity, he emphasizes (in line with Rawls' notion of social cooperation) the 'pleasure' of cooperative activity (p. 123), and if I may say so, this shows that Sangiovanni essentially argues from the perspective of an *Aristotelian Rawlsian*, one who believes that forms of solidary, reciprocal cooperation are an important part of individual and collective human *flourishing* (cf. also pp. 104–11).

It is important, however, that his Aristotelian Rawlsianism commits Sangiovanni to relativize his thesis about the non-instrumental value of acting in solidarity as a collective virtue. For in arguing that the solidarity we find in Mafia groups, for example, does *not* convey that kind of virtue, as it is '*conditional* on the value of the ends it promotes' (p. 111), Sangiovanni confirms my interpretation that the value of solidarity is based on *other* principles and values and thus is not normatively independent. Hence this questions the interpretation of solidarity as an independent, non-instrumental value for us as cooperative beings.

This, however, brings Sangiovanni into conflict with his following discussion of the relation between justice and solidarity. For if (as I believe) the value of solidarity depends upon justifiable principles and values at its basis then it can only demand 'more than merely justice' (p. 113) if it rests on *another* value such as loyalty to a colleague (as in the example on p. 113). One always needs to add what particular kind of solidarity can conflict with the solidarity required by justice, and it is normatively underdetermined to use a notion of solidarity as free-standing to analyze such a conflict, as Sangiovanni suggests.

This is also true when persons give partial communal solidarity priority over the solidarity demanded by justice (p. 113). This is how we should describe such a conflict, not as one between 'justice' and 'solidarity', as there is no such thing as solidarity without a further ground. It always needs to be grounded; it can be grounded in justice, or something else, or both; and then the two may conflict (as in a conflict between socialist and nationalistic solidarity).

But we may also have arrived at a point at which Sangiovanni actually defends a different view, and maybe he has done so all along. So far, I have assumed that justice, as well as other principles or values, can provide grounds for solidarity (for social movements especially, socialist or other), and I have also assumed that Sangiovanni agrees when he says, for example, that solidarity can exhibit 'the *internal* aspect of justice' (p. 114), that is, 'the attitudes, relations, commitments, and structure of deliberation that ought to lie behind and support a sincere affirmation and realization of principles of social justice' (p. 114). But when he goes on to argue that solidarity 'can be seen as a crucial *motivating* factor in realizing principles of justice' (p. 115), he emphasizes that this means that 'identification with others on one or more of the bases we have discussed gives people reasons to engage in justice-promoting collective actions that are independent of justice' (p. 115) and merely 'reinforce reasons of justice'. While I think that reasons of solidarity in contexts of (in-)justice *are* reasons of justice promoting a *particular* project and community aiming to realize justice, thus combining justice and a common bond, Sangiovanni separates the two and argues that solidarity here provides *independent* practical reasons apart from justice based on communal identification. But what would the content of such reasons be? It cannot be 'solidarity', as it has no content without supporting principles and values. Yet the argument here seems to suggest precisely such a content. If Sangiovanni means the considerations that stem from a *different* substantive bond of solidarity, one that is different from justice, such as some form of national cohesion, then this needs to be added here (and could lead to further problems). In any case, solidarity always needs a further adjective, otherwise talk of it remains too abstract.

Or else, it remains too concrete, as in Sangiovanni's argument that 'the normative, epistemic, and affective degree of commitment required by solidarity far outstrips what is required – *by way of our attitudes rather than our actions* – to meet the demands of justice' (pp. 116–7.). At this point, the Aristotelian Sangiovanni wins out against the Rawlsian, as Rawls' idea of social cooperation did include the required forms of solidarity and 'fraternity' (Rawls 1971, §17).[7] Hence, when Sangiovanni stresses that '[t]he nature

---

7 See also Sangiovanni at pp. 107–8 and n. 219.

of our identifications is intimate and personal' (p. 117), he falls prey to taking a certain *conception* of solidarity in personal contexts for the whole *concept*, excluding conceptions of solidarity based on justice. The distinction he goes on to suggest between justice focusing on '*principles*', while solidarity focuses on '*practices* with normative and evaluative significance' (p. 117) thins out the meaning of justice far too much, as if it were only concerned with principles embodied in abstract institutions and not with practices. This also goes against Sangiovanni's own view of practice-based accounts of justice (Sangiovanni 2008, p. 2014).

In sum, the final attempt to subsume the notion of solidarity, after it has become obvious that it is dependent on other principles and values to gain content and motivational force, under a category of '*associational* ethics' (p. 117) is doomed to fail. Solidarity is a term of relational ethics and politics which highlights the particular projects and collective aims people have, but it cannot be relegated to the realm of personal or communitarian social ethics. This reifies the meaning of solidarity and reduces the plurality of its forms as we learn to appreciate them from Sangiovanni's great treatise.

References

Alcoff, L. and E. Potter, eds. (1993), *Feminist Epistemologies* (New York: Routledge).
Derpmann, S. (2013), *Gründe der Solidarität* (Münster: Mentis).
Forst, R. (2012), *The Right to Justification: Elements of a Constructivist Theory of Justice* (New York: Columbia University Press).
Forst, R. (2013), *Toleration in Conflict: Past and Present* (Cambridge: Cambridge University Press).
Forst, R. (2017), *Normativity and Power: Analyzing Social Orders of Justification* (Oxford: Oxford University Press).
Forst, R. (2022), 'The Justification of Trust in Conflict. Conceptual and Normative Groundwork', *Contrust Working Paper* 2. (Frankfurt am Main: ConTrust – Trust in Conflict), https://contrust.uni-frankfurt.de/files/2022/10/ConTrust-WorkingPaper-No2_Forst.pdf (accessed 13 May 2023).
Forst, R. (forthcoming), 'Solidarity: Concept, Conceptions, and Contexts', in *Solidarity*, eds. Andrea Sangiovanni and Juri Viehoff (Oxford: Oxford University Press).

Habermas, J. (1971), *Theorie und Praxis* (Frankfurt am Main: Suhrkamp).
Jaeggi, R. (2001), 'Solidarity and Indifference', in *Solidarity in Health and Social Care in Europe*, eds. Ruud ter Meulen, Wil Arts, and Ruud Muffels (Dordrecht: Kluwer), pp. 287–308.
Jay, M. (1986), *Marxism and Totality* (Los Angeles: University of California Press).
Kallscheuer, O. (1986), 'Marxismus und Sozialismus bis zum Ersten Weltkrieg', in *Pipers Handbuch der politischen Ideen*, vol. 4, eds. Iring Fetscher and Herfried Münkler (Munich: Piper), pp. 515–44.
Kruse, W., ed. (1997), *Eine Welt von Feinden. Der große Krieg 1914–1918* (Frankfurt am Main: Fischer).
Mommsen, H. (1979), *Arbeiterbewegung und nationale Frage* (Göttingen: Vandenhoeck und Ruprecht).
O'Neill, O. (1996), *Towards Justice and Virtue* (Cambridge: Cambridge University Press).
Rawls, J. (1971), *A Theory of Justice* (Cambridge, MA: Harvard University Press).
Sangiovanni, A. (2007), 'Global Justice, Reciprocity, and the State', *Philosophy and Public Affairs* 35(1): 3–39.
Sangiovanni, A. (2008), 'Justice and the Priority of Politics to Morality', *Journal of Political Philosophy* 36(2): 137–64.
Schmitz-Berning, C. (2007), *Vokabular des Nationalsozialismus* (Berlin: de Gruyter).
Tönnies, F. (1957), *Community and Society* (East Lansing: Michigan State University Press).

6

Solidarity and structural injustice

Catherine Lu

Introduction

A few weeks after COVID-19 began its deadly embrace in Italy, prompting a lockdown that severely disrupted social life and the economy, a couple of community activists lowered 'solidarity baskets' in the city center of Naples, with the note, 'Those who can, put something in, those who can't, help yourself' (Poggioli 2020). In the face of isolating and uncertain circumstances, as well as various kinds of hardships wrought by the pandemic, there have been many such examples of people and communities devising creative ways of coming together to offer mutual aid and assistance to those in need.[1] At the same time, globally, the lack of solidarity on ensuring equitable access to COVID-19 vaccines is blatant. Although effective global vaccination would help to halt virus transmission and mutations, by the end of 2021, only '2.6 per cent of people in low-income countries were fully vaccinated against COVID-19, compared to 66.6 per cent of people in high-income countries' (United Nations 2021, p. 4). At the time of writing, six months later, it is not much better: 2.8 billion people in the world still have not received even one shot of the COVID-19 vaccine, making them more vulnerable to severe illness and death, and disproportionately increasing hardships in low-income countries, including major economic setbacks and political disruptions (United Nations 2022).[2]

1   See The International Observatory on Participatory Democracy (IOPD): https://oidp.net/en/covid19/page.php?id=46 (accessed August 18, 2022).
2   For data, see the Global Dashboard for Vaccine Equity: https://data.undp.org/vaccine-equity/ (accessed August 6, 2022).

These examples of successes and failures of solidarity in the struggle to alleviate the toll of the pandemic generate perplexing and urgent questions about the value of solidarity as a social practice. On the one hand, solidarity seems like a reliable and virtuous social practice that affirms the bonds of social identification and attachment in contexts of adversity, generating collective action that extends the boundaries of social obligation, and may even prompt their transformation towards greater equity and inclusion. The solidarity baskets in Naples affirm to poorer residents that they do not suffer alone, that the fate of the disadvantaged is of common concern to the whole, that everyone is in it together. On the other hand, solidarity seems most rare and fickle where it is most needed, that is, in contexts of adversity marked by deep structural injustice, where the bonds of communal attachments or identification are rigidly segregated, demotivating action that could aid in dismantling the barriers posed by structural domination or oppression. 'Vaccine nationalism' on the part of wealthy nations since the start of the pandemic has pointedly exposed the limits of solidarity, and the role of exclusionary identification in stymying wider cooperation, despite the fact that global vaccination would produce a win-win outcome of minimizing virus mutations (Bollyky and Brown 2020).

Andrea Sangiovanni's essay provides us with a clear and compelling analytic account of the concept of solidarity, focusing on its two core elements of identification and joint action. His account is useful for identifying practices of solidarity empirically, and distinguishing them from acts of charity/altruism, love, and justice. His essay also provides a lucid account of the potential normative role of solidarity in contemporary moral, social, and political life, highlighting its instrumental and non-instrumental value to agents' flourishing in associational life. In this short commentary, I build on Sangiovanni's account to address some issues that arise when considering the value of solidarity in contexts of structural injustice. Although he does not address this question directly, Sangiovanni's analysis of the concept of solidarity can help to explain why, despite its potential to be instrumental for achieving greater justice, solidarity as a social practice often fails to materialize effectively to dismantle deep and pervasive structural injustice. The reasons, I posit, have to do with how structural injustices affect agents' intersubjectivity and the contours of their schemas for identification, with implications for their opportunities and capacities for joint action. If solidarity as a social practice is predicated on social structural processes that mediate identification and joint action, we can locate the reasons for morally objectionable failures of identification and joint action in unjust social structures.

Focusing on the social structures that mediate, enable, and constrain identification and joint action allows us also to make sense of the structural reasons why individuals may be inhibited from forming the epistemic, affective, and normative attitudes that would ground their joint action with others resisting injustice, oppression, or domination. In this light, I think we can understand better how calls for solidarity by various social movements are related to calls to dismantle structural injustice. While Sangiovanni aptly distinguishes the demands of solidarity and justice (with the latter understood as institutional morality or enforceable duties), I consider how the demands of solidarity can themselves be constitutive of social structural justice, and how showing a lack of solidarity can itself be morally objectionable or blameworthy. This is because lack of solidarity with the oppressed may be based on a moral failure to acknowledge the oppressed as agents who have interests in and entitlements to equal freedom, dignity, and/or respect. In such cases, even if members of a privileged group share in solidaristic associational life towards a good end, the non-instrumental value of such solidarity is necessarily limited, and even questionable. Although I am sympathetic to Sangiovanni's account of the instrumental and non-instrumental value of solidarity (for an assumed good end), assessing solidarity's value in contexts of structural injustice is more complicated than his analysis suggests. Ultimately, one may be more ambivalent about the instrumental or non-instrumental value of solidarity as a social practice in contexts of deep and pervasive structural injustice.

Structural injustice and the instrumental value of solidarity

According to Sangiovanni, solidarity is a part of '*associational* ethics – the ethics of life in associations and within social relationships that extend beyond relations among intimates' (p. 117). While fellow-feeling may motivate solidarity, the nature of solidarity consists of '*joint action* characterized by a typical profile of commitments, intentions, and attitudes, and triggered by, *inter alia*, an identification with others on the basis of a shared cause, role, way of life, condition, or set of experiences' (p. 5). Distinct from altruism/charity, love, and justice, solidarity is

> a form of acting together to overcome significant adversity grounded in identification. We act solidaristically when, that is, (a) we identify with one another on the basis of a shared way of life, cause, set of experiences, condition, or role, (b) we are, as a result, committed to doing our part in overcoming significant adversity and to setting aside, in a range of cases, narrow self-interest in its pursuit, (c) we have a settled, reliable disposition to come to others' aid in support of our goal, and (d) we trust one another with respect to (b) and (c) (where trust is reliance plus a normative expectation that others will indeed be committed and come to our aid when necessary). (p. 66)

As Sangiovanni notes, his concept of solidarity is a unified account that is meant to be useful for distinguishing practices of solidarity from other phenomena such as love, charity, or justice, as well as for developing normative and empirical conceptions of solidarity. With his account, we can better describe and explain solidarity as a social practice in the empirical world, and also better evaluate or make sense of its normative function and value in moral, social, and political life.

When considering the value of solidarity as a social practice, however, a puzzle arises. As Sangiovanni observes, although solidarity as he has conceptualized it may not always have normative value, especially when it is practiced to promote wicked ends, contemporary social movements typically call for solidarity on the expectation that it can be 'a crucial *motivating* factor in realizing principles of justice' (p. 115). The puzzle is why solidarity does not work, or become operational, as an instrumentally effective practice in all contexts or against all forms of structural injustice. What are the conditions in which solidarity gains emancipatory or egalitarian potential to reform or revolutionize social relations towards greater social justice? Sangiovanni's clarification of the main components of solidarity – identification and joint action – is helpful not only for identifying solidaristic practices empirically, but also for understanding why solidarity may or may not be forthcoming in response to various social and political crises. Understanding the reasons for failures of solidarity, however, raises questions about the instrumental value of solidarity in contexts of structural injustice.

To get at these questions about the relationship between solidarity and structural injustice, we can revisit the historical practices of solidarity that Sangiovanni describes in section 2. To construct his account, Sangiovanni engages with solidarity as a historical social practice, 'a lived system of norms, rules, and expectation that gives rise to new self-understandings, new concepts, and new possibilities for collective action and social relation within complex, modern societies' (p. 33). Historically, 'solidarity names an egalitarian, mutualistic, and cooperative practice among strangers, whose aim is to overcome significant forms of adversity in an era when traditional social ties […] have weakened' (p. 34). The 'language of solidarity emerges as a response to growing anxiety regarding the expansion of commercial society, large-scale industry, and perceived collapse of traditional communities' (p. 35). It called on citizens to identify 'with one another on the basis of their role in sustaining and reproducing the division of labor' (p. 38). Solidarity, historically, was about joining together with others, based on a shared, common, or joint affinity or identity, to solve collective social, economic, and/or political problems in mutually supportive or reciprocal ways.

Sangiovanni rightly argues that the value of solidarity is 'deeply bound up with the history of egalitarianism as a collective struggle' (p. 62). The historical and contemporary cases he discusses – solidarism, socialism, nationalism, Christianity, and social movements such as feminism and civil rights – can all be described as engendering 'collective agency and transformative mobilization' (p. 65) among strangers. These 'core' cases, for Sangiovanni, are paradigmatic examples of the social unity that solidarity as a social practice engenders:

> This social unity has, at its core, a common recognition that our individual flourishing inevitably depends on the actions of myriad others in an extensive division of labor, and hence that the flourishing of all is necessary for the flourishing of each. This aspect of solidarity is evident, as we have seen, in each of the main sources of our thinking on solidarity, namely solidarism, socialism, liberal nationalism, Christianity, and the social movements of the twentieth century. (p. 107)

While Sangiovanni implicitly evaluates his 'core' cases of solidarity as normatively valuable, and shows convincingly that the history of solidarity as a social practice is bound up with the history of egalitarian struggle, one interesting part of the history of egalitarianism that is not really mentioned in his account is their limited or selective nature. Although he is right that normatively, solidarity is valuable when the social unity it expresses is based on a common recognition that the flourishing of all is necessary for the flourishing of each, this normative aspiration was not instantiated by any of Sangiovanni's core historical cases. Including the inegalitarian history of egalitarianism, I think, is instructive for illuminating the barriers posed by structural injustice to solidaristic practices. Doing so also exposes the limits of the transformative potential of solidarity as a social practice, especially in the face of deep structural injustice.

Perhaps most obviously, nationalism as a shared identification in an imagined community is a morally complicated expression of solidarity in the modern world. While Ernst Renan described the nation as 'a great solidarity' (une grande solidarité), he and other nineteenth-century nationalists were also known to have fused national identification with racial hierarchy: 'nature has made a race of workers, the Chinese race ... a race of tillers of the soil, the Negroes [sic]; a race of masters and soldiers, the European race'.[3] Even the history of liberal nationalism cannot be told without the context of global White supremacy (Mills 2019, p. 103).

Consider also the French Revolution, a paradigmatic case of egalitarian struggle that called for a new egalitarian basis of fraternity and solidarity in the face of the collapse of the *ancien régime*. Yet the African-American scholar Anna Julia Cooper noted in her historical study that the French revolutionists had not considered extending their liberatory struggle to enslaved Blacks in France's most lucrative colony of Saint-Domingue (Haiti). Cooper shows that Blacks in Haiti had engaged in several slave revolts, in 1679, 1691, 1703, and 1758, that preceded the French and American revolutions. Yet politicians in France and White colonists in Saint-Domingue consistently overlooked and underestimated the capacities of the Blacks and the *gens de couleur*, and could not believe that the enslaved Blacks would revolt, even when it was happening everywhere.[4] Why

---

3 See Renan 1929, quoted in Césaire 1950, pp. 37–8.
4 See Cooper 2006 [1925] and May 2021.

did the French revolutionists not engage solidaristically with the enslaved to deepen the revolution?

One reason seems to be that they did not see Blacks as equals or even as agents, who are capable of sharing in a republican political project, a convenient belief that made the French republic consistent with slavery and empire.[5] If solidarity as a social practice holds the potential to transform social relations in a more inclusive, egalitarian direction, the case of the French revolutionists on slavery shows that deep structural injustices of racial hierarchy and anti-Black racism can pose a barrier to developing any identification based on shared experiences, conditions, and fates, cutting off the prospects of solidarity across the racial divide. Recovering this history of egalitarian struggle may generate more ambivalence, not only about the value of solidarity but, more significantly, about its potential to support radical structural transformations. For how can solidarity as a form of joint action grounded in identification be transformative of unjust social relations, when those relations and their attendant schemas of identification are embedded in unjust structures that deny the very agency of the oppressed? If solidarity is a special form of joint action grounded in identification, then to be operationalized, it already presupposes some level of equality between those who identify, or some level of recognition of others as the kinds of agents with whom one can engage in joint actions.

Sangiovanni's account helps us to focus on identification as a fundamental component of solidaristic practices and, for my purposes, raises the question of why building identification among agents in different social positions is so difficult in contexts of deep structural injustice. If solidarity is grounded in identification, but identification itself is produced and grounded in social structures, then the challenging question is how solidarity can motivate individuals to dismantle the structural injustices that mediate and condition their identification or their boundaries. It may be that for solidarity to serve any emancipatory role, it must not only broaden notions of self (beyond narrow self-interest), but must involve disorienting and even destroying the social identities that entrench certain structures of injustice and their attendant barriers to shared identification. For example, BLM is a slogan that aims not for inclusivity of Black

---

5 See Césaire 1950 on 'thingification'.

people in the social order but, more provocatively, to reveal and counter the racial logic of White supremacy underlying the current social order (in which Black lives are dispensable). Sangiovanni argues that solidarity 'gives rise to new self-understandings, new concepts, and new possibilities for collective action and social relation within complex, modern societies' (p. 33), but it seems that before solidarity can forge new identities, it needs some old identities to be destroyed. Solidarity against racism and for a racially just society and world, for example, would require repudiating the ideology of White supremacy, just as solidarity with the poor requires endorsing a shared understanding of poverty as a political problem of oppressive or unjust social structures, and of the poor as agents rather than passive recipients of aid (Deveaux 2021, p. 201).

Such transformations of intersubjectivity are harder to accomplish than one might think. As Sangiovanni observes, identifying with others is a transformative endeavour: 'When I identify with another, my imagining and sympathizing with their life is not just a way of learning about them but a way of modifying or transforming myself in the process' (p. 12). To identify with Indigenous peoples and their struggles, however, may require imagining myself as a settler in a settler-colonial society, and giving up my self-image as an immigrant who successfully integrated into a liberal egalitarian and multicultural society, which can be a deeply unsettling and painful transformation. To identify with the poor and their struggles may require imagining myself as a beneficiary of global and domestic social structures that produce their subordination, and giving up my self-image as a hard-working person whose gains are largely attributable to my own ambitions and efforts.

Sangiovanni is right to argue that identification does not require sharing interests or values (p. 102), but as Iris Marion Young noted, 'for every structural injustice there is an alignment of powerful entities whose interests are served by those structures' (Young 2011, p. 148). A significant method of entrenching structural hierarchies of domination is to socialize agents into being attached to ideologies and narratives that produce epistemic distortions and biases which combine to rationalize the denial, dismissal, or inhibition of the agency of those who are marginalized, dominated, or oppressed by the social structure. One salient effect of structural injustice is thus to stymy agents' capacities to foster identification as a basis for joint action against structural injustice.

Indeed, the kind of identification required to foster solidarity may even be hard to establish among those who are victims of structural injustice. Although Sangiovanni is right that victims of oppression can identify with their oppression, such identification can be crippling or burdensome rather than empowering. As Judith Shklar noted, 'Most people hate to think of themselves as victims; after all, nothing could be more degrading. Most of us would rather reorder reality than admit that we are the helpless objects of injustice' (Shklar 1990, p. 38). For this reason, building solidarity as a sustainable social practice among the oppressed is a real political achievement, and requires critical political conscious-raising as a precondition (Deveaux 2021, pp. 113–26).

To take seriously the social structural processes that shape individual and group identification generates a conundrum for those who seek to build solidarity in contexts of structural injustice. To produce solidarity, understood as joint action grounded in identification, agents need to identify with each other; but structural injustice precisely produces social positions that obstruct identification with the causes or conditions of those vulnerable to or suffering from structural injustice. In this sense, structural injustice produces forms of identification-based joint action that tend toward the reproduction of domination and oppression. Understanding how solidaristic practices are embedded in and fortify structural injustice generates a more sober view of the instrumental potential of solidarity in struggles against deep and pervasive structural injustice.

Structural injustice and the non-instrumental value of solidarity

While Sangiovanni understands solidarity to refer to 'a social, interpersonal relation, constituted [...], by a characteristic set of other-regarding attitudes, behaviours, norms and dispositions' (p. 9), he notes that solidarity is not the same as justice, whether justice is understood as the 'domain of institutional morality [...] or of enforceable duties' (p. 112). Indeed, he offers several ways in which solidarity may go beyond justice, as well as assist or motivate justice;

in addition, he also offers some ways in which the normative demands of solidarity may be more narrow than justice, and even go against justice. As a part of associational ethics, solidarity may or may not be instrumental for justice, in the same way that the associational ethics of friendship may or may not be consistent with the demands of justice.

Sangiovanni asserts that part of the reason why solidarity cannot be an enforceable duty is that the 'nature of our identifications is intimate and personal' (p. 117); for this reason, 'there is very little non-prudential normative pressure that we can put on another to identify' (p. 116). He argues that 'the normative, epistemic, and affective degree of commitment required by solidarity far outstrips what is required – *by way of our attitudes rather than our actions* – to meet the demands of justice' (p. 117). While true, I think Sangiovanni misses an opportunity to confront the problem of lack of solidarity as a problem of justice, and not only of associational ethics.

Understanding the lack of solidarity as a failing of justice helps to make sense of many contemporary calls for solidarity by progressive social movements. Some calls for solidarity consider it a vital instrument for achieving greater justice or overcoming injustice. For example, Carol Gould has argued that calls for solidarity in bioethics and healthcare literatures have not sufficiently taken into account the impact of structural injustices: 'Systemic forms of injustice militate against adequate healthcare for all, and suggest the need for solidaristic action to struggle against and to remedy existing entrenched inequalities' (Gould 2018, p. 542). In addition to this instrumental view of solidarity, some calls to take 'political responsibility for solidarity' with the oppressed imply that solidarity is itself constitutive of justice (Young 2011; Deveaux 2021, pp. 129–202). They are appeals to identify with others, often those who are oppressed, dominated, marginalized, or exploited, *as a matter of justice*, and to commit to joint actions to support their claims or causes, in ways that recognize them as agents with whom one can engage in jointly reciprocal action (Gould 2020; Deveaux 2021). The conception of justice in social movement discourses refers not mainly to institutional morality or enforceable duties, but to a broader conception of justice that goes beyond formal rules and institutions, and engages with 'all social processes that support or undermine oppression, including culture' (Young 1990, p. 149).

As Iris Marion Young argued, structural injustices such as racism and sexism are not only instantiated in formal or discursive discriminatory practices. Rather, they structure and mediate the way that individuals' intimate and personal identifications are constituted, thus 'unconscious reactions are more widespread than discursive prejudice. Judgements of beauty or ugliness, attraction or aversion, cleverness or stupidity, competence or ineptness, and so on are made unconsciously in interactive contexts and in generalized media culture, often mark, stereotype, devalue, degrade some groups' (Young 1990, p. 151). While attitudinal changes cannot be compelled through enforceable duties, I think Young's account of structural oppression can help supplement Sangiovanni's argument by pointing out that lack of solidarity is a moral failing in contexts where it is a symptom of the effects of structurally unjust schemas of identification. Young's call for political responsibility for structural justice includes changing 'cultural habits'. Taking such responsibility requires individuals to become aware of and change their 'actions, habits, feelings, attitudes, images, associations'; thus, to call on individuals to contribute to dismantling structural injustice 'is to ask the person from now on to submit such unconscious behaviour to reflection, to work to change habits and attitudes' (Young 1990, p. 151).

Structural injustice also complicates the assessment of solidarity's non-instrumental value. Sangiovanni argues that solidarity 'instantiates a form of non-instrumentally valuable cooperation in which we each participate in the complementary excellences of all, and take pleasure in the collective realization of ends that none of us could achieve alone' (p. 123). In the right conditions, 'solidarity is non-instrumentally good, but it is non-instrumentally good *for* us, by which I mean that, in the right conditions, solidarity makes our life better' (p. 105). At the same time, when discussing this non-instrumental value, he notes that 'the non-instrumental value of the trusting, cooperative you-and-me reciprocal activity constitutive of solidarity is ... *conditional* on the value of the ends it promotes. If the ends are wicked – as we are assuming the ends of the Mafiosi are – then the solidarity enacted to realize them becomes disvaluable as well. This goes for all forms of solidarity bent to wicked ends: racist groups, terrorist cells, xenophobic nationalists, and so on' (p. 111). Furthermore, 'If solidarity's ends are good, the non-instrumental value is all the greater; if they are bad, then its non-instrumental value is all the worse' (p. 112). The non-instrumental value of solidarity, then, is normatively parasitic on the value of the ends it promotes.

Sangiovanni implies that if the ends of associations are morally permissible or good, then solidarity has non-instrumental value. The impact of structural injustice, however, may complicate this assessment. Can the ends of associations be considered good without an examination of the larger structural contexts in which they are embedded? What are the conditions in which solidaristic associational life is non-instrumentally good for us? Is solidarity (for an assumed good end) non-instrumentally good for those who participate in it, even in contexts of structural injustice?

Consider the Catholic Church and its members in Canada. After a week-long 'penitential pilgrimage' of reconciliation between the Catholic Church and Indigenous peoples in Canada in July 2022, Pope Francis called the Indian Residential School system and forced assimilation policies 'genocide',[6] and apologized for the Church's participation in running the schools in Canada. In the 2006 court-mandated settlement, the Church promised to contribute to healing and reconciliation efforts through a fundraising campaign for $25 million.[7] The campaign raised only $3.7 million. Over the same period of the fundraising campaign, the Church paid $128 million to renovate St. Michael's Cathedral Basilica in Toronto, '30 times what was raised for residential school survivors' healing programs'.[8] Catholics express a robust solidarity within their own community in ways that are admirable and fulfill the criteria of other-regarding joint action, but as a group, their lack of solidarity with Indigenous peoples reveals something less praiseworthy about the mutuality of Catholic associational life. In settler-colonial contexts of longstanding anti-Indigenous structural injustice, what can the lack of solidarity

---

6 See Deer 2022.

7 The court-mandated settlement was agreed to by the legal counsel for former Residential School survivors, the Assembly of First Nations, and other Indigenous organizations, as well as church bodies, and the Canadian federal government. See 'The Indian Residential Schools Settlement Has Been Approved,' Residential School Settlement, www.residentialschoolsettlement.ca (accessed September 8, 2022).

8 For a damning investigative report on the Catholic Church in Canada, see Grant and Cardoso 2021.

shown by Catholics to the plight of Indigenous peoples in Canada reveal other than a fundamental lack of acknowledgment of Indigenous people as the kind of agents who are entitled to equal worth, dignity, and respect?

Although the Catholic Church and Catholics arguably can be said to be promoting good ends, it would be difficult to argue that the solidarity of Catholics is morally commendable or non-instrumentally valuable, except from the internal perspective of those who benefit from the association. From an external point of view, the benefits of such solidarity may even be viewed as morally blameworthy. When assessing the non-instrumental value of solidarity, then, in addition to the condition identified by Sangiovanni – that associations do not promote bad or wicked ends – we should also add the condition that the solidaristic practice is at least not perpetuating structural injustice.

Perhaps Sangiovanni would respond that Catholics have moral reasons, even duties, to support collective actions of repair, whether or not they identify with Indigenous peoples and their struggles. If the Catholic Church were ordered by the courts to pay compensation or reparations, for example, such action could be required by justice and the duty to pay would be enforceable, but would not constitute solidarity. I agree with this assessment that solidarity is not an enforceable duty, but my point is that we cannot straightforwardly evaluate Catholic solidarity in these circumstances as non-instrumentally valuable. Even though such solidarity is not promoting a wicked end, its selective basis perpetuates the structural indignity[9] of Indigenous peoples, which thus nullifies its value. It is due to Sangiovanni's lucid account of the egalitarian ethos of solidarity as a social practice that we can see more clearly how deep a moral failure the lack of Catholic solidarity with Indigenous peoples is.

Conclusion

Wherever groups face adversity, especially in conditions of injustice, oppression, or domination, we hear calls for solidarity. I have argued

---

9 For a discussion of the position of structural indignity of Indigenous peoples within settler-colonial domestic and international orders, see Lu 2017.

that such calls for solidarity can be understood as components of a wider conception of social structural justice. Clarifying the relationship between solidarity and structural injustice helps us to understand why solidarity in practice may buttress social justice claims in some contexts, while stymying such efforts in others. Structural injustice is a major reason why individuals are inhibited from forming the epistemic, affective and normative attitudes that would ground their joint action with others resisting injustice, oppression, or domination. In addition, by focusing on the structural conditions in which solidarity is practiced, we can better assess the value of solidarity as a social practice, which is based not only on the worthiness of an association's ends, but also on its contribution to the perpetuation or dismantling of structural injustice.

The paradox of solidarity is that for it to be a virtuous social practice, it would presuppose largely just social relations, but if social relations were just, then solidarity in social relations would not be fundamentally transformative but merely expressive of the moral reciprocity instantiated in a just society. In contexts of structural injustice, however, associational life will be distorted or corrupted in ways that also undermine the value of solidarity as a social practice. Thus, while valuable to some, solidarity will precisely fail where structural injustice is deep and pervasive enough to sever the bonds of identification that are needed to ground solidarity as an emancipatory social practice.

In assessing the instrumental value of solidarity for dismantling deep and pervasive structural injustice, I have raised the concern that empirically, solidarity as a social practice is likely to disappoint, given that the grounds of solidaristic collective action in identification are likely structured to reproduce structural injustice, rather than its dismantling. Sangiovanni's account of the concept of solidarity helps to pinpoint what political efforts need to focus on in order to construct effective solidaristic movements against structural oppression or domination. In assessing the non-instrumental value of solidarity, I have raised the challenge that contexts of structural injustice may undermine the non-instrumental value of solidarity as a social practice, even when the group's ends are not wicked. Structural justice thus is a condition for both the instrumental and non-instrumental value of solidarity, understood as a special form of joint action grounded in identification. In this way, the value of solidarity as a social practice is ultimately parasitic on visions of and struggles for structural justice.

Acknowledgment

I am grateful to Maria Laura Chobadindegui and Brian Isaac for their research assistance.

References

Bollyky, T. and C. P. Brown (2020), 'The Tragedy of Vaccine Nationalism: Only Cooperation Can End the Pandemic', *Foreign Affairs* 99(5): 96–108.

Césaire, A. (2000 [1950]), *Discourse on Colonialism* (New York: Monthly Review Press).

Cooper, A. J. (2006 [1925]), *Slavery and the French and Haitian Revolutionists*, trans. and ed. Frances Richardson Keller (Toronto: Rowman & Littlefield).

Deer, K. (2022), 'Pope says genocide took place at Canada's residential schools', Canadian Broadcasting Corporation (CBC), July 30, www.cbc.ca/news/indigenous/pope-francis-residential-schools-genocide-1.6537203 (accessed September 8, 2022).

Deveaux, M. (2021), *Poverty, Solidarity, and Poor-Led Social Movements* (Oxford: Oxford University Press).

Global Dashboard for Vaccine Equity, https://data.undp.org/vaccine-equity/ (accessed September 18, 2022).

Gould, C. (2020), 'Motivating Solidarity with Distant Others: Empathic Politics, Responsibility, and the Problem of Global Justice', in *The Oxford Handbook of Global Justice*, ed. Thom Brooks (Oxford: Oxford University Press), pp. 122–38.

Gould, C. (2018), 'Solidarity and the Problem of Structural Injustice in Healthcare', *Bioethics* 32(9): 541–52.

Grant, T. and T. Cardoso (2021), 'The Catholic Church in Canada Is Worth Billions, a *Globe* Investigation Shows. Why Are Its Reparations for Residential Schools So Small?' *The Globe and Mail*, August 7 (updated October 25), www.theglobeandmail.com/canada/article-catholic-church-canadian-assets-investigation/ (accessed 23 April 2023).

The International Observatory on Participatory Democracy (IOPD), https://oidp.net/en/covid19/page.php?id=46 (accessed August 18, 2022)

Lu, C. (2017), *Justice and Reconciliation in World Politics* (Cambridge: Cambridge University Press).
May, V. (2021), 'Anna Julia Cooper on Slavery's Afterlife: Can International Thought 'Hear' Her 'Muffled' Voice and Ideas?', in *Women's International Thought: A New History*, eds. Patricia Owens and Katharina Rietzler (Cambridge: Cambridge University Press), pp. 29–51.
Mills, C. (2019), 'Race and Global Justice', in *Empire, Race and Global Justice*, ed. Duncan Bell (Cambridge, Cambridge University Press), pp. 94–119.
Poggioli, S. (2020), 'In Naples, Pandemic 'Solidarity Baskets' Help Feed the Homeless', *NPR*, April 7, www.npr.org/2020/04/07/828021259/in-naples-pandemic-solidarity-baskets-help-feed-the-homeless (accessed August 18, 2022).
Renan, E. (1929), *La Réforme intellectuelle et morale* (Paris: Calmann-Levy).
Residential School Settlement (2006), 'The Indian Residential Schools Settlement Has Been Approved', www.residentialschoolsettlement.ca (accessed September 8, 2022).
Shklar, J. N. (1990), *The Faces of Injustice* (New Haven, CT: Yale University Press).
United Nations (2022), 'UN Analysis Shows Link Between Lack of Vaccine Equity and Widening Poverty Gap'. March 28, https://news.un.org/en/story/2022/03/1114762 (accessed August 18, 2022).
United Nations (2021), 'United Nations Comprehensive Report to Covid-19: Saving Lives, Protecting Societies, Recovering Better – 2021 Update', www.un.org/sites/un2.un.org/files/2021/12/un-comprehensive-response-covid-19-2021.pdf (accessed September 8, 2022).
Young, I. M. (2011), *Responsibility for Justice* (Oxford: Oxford University Press).
Young, I. M. (1990), *Justice and the Politics of Difference* (Princeton: Princeton University Press).

Part III

Reply

7

Response to critics

Andrea Sangiovanni

I am very grateful to Avery Kolers, Jared Holley, Sally Scholz, Rainer Forst, and Catherine Lu for writing such thoughtful and careful responses to 'Solidarity: Nature, Value, and Grounds'. It is a humbling task to respond, which requires one to come face to face with how one's work appears to others, and to see, often quite clearly, how one could have done better. But it also offers an opportunity to try to make progress together even if, in the end, we decide to take different paths to the same destination. I take each response in the order in which it appears in this volume. To keep this exchange readably short, I have refrained from trying to answer every point or challenge made. Instead, I have tried, to the best of my ability, to choose the lines of argument that struck me as most salient and most instructive.

Avery Kolers

Avery Kolers' careful and probing remarks challenge whether solidarity should really be understood, as I claim, as a special form of joint action. To make the argument, he gives a fruitful example from early twentieth-century colonial Trinidad. The example involves the famous Trinidadian cricket player, Wilton St. Hill. In an earlier stage of his career, St. Hill faced a choice: he could either play with the 'higher caste', lighter-skinned, bourgeois team – Maple – or with the working-class, darker-skinned team – Shannon. Maple, however, actively excluded dark-skinned blacks. (St. Hill's skin is deemed light enough, and his play good enough, that it doesn't matter in his case.) St. Hill decides to throw his lot in with Shannon, despite the greater advantages, both social and athletic, that a career playing for Maple might offer him. The reason that St. Hill gives is that Maple would 'not have accepted his brothers'. Kolers says that St. Hill's act of identification *as such* counts as an act of solidarity. And so, Kolers concludes, there can be solidarity *without* joint action. This is because St. Hill's taking sides with the more disadvantaged is a purely individual action, and therefore cannot be understood as part of a wider joint action in which, say, Black Trinidadians, let alone his fellow team players, oppose the racial and colonial caste order.

But is this really true? I agree with Kolers that St. Hill's throwing his lot in with Shannon counts as an act of solidarity, but I disagree that it cannot be understood as part of a wider, ongoing joint action. I want to argue that what makes it such a powerful example of solidarity is precisely the fact that, in deciding to go with Shannon, St. Hill *does his part* in a collective act of resistance to the colonial and racialist order. Indeed, part of the point of C. L. R. James's *Beyond a Boundary*, from which the example is drawn, is to bring out how the West Indian cricket of the time is a central stage[1] in which everyday Trinidadian resistance to colonialism is played out (and, often, as in James's own more ambivalent case, only *half*-played out). The teams are the lived embodiment of both a spiritual and a physical resistance; in them, among other things, Black Trinidadians place their hopes for transcending the categories of racialism and colonialism. James writes:

> I do not know of any West Indians in the West Indies to whom the success of a cricketer meant so much in so personal a way. There may be some among the emigrants, but I know that to tens of thousands of colored Trinidadians the unquestioned glory of St. Hill's batting conveyed the sensation that here was one of us, performing *in excelsis* in a sphere where competition was open. It was a demonstration that atoned for a pervading humiliation, and nourished pride and hope. Jimmy Durante, the famous American comedian, has popularized a phrase in the United States: 'That's my boy.' ... Wilton St. Hill was our boy (James 2013 [1963], p. 93).

When St. Hill takes the field for the West Indian team as a Shannonian he acts *on behalf of* and *for the people*, where *the people* is understood as a collective agent who has placed their hopes for

---

1 See, e.g., James 2013 [1963], p. 66, where he describes cricket as a 'stage ... charged with social significance'.

beating the English at their own game in one of their own. His act of throwing in his lot with Shannon, then, makes most sense in terms of an expression not just of loyalty to his own but also of protest against the order. As one of many such acts, each of which needs to be understood in terms of all the others, it is part of a much wider set of coordinated, mutually supportive acts through which, we might say, the *Trinidadian people resist*. They resist not separately and accidentally, but jointly and intentionally; they resist, that is, *together*.

To draw the contrast, compare a Black Trinidadian man living abroad, who is watching a cricket match between Maple and Shannon on television and decides, that afternoon, to side with Shannon because he wants to be on the side of the people. Let us imagine that this is a purely individual act and that his commitment will last. Now further suppose that no one knows of his decision, his decision has no public or social meaning (and is not intended to have any such meaning), and that it therefore affects no one. Suppose, that is, that there is no plausible way in which his decision can be taken as *playing his part in a larger-scale, collective act of resistance*. Is this an act of solidarity? It looks too lonely, too *disengaged*, to count. Perhaps, one will object, the problem here is that his decision is *costless*. But let us suppose he must pay some personal cost to side with Shannon (that, once again, affects no one but himself and remains private). I submit that this makes no difference. Without the sense that, by acting, he is *playing his part in a larger cooperative activity of resistance* – and, just as importantly, without the mutual commitment to the cause and to each other that comes (most often implicitly) in the wake of such decisions – this cannot be an act of solidarity.[2] Mikhail Bakunin refers to the 'single law of solidarity' in his 1873 pamphlet *Solidarity in Liberty: A Workers' Path to Freedom*: 'No man can emancipate himself save by emancipating with him all the men about him' (Bakunin 1873). Solidarity, when it is a virtue, is a virtue of *association*, which therefore requires *cooperation*. While of course solidarity requires individual action, it is individual action that is intentionally aimed – via the cooperation of others to whom one has committed and who are committed in return – toward the collective end of overcoming some significant adversity.

---

2 For more on why 'silent' forms of solidarity should not count, see pp. 119–20.

Kolers goes on to worry about the role of deference in my account. Kolers says that I cannot explain how a group like 'White Coats for Black Lives' can be in solidarity with BLM if they defer to BLM in how, when, and whether to conduct their protest activities. But this is to misunderstand my view on deference. To see this, we need to draw a distinction between three types of deference: moral, epistemic, and practical. When I say that the egalitarian attitudes intrinsic to relations of solidarity rule out deference, I mean *hierarchical* deference – namely the deference of a socially inferior caste, order, or group to one deemed superior. This is the deference of the slave and servant to the master, the servile wife to the husband, and so on. This is evidently not the case with the 'White Coats'. Rather, the 'White Coats' defer in two further senses, both of which – as I explain in the lead essay at p. 57 – are compatible with the account I have provided of solidarity.

The first sense of deference is *epistemic*. One defers epistemically when one puts aside one's first-order beliefs about some matter – say, regarding health – and takes the doctor's say-so as a reason to believe a contradictory proposition. One defers in this sense because the doctor knows better. Anyone who is an 'outsider' to a particular struggle – i.e., who is not directly implicated in the adversity against which the struggle is directed – should defer epistemically to those within the struggle who know better for analogous reasons. This will often be the case because those within the struggle have first-hand acquaintance with the structure and character of whatever adversity is at stake – an acquaintance that, therefore, gives them privileged epistemic access to truths about that adversity (and hence, potentially, what to do about it) (Bettcher 2009). When conjoined with the fact that, given one's structural position, one may be blinded to features of the adversity at stake because of one's privilege, epistemic considerations give powerful reasons to defer.[3]

The second sense of deference is *moral*. Once again, this is a deference appropriate for members of outgroups who participate in solidaristic action with an ingroup. One defers morally when one sets aside a range of first-order objections to *X*ing and does *Y* instead, just because members of an ingroup have issued a directive

---

3 Cf. Anderson 1995.

to Y.⁴ This is not because one deems members of the ingroup to be in an epistemically privileged position to make a decision, or because doing so will promote better coordination of ends. Rather, one does so out of *respect* for what is at stake for members of the ingroup.

Both forms of deference would be appropriate, in different contexts and for different members, for a movement like 'White Coats'. Kolers agrees. So where is our disagreement on the role of deference? There are two. First, for Kolers, deference is *essential* to solidarity. Paradigmatic forms of solidarity all exhibit, he argues, the forms of deference we have just discussed. On my account, this is too strong. Indeed, foregrounding deference has the effect of making the relationship of outgroup members to ingroup members the central, defining characteristic of solidarity, while perversely making it difficult for *ingroup* members (who do not defer to one another) to be in solidarity.⁵ On my account, by contrast, deference is appropriate in the cases we have discussed, but it is not a central, let alone defining, feature of solidarity itself. Looking at the long history of solidarity, deference of this kind looks peripheral: it only makes an explicit⁶

---

4 Cf. the 'Letter to White People' issued by Krys Foster in the context of the US medical profession's involvement in BLM, available at www.annfammed.org/content/annalsfm/19/1/66.full.pdf (accessed May 15, 2023). As a doctor within a large health organization, she recommends that White people listen to Black people and people of colour; support leaders and advocates of vulnerable communities with time, expertise, and voice; identify, sponsor, and mentor colleagues of colour to serve as leaders; explore and uproot biases; and use privilege to advocate for changes designed to address systemic racism and health inequalities.

5 Kolers suggests, in response, that ingroup members defer to the *group* as such. See main essay, pp. 57–9 and Kolers 2016, p. 62. For example, union members defer to the union in deciding what to do. But this solution only works for organized groups with clear authority structures, where it is clear what the 'marching orders' are. In looser groups, such as a protest or in a wider social movement, there may not be a single, generally recognized authority issuing orders in the name of the group. In such cases, is solidarity impossible? Or consider just two people who stand in solidarity against some adversity. It would be odd to say that they defer to 'the group', or that they cannot stand in solidarity unless they do so.

6 It is likely that such practices have been widespread (though not theorized) whenever outgroups have been involved. Perhaps the international brigades during the Spanish Civil War can provide earlier examples (though I have not been able to find any). Explicit practices and politics of deference and

appearance in much more recent social movements, and only when outgroups are concerned.

Second, for Kolers, the fact of deference shows that relations of solidarity can be *asymmetrical*, in the sense that members of the outgroup can be expected to defer and to sustain costs on behalf of the ingroup in ways that the ingroup is not toward the outgroup. Solidarity requires *uptake* by the ingroup but not *reciprocation*. As Kolers writes, this makes it possible for the 'b_i [to] be in solidarity with a even if it would be strained, at best, for a to claim to be in solidarity with the b_i'. The problem with Kolers' view is that it cannot distinguish *support for a noble cause* from *solidarity*. The key differentiating example is the following one. Suppose that there is an outgroup – such as 'Asians for Black Lives' – who protest on behalf of and alongside core members of BLM. Suppose that BLM welcomes their support. But further imagine that, while the Asians for Black Lives are willing to take on significant costs for the core members – for example, imagine they are willing to stand up to police should there be violence, accept risks of imprisonment to defend other Black protesters, and so on – the core members are not disposed to take on *any* such costs in return. Suppose further that, while they welcome their support, the core members do not identify in any way with the Asians for Black Lives. As described,[7] I do not believe there is any solidarity between the Asians for Black Lives and the core members: this is because they are not *mutually* willing to share one another's fate in ways related to the end toward which they are working. Solidarity always requires mutuality and reciprocity, and here both are missing. All that remains is cooperation, but that is not enough, and we have other concepts (e.g., support for a noble cause) to explain what is happening.

Kolers is, however, right to query *whether and what kind of asymmetry* is compatible with my account. In this response, I extend

---

allyship seem to trace their origin (as far I can tell) to support for the miners in the UK in the 1980s (including, as made famous in the 2013 film *Pride*, the group 'Lesbians and Gays for the Miners'). Practices of deference seem irrelevant in civic and nationalist forms of solidarity.

7 I very much doubt this was the case between the *real-world* members of Asians for Black Lives and core members of BLM.

the account. In the main text, I defended the idea that there must be symmetry between participants in their mutual commitment, willingness to share one another's fates, dispositions not to bypass others' wills, and trust. But how strong or perfect must this symmetry be? We have already discussed how symmetry is compatible with deference. But even in the absence of deference, different participants in any ongoing solidaristic action will have *varying degrees* of commitment, trust, and willingness to share others' fate and not bypass others' wills. Is such variance compatible with solidarity? I believe it is. The key is to see that the related ideas of mutuality, reciprocity, and mutual commitment undergirding my account spell out a *threshold* above which variation doesn't matter. As long as participants are mutually committed *enough*, disposed to share each other's fate *enough*, and so on, then they can count as acting in solidarity, even if their absolute level of each of these elements varies. This allows, then, for solidarity among core and more peripheral or occasional members, as long as there is *some* mutual commitment, reciprocity, and mutuality (which was, by design, missing in the previous example discussed). It will be difficult to say, of course, where that threshold will lie, and the threshold will vary itself across different types of solidarity groups. But the important thing is to see that the logic of the account allows for variation in a way that seems plausible, given the value, practice, and history of solidarity across each of our paradigmatic contexts.

Jared Holley

Jared Holley's insightful response urges us to reconsider the role of solidarity in the French late nineteenth-century colonial context in which it emerged. He worries that accounts like mine exhibit a 'methodological nationalism' such that solidarity is worked out as a response to and engagement with solely domestic issues (for example, the class conflict endemic to the Third Republic in which solidarism was born). This is a mistake because it obscures how solidarity emerged (in part) as a response to and in engagement with a much more international, and in the French case, *colonial* (and postcolonial) context. I believe that Holley raises an important point with respect to the history of solidarity in an international, and especially colonial, context. That history has yet to be written.[8] But I believe that Durkheim (and the Durkheimians) had a more complex relationship to France's colonialism than Holley allows; they were not blind supporters of France's *mission civilisatrice*. I will say more about this first, and then turn to Holley's discussion of postcolonialism.

It is first worth reflecting on the relationship of Durkheim's division between mechanical and organic solidarity, on one side, to colonialism and colonial ideology, on the other. There can be no doubt that Durkheim based his account of mechanical solidarity – adequate to so-called 'segmented' or 'inferior' societies – to a large extent on the societies described by contemporary ethnographers – themselves often colonial settlers. Such societies included, for example, the Iroquois and Kabyle. But did Durkheim portray modern societies as *morally superior* to premodern societies? And, relatedly, did he advocate the colonization of the latter by the former? Holley suggests a tentative answer in the affirmative to both questions. I don't think it is so clear.

There are two reasons to doubt that Durkheim put modern and premodern in any kind of value hierarchy; indeed, I think he is better read as actively *resisting* any such attempt. The first reason is that he is everywhere adamant that moral systems are functional responses to a society's underlying organization. There is no 'best' morality *sub specie aeternitatis*, only moralities that serve (and do not serve) to stabilize and coordinate the societies in which they operate. As he writes in *Sociology and Philosophy*, 'History has established that, except in abnormal cases, each society has in the main a morality suited to it, and that any other would not only be impossible but also fatal to the society which attempted to follow it' (Durkheim 1953 [1924], p. 28). 'We cannot aspire', he continues, 'to a morality other than that which is related to the state of our society. We have here an objective standard with which to compare our evaluations' (Durkheim 1953 [1924], p. 30).[9] Now, to be sure, Durkheim often talks of 'higher' and 'lower' societies, 'more' and 'less' complex ones,

---

8 For a history of the impact of French solidarism on international law, see Koskenniemi 2002.
9 See also Durkheim 1984 [1893], p. 311; 1982 [1895], p. 86.

'superior' and 'inferior' groups, and so on. But in all such cases, it seems more plausible to maintain, given his general organicism, that he means 'higher' and 'lower', 'superior' and 'inferior', not in *ethical* terms but in *taxonomical* terms. Just as the biologist speaks of higher and lower orders, more and less complex organisms, and so on, so Durkheim speaks of societies.[10] And nor does he think that 'more primitive' societies are bound to develop, by an inner logic or impulse, into 'higher' ones (on this he disagrees with sociologists like Herbert Spencer). He is clear that it is only in a given set of circumstances – for example, an increase in population, competition, and social interaction – that more 'primitive', less complex societies will develop a more specialized division of labor.[11] In the absence of such forces, segmentary societies are very stable.

The second reason why we ought to resist the idea that Durkheim placed societies in a value hierarchy is that he often emphasizes an essential *continuity* between modern and premodern. Modern religions like Christianity, for example, are more complex and articulated combinations of the very same elements as 'primitive' religions. As he writes in *Elementary Forms of the Religious Life*,

> But howsoever real this greater complexity and this higher ideality may be [the greater complexity and higher ideality of modern religions], they are not sufficient to place the corresponding religions in different classes. All are religions equally, just as all living beings are equally alive, from the most humble plastids to man. So when we turn to primitive religions it is not with the idea of depreciating religion in general, for these religions are no less respectable than others. They respond to the same needs, they play the same role, they depend on the same causes ... (Durkheim 1995 [1912], p. 15).

Indeed, the suggestion that there was no essential difference in nature between Christianity and the animist, totemic religions studied by Durkheim and the ethnographers is what made the *Elementary Forms* so controversial in his time.

But, if this is all true, then how do we read the enigmatic final passages of the *Division* quoted by Holley? Doesn't Durkheim say there that modern morality – embodied in the cult of the individual – is both more *human* and *rational* than its predecessors? And

---

10 On this point, see also the instructive discussion in Fields 2005.
11 See, e.g., Durkheim 1984 [1893], p. 197.

doesn't he also seemingly applaud the assimilation of premodern peoples into the modern metropolitan way of life? Doesn't he, that is, outspokenly advocate France's civilizing mission? It is worth quoting the two passages in full; it is also essential to put them in context. In the last passages of the *Division*, Durkheim is reflecting on the fact that our morality is 'in the throes of an appalling crisis' (Durkheim 1984 [1893], p. 317). The new, more specialized and advanced division of labor – with factories, large cities, and large numbers of workers, each of whom must compete for jobs that are ever more specialized – has outstripped our morality, and, more specifically, our sense of *justice*. As discussed at much greater length in Part III of the *Division*, modern class struggle and the ensuing social breakdown is due, in part, to the fact that workers have come to feel that they are mere 'cogs in the machine'. Seeing what seem like idle entrepreneurs and rentiers (often from aristocratic backgrounds), they have come to the belief that they are not receiving a just reward for their labor and merit. Finally, growing unemployment in the absence of a secure safety net has given workers the sense that there is not enough work available to make ends meet. In the face of these threats, Durkheim calls on his readers to 'fashion a new morality'. It is against this background that we should read, I believe, the following passage:

> But the mere existence of rules is not sufficient: they must also be just. For this the external conditions of competition should be equal. If, on the other hand, we call to mind that the collective consciousness is increasingly reduced to the cult of the individual, we shall see that the characteristic of morality in organized societies, as compared to segmentary societies, is that it possesses something more human [*plus humain*], and consequently more rational, about it. It does not cause our activity to depend upon ends that do not directly concern us. It does not make us the servants of some ideal powers completely different in nature from ourselves, powers that follow their own course without heeding the interests of men. It requires us only to be charitable and just towards our fellow-men, to fulfil our task well, to work towards a state where everyone is called to fulfil the function he performs best and will receive a just reward for his efforts. The rules constituting this morality have no constraining power preventing their being fully examined. Because they are better made for us and, in a certain sense, by us, we are freer in relation to them. We seek to understand them and are less afraid to change them. (Durkheim 1984 [1893], p. 317).

When Durkheim says that our morality is *plus humain*, I think what he means is that our morality is more 'down-to-earth', not that it is morally superior. The idea he is trying to convey is that our morality is more down-to-earth because it no longer relies on the backing of fixed and distant god-legislators (or ancestors or spirits) who punish but about which we can do nothing. We are now (especially after reading Durkheim's own work) in a position to know that morality is *made by us* to suit our ends. This gives us an opportunity that other societies lack: we can act to change our morality as circumstances require. Indeed, at the end of that passage, he is anxious to calm the reader that, just because it lacks transcendental backing, our morality is not in fact any *less* worthy of commitment and support. He also says, to be sure, that our morality is 'more rational', but again, I think here he meant that, because of its reflexive character, it is capable of modification in light of rational reflection, not that it is in some sense, from an 'absolute' point of view, better. This passage is meant to encourage the reader to see the possibilities in *refashioning* a morality of justice – a new morality of *solidarity* – to undergird the new division of labor, and to shore up the anomie that has broken out across all European societies. It is meant to reflect on what kind of morality is required by us here and now, not to assert its superiority over the moralities of segmentary societies.

Where does this leave Durkheim with respect to France's late nineteenth and early twentieth-century colonial projects? Durkheim says very little with respect to the colonies. But what he does say seems, if anything, critical. In 'The Concept of the State', he writes that the 'State must ... increasingly strive, not to base its glory on the conquest of new territories, *which is always unjust*, but to bring about the reign of greater justice in the society that it personifies' (Durkheim 1986, p. 50).[12] In *Moral Education*, he bemoans the meeting of 'unequal cultures':

> Wherever two populations, two groups of people having unequal cultures, come into continuous contact with one another, certain feelings develop that prompt the more cultivated group – or that which deems itself such – to do violence to the other. This is currently the case in colonies and countries of all kinds where representatives

---

12 Many thanks to Rouven Symank for the reference.

of Europe and civilization find themselves involved with underdeveloped peoples. Although it is useless and involves great dangers for those who abandon themselves to it, exposing themselves to formidable reprisals, this violence almost inevitably breaks out. Hence that kind of bloody foolhardiness that seizes the explorer in connection with races he deems inferior.[13]

His ironic qualifications – 'deem themselves more cultivated', 'deems inferior' – signal that he is sceptical that Europeans' claims to superiority justify violence – such violence, in addition, is 'useless' and 'dangerous'. It is in this light that we should read the following passage from the *Division*, quoted by Holley:

> There is nothing that demonstrates that the intellectual and moral diversity of societies is destined to continue. The ever greater expansion of higher societies, whereby the absorption or elimination of less advanced societies occurs, is tending in any case to lessen that diversity. (Durkheim 1984 [1893], p. 319n6)

The footnote occurs in the context of a discussion regarding the possibility of a global organization designed to secure peace and regulate the division of labor at a supranational level. Durkheim worries that, given vastly different levels of development (which correspond to different moral systems), such a global organization has no hope of emerging. He notes, however, that European societies (which do share a similar level of development, and hence a moral system) are beginning to cooperate in this direction.[14] But can such an organization ever become truly global? Here Durkheim notes that there is no reason to think that it can't be (and includes the footnote cited above). Given the passages I have cited, I think we can (tentatively) conclude that Durkheim was not *celebrating* the absorption or elimination of less advanced societies (e.g., via colonialism), but merely noting it as an inevitable fact about the current world order.

This does not make Durkheim an *anti*colonialist. His position was most likely similar to his (Durkheimian) successors, including,

13 Quoted in Kurasawa 2013, p. 198.
14 Durkheim presumably had in mind precursors to the League of Nations, such as the Inter-Parliamentary Union (1889) and possibly the Concert of Europe. The *Division* was published in 1893.

most famously, his nephew Marcel Mauss. The Durkheimians were against the universalistic mode of French colonization.[15] According to this 'Jacobin' ideology, the natives were considered to have no history or culture worth preserving; the point of French colonialism was to replace their backwards (morally) inferior culture with the modern, rational, universal French way of life. As we have seen, the Durkheimians believed that this was not only counterproductive but also wrong-headed: native ways of life were neither superior nor inferior to the French way of life; their moral systems were adapted to their societies, and simply to replace them with a foreign system would destroy the fragile fabric of their society. But what was the Durkheimian response? It was *not* to challenge the colonial system wholesale, or to advocate for the self-determination of subject peoples. Rather, the response was to encourage the French authorities to engage with and to respect native ways of life *in running the colonies*. The colonies offered a key natural resource for the ethnographer, namely their Indigenous populations. There is a 'key interest', Mauss wrote, 'in having an exact and thorough knowledge of [the Indigenous population's] languages, its religions, and its social frameworks, which it is unwise to thoughtlessly destroy'.[16] The proposal, that is, was for a 'kinder, more gentle' colonialism – but colonialism it still was. There is no doubt that the Durkheimians had much to gain from this position. In 1925, the Colonial Ministry funded a new Institute of Ethnology at the University of Paris, founded by Marcel Mauss and several Durkheimian collaborators.[17] The purpose of the institute was scientific, but it also had another function: to train future colonial administrators – doctors, governors, missionaries – about the culture and mores of the colonies they were going to rule.[18]

What conclusions should we draw? It is clear that Durkheim and the Durkheimians had a definite place in France's colonial project, and hence served to reproduce and reinforce patterns of structural

---

15 For this point, see the discussion in Kurasawa 2013, p. 191; Conklin 1997, pp. 279, 310; Fournier 2005, pp. 235–6.
16 Quoted in Fournier 2005, p. 237.
17 For this history, see Fournier 2005, pp. 234ff.
18 See Conklin 1997, pp. 196ff; Fournier 2005, p. 237.

inequality and violence between settler and colonized. What is less clear is how the idea of solidarity *itself* was shaped and shaped this project. On one hand, the idea of categorizing 'primitive' societies as exhibiting one kind of solidarity – characterized by homogeneity in thought and way of life – and 'higher' societies as exhibiting another kind – characterized by heterogeneity and diversity – served to support the French adoption of its own form of indirect rule.[19] Such indirect rule, it is important to remember, was often promoted alongside of a *denial* of the superiority of Western societies (and so very much in a Durkheimian spirit).[20] Furthermore, the language of solidarity – including specifically European solidarity – was later used to support plans for integrating not just Europe but also its colonies into a single 'Eurafrican' empire.[21] But, on the other hand, is the distinction between organic and mechanical solidarity essential to the idea of solidarity itself? Must an invocation of European solidarity *necessarily* be yoked to colonialism (or neocolonialism)? (Can't the idea of solidarity be used for counter-hegemonic purposes [as it often has been and as Holley himself grants]?) The kind of ideology critique that would be required to complete the debunking argument has yet to be written.

I now turn to the second part of Holley's response, which focuses on the anticolonial solidarities, for example, of the First Nations in Canada. His main claim is that the divergences and disagreements about solidarity within Indigenous anticolonial movements undermine my attempt to identify a unified concept of solidarity. In response, I want to suggest that Holley's examples can be used to *reinforce* my account. Take the distinction, as used by Holley, between *resurgence* and *reconciliation* within Canadian anticolonial Indigenous solidarities. Resurgence theorists are more radical: they argue that pressure to adopt and adapt to Western norms of constitutionalism and self-governance reproduce, at a structural level, the same settler violence that characterized the displacement of the First Nations in the early

---

19 See Conklin 1997.
20 See, e.g., Wagner 2022, ch. 7. Malinowski, for example, presented two papers at the 1938 Volta Congress – organized by Italian fascists, and which brought together all the European colonial powers to discuss integration and better management of the colonies – in which he compared, non-hierarchically, the rationality of Indigenous societies with modern ones.
21 See Hansen and Jonsson 2014.

modern and modern periods. Solidarity requires movement against and often outside of the current order, a non-Western understanding of communal/national self-determination, and limited interaction with settler communities. By contrast, reconciliation theorists demand greater recognition of land, cultural, and self-governance rights, and argue for greater engagement with, and inclusion in, the Canadian constitutional order, and hence greater engagement with settlers. Solidarity here requires rebuilding relationships not just among the First Nations, but among settlers, the First Nations, and the wider natural environment on which they all depend.[22] Holley writes that, in both cases, *contestation* about what solidarity is (e.g., land-based, aim-based), what it requires (e.g., working within/without the constitutional order), what it opposes (e.g., hegemonic discourses, strife, and conflict), and who it includes (e.g., settlers, other Indigenous groups) is central to the way practitioners use and understand the concept.

Is this account of disagreement among Indigenous activists incompatible with my account? I don't think it is. As Holley recognizes, explaining the possibility (and character) of meaningful disagreement about the aims, scope, content, and basis of solidarity is central to my account. Seen from the perspective of the resurgence–reconciliation debate, my account gives a conceptual framework within which to understand what is at stake in the disagreement. (NB: It does not aim to determine how the disagreement should be resolved.) For example, the disagreement regarding whether to claim greater recognition from the constitutional order or to go outside of it is a disagreement about what the *shared goals* of the movement should be. Disagreement about whether solidarity is grounded in membership of a particular First Nation (say, the Mohawks), or whether it should span across Nations, or whether it should also include settlers is a disagreement about the *basis of identification* undergirding solidarity. Across Nations, the basis is a *condition* as oppressed by settler colonialism. Within a Nation, it is based on what counts as sharing the *way of life* (and therefore who counts

---

[22] For an overview of this debate that canvasses a variety of different positions within each of these camps, see Asch et al. 2018. For powerful statements of the resurgent view, see Coulthard 2014; Alfred 2005.

as a member of the relevant group[23]).[24] With respect to settlers, the basis is a *shared cause*.[25] Disagreement about what is required by way of sacrifice for the cause is a disagreement about what counts as *sharing others' fate*. In short, I don't see why there is any tension between the divergent self-understandings of the groups in question and the categories I lay out for analyzing the structure of those disagreements. There is nothing I say that rules out contestation over the core features of solidarity.

Sally Scholz

Scholz's insightful and inspiring response urges us to reconceive of solidarity less as a kind of *action* and more as a transformative set of *relationships* that evolve over time. Rather than merely *act* in solidarity, she pushes us to *live* in solidarity. Solidarity, she claims, is transformative in two senses: internal and external. It is *externally* transformative in the sense that it aims at radical societal and political change. It is *internally* transformative in the sense that it encourages us to rethink and rework our relationships to ourselves and to others. With respect to ourselves, being in solidarity compels us to overcome bias, prejudice, isolation, and self-interest; with respect to others, being in solidarity sparks care, concern, and mutual understanding while also generating the possibility of new kinds of cooperative association.

I find myself in agreement with almost all of what Scholz writes. I, too, believe that solidarity is transformative. Although I only

---

23 Here the criteria for membership of, say, the Mohawks is relevant. There have been important disagreements within the community about what the basis of such membership should be. Should it be based on traditional understandings that emphasize matrilineal descent and practices of adoption? Or should it be based on settler ideas about whether a person has a 'quantum of blood'? These disagreements determine who should be included in the way of life that defines the Nation, and hence with whom one identifies *as a Mohawk*. See, e.g., Dickson-Gilmore 1999.

24 Of course, what counts as the way of life that solidarity aims to protect can also be the site of protracted disagreement, including what counts as desirable forms of self-government. See, e.g., the conclusion of Coulthard 2014.

25 The Dakota Access Pipeline protests, cited above, are a good example of all three modes of solidarity.

emphasized the external dimension, I also believe that sympathy, shared understanding, shared normative orientation, and mutual concern (embodied in the disposition to share another's fate) can be, in certain circumstances, transformative. (Recall that the first three in this list for me characterize *identification with another*, which is a core component of solidarity.) I also believe that solidarity is essentially relational: it is only present when the identification, dispositions, and intentions constitutive of it are *mutually directed*, only when, that is, you identify with me, and I identify with you, you are disposed to share my fate, and I am disposed to share yours, I trust you and you trust me, and so on, and this is all out in the open between us.

But it is also true that I write about solidarity as a form of *action*, and not as a *way of living*. I think this marks an important difference; this difference, however, is not as stark as it may at first seem. Sometimes Scholz writes as if solidarity names an open-ended virtue that is displayed by anyone who shows a disposition to enter into the kinds of transformative relationships with others in many (perhaps all?) areas of their life. For me, this is not necessary. Solidarity is present whenever there is the kind of collective action undergirded by identification that I outline in the main text; solidarity does not name, then, a general disposition of an agent, displayed when the person acts and relates with others in the ways indicated across many domains of their life. Someone could end up experiencing solidarity with others, on my view, only once in their life, or only intermittently. While one might talk, derivatively, of a solidaristic person – as someone who is disposed to act in solidarity with others consistently across many domains of their life – this usage is not central. It does not refer to the social kind, but derives from it. An analogy: one might be a cooperative person, but being a cooperative person is a different kind of thing than cooperation itself.

Speaking of solidarity as a form of action may give rise, however, to the following Scholz-inspired objection. Answering the objection will help us to see that the general idea of *living* and *acting* in solidarity are not as far apart as they may at first seem. The objection is this: solidarity seems to name a relation that *persists beyond* and *independently* of any particular actions to which it may give rise. For example: Isn't Malcolm X in solidarity with other Black people even when he is not acting together with them? Is Malcolm X really in solidarity with other Black people only when he is giving a speech, or at a protest (and only with the people attending)? In response, I think the key is to identify the correct description of the collective action. This can be more or less fine-grained. In the examples given, we can say that the collective action at stake is the civil rights movement, which is composed of many thousands, perhaps millions, of smaller-scale individual and collective actions, each of which is intentionally and jointly directed at overcoming racial oppression. Each person in each one of these smaller-scale actions can be understood as *doing their part* in the broader action of overcoming racial injustice. As long as they are appropriately responsive to one another's actions, have overlapping satisfaction conditions, each intend to do their part, and this is all common knowledge, they count as *acting together*. And they count as acting in *solidarity* if the further conditions for solidarity are present. (Are they disposed to share one another's fate, should this be required? Do they trust one another? And so on.) If we think of the overall action in this way, we can also think of a map or graph, where each person is a node connected to others via their dispositions, identifications, and intentions in acting. Conceived in this way, there will be more and less dense regions of connection relevant to solidarity, varying with, among other things, the degree of interaction among persons in achieving more proximate goals (for example, a protest, an action of everyday resistance, support for a political candidate, and so on). As long as there are connections among all the regions, then the smaller-scale actions can combine to produce the larger-scale one, which, in our case, is the civil rights movement as a whole. We can then think of the action as distributed not just across space but also across *time*. Perhaps it is best, then, to describe it as an *activity* rather than an *action*. Described in this way, Malcolm X is in solidarity with all those who identify with one another (perhaps on different grounds), who resist, together, anti-Black racism, who trust one another, and who are disposed to share one another's fates and not bypass each other's wills. Once we allow for such unfolding, developing joint activities over time – distributed through many smaller-scale actions – then it is possible to see *acting in solidarity* as much more similar to, though not the same as, what Scholz means by *living in solidarity*.

Rainer Forst

Forst's rich and penetrating analysis raises two main sets of concerns.[26] The first set of concerns lays out a series of challenges designed to show that solidarity can exist in the absence of action and can be unilateral. The second set of concerns queries the normative structure of solidarity, and especially its relation to justice. I address each in turn.

In the text, I give the example of Marie.[27] In the silence of her living room, Marie, an East German, is watching television on November 9, 1989, and sees a group gathering together on the Berlin Wall to sing the *Deutschlandlied*. She begins singing along with them. Is she singing in solidarity with them? The example seems to challenge my view because there is no joint action. Her singing *along* is not singing *together*, given that the group is not responsive in any way to her singing (in the same way as each member of the group on the wall is with respect to each other). In the text, I say that we can conceive of her singing as an act of solidarity but only in a limit, or borderline, sense. It is only because we conceive of her singing *as if* it were joint, it is only because we *imagine* her to be disposed to share the others' fates should that be necessary, just as they would be disposed to share hers, and so on, that we can rightly call it acting in solidarity.[28] (This is why I say that her singing counts as solidarity because it is *in the shadow of a nearby joint action*.) If she had merely raised a glass, or shouted 'hurrah' at the television, or merely inwardly felt the warm glow of community, this would *not* have been an act of solidarity.

---

26 Forst also raises a third set of concerns regarding the conceptual structure of the account, but I think here there really is no disagreement between Forst and me, so I leave them aside.
27 I draw the example from Zhao 2019.
28 I note, in passing, that had the group on the Berlin Wall known that there would be people at home watching their televisions, singing with them, and had people at home known that they knew this (and had this knowledge been in common among them), then this *would* have been an instance of singing together. There would have been, in this case, mutual responsiveness: for example, if the group had known that the television connection had cut out, then they would have waited to start singing until it was on again.

Forst, in response, says two things. First, if I grant that this is a borderline, or limit, case, then doesn't this mean that I don't hold joint action to be necessary, and so contradict myself? No. Nearly all concepts have borderline cases about which we are uncertain whether a given object is within the extension of the concept or not. This explains why I use the language of 'core' and 'penumbra' and don't speak of necessary and sufficient conditions. The criteria I set out for identifying what solidarity as a social kind is are meant to pick out *core* features; this leaves it open for some of the core features to be missing in certain cases *as long as we can explain why the fact that they are missing makes the case a borderline case.* If a counterexample looks central, then the account would fail. But Marie's case is, I have argued, clearly peripheral. Why? For two reasons. First, as we have just seen, the case only counts as solidarity if we think of it as occurring in the shadow of a nearby joint action. Merely shouting 'hurrah' wouldn't count. Second, as I explain in more detail in the text, Marie's action lacks the cooperative values that make solidarity distinctive and worthy of our attention. It is no surprise that cases like Marie are not central to any of the main traditions of thinking about solidarity. To see the contrast, let us take the 'hurrah' version again. Merely shouting 'hurrah' at the television is an expressive act of support without any gesture toward cooperative activity, sharing others' fate, being committed to a cause, and so on. The plausibility of Marie's case *trades on* the similarity between singing *along* and singing *together*, and puts us in the mind that she would have, if only she could have, been up there on the wall with her fellows, tearing it down, and so on.

Forst, on the other hand, wants us to adopt a view of solidarity according to which a mere *willingness* to act is sufficient. Forst writes: solidarity 'is a practical attitude of the willingness to act with and/or for others on the basis of a *common bond* grounded in a common cause and/or identity'. Note that being *willing* to do something is weaker than both *desiring* it and *intending* it. One might be willing to do something that one neither has a desire to do nor intends to do. Someone might be *willing*, say, to clean the house (if only the conditions were right ...), but also have no intention or desire to do so. There are two problems. The first is that merely being willing looks too weak. If you are merely willing to take action with others, but do not ever actually do so (because, say, there might always be some other moment or because one is weak-willed), then one is not in solidarity with others. Solidarity requires *commitment* (which I capture via the idea of intention [on which more below]). The second is that this makes cases like Marie *paradigm* cases of solidarity rather than *peripheral*. Marie, on Forst's view, is just as much in solidarity with other East Germans as workers in the shipyards at Gdansk are with each other. This is the case even if she never takes up the opportunity to act together with anyone to accomplish anything – being willing, Forst says, is enough.

Forst then wonders why – since I refer to intentions, dispositions, and other attitudes throughout – I require *action*. Why wouldn't the intention be enough (on a par with Forst's mere willingness)? The reason is simple: intentions connect very tightly with action, and it is for this reason that it is standard in the literature to refer to actions as constituted by sets of interlocking, joint intentions (e.g., Bratman). If one has an intention to X, one assumes that, absent special conditions, X will be forthcoming. This is in part because intentions require what is called a 'settle condition': one must take oneself to be able to settle whether X will occur for one to act with an intention that it occur.[29] I cannot intend to do things that I do not believe are within my power to settle. I might *try* to do them, or *wish* to do them, or *desire* to do them, or be *willing* to do them but I cannot *intend* to do them. So what might thwart my intention to X? I might take myself to be able to settle some matter, but not actually be able to settle it. Or someone might prevent me from Xing either by stopping me or not fulfilling some condition necessary for me to succeed. But these will be special cases, and I will (normally) still be doing *something* in the pursuit of X. So, suppose we each intend to do our part in the protest, but the police stop us from ever getting started. Note that there will be all kinds of joint action on the way to the protest: the joint planning, mutual coordination of activities, and so on. This is sufficient for solidarity (under the usual conditions). We can imagine, of course, limit cases: each of us intends, on her own and without any knowledge of what others are doing, to go to the first planning meeting, announced in an uncoordinated way on social media, but we are blocked before we even start. Did we act in solidarity? The answer

---

29 See, e.g., Harman 1976; Bratman 1987.

will be mixed. Yes, because we all intended to go to the meeting, identified with one another, were disposed to share one another's fates, and so on. No, because while we intended to *begin* our joint activities on the way to overcoming some significant adversity, we were stopped before we ever got started. Our solidarity, we might say, was only incipient.

Forst also challenges whether solidarity must be *omnilateral*, with examples in which people act *on behalf of* a group 'blindfolded by ideology', but in which the target group themselves do not act (indeed, they may resist the need for any such action). Forst illustrates the point with the women's movement, which, he claims, can rightly be regarded as acting in solidarity not just with other women who participate in the movement, but with women everywhere, and with the workers' movement, where socialist workers have often thought of themselves as fighting for both striking workers as well as those workers who remain misled by capitalist ideology. My response is similar to the response I gave to the example of refugees and prisoners in the main text. The key distinguishing feature of such cases is that, to count as solidarity, activists must aim *to engage the agency* of those on whose behalf they fight. This includes not only deliberating with them but also respecting their autonomy (even if they disagree with their point of view). If the activists either do nothing to engage those on whose behalf they fight (say, by ignoring them), then they fail to act on solidarity. Why is this a plausible requirement? Solidarity, once again, is essentially *cooperative* and *relational*: core cases involve individuals acting *together*. In cases where this is *not possible* (as in my refugee and prisoner cases), individuals can still act in solidarity with the target group if they act *as if* the agency of those involved is engaged, or *with the aim* of engaging that agency. That is why I called such solidarity *latent*. But in cases where such engagement *is* possible, and activists *do* seek to engage the agency of a target group, but this group outright rejects their entreaties, then the activists can act *on behalf of* but not *in solidarity with* those who have rejected them. Solidarity – as a form of cooperation – requires mutuality in the exercise of autonomy and unity in the exercise of agency. Without such mutuality and unity, one has *humanitarian aid* or *acting on behalf of*, not solidarity. As becomes clear in Forst's discussion of Christian charity *qua* humanitarianism, his view – which allows merely unilateral forms of action and aid (as long as such action and aid is grounded in identification) – cannot make this distinction.

I now turn to the second set of concerns. Forst wonders whether identification – whether on the basis of a role, cause, way of life, set of experiences, or condition – can ever give a *normatively independent* ground for acting in solidarity. Forst grants that, for example, an injustice, or the continued existence of, say, a certain community, or the value of a profession can all provide grounds for acting in solidarity; but what, then, to say of identification *as such*?[30] In answer to these questions, we can use the distinction between personal and impersonal reasons, where personal reasons are reasons that I have in virtue of special features of my situation, and impersonal reasons are reasons that everyone has, whatever their particular situation. My claim in the text is that *personal* reasons can give one special reasons to act in solidarity with others that merely *impersonal* ones do not. For example, the injustice that the Roma experience across Europe gives everyone (impersonal) reasons to join together in solidarity to fight the injustice. But the fact you are Roma gives you a special reason that someone who is not Roma lacks. The special, personal reason derives from the fact that you identify with other Roma, and, on the basis of that identification, also feel special concern and attachment to other Roma, and a special indignation when it is your fellows that suffer. These are reasons to join in solidarity that those who are not Roma lack. The same thing applies to identification based on a cause. Suppose you have invested much of your life and time in fighting climate change; it is one of your ground projects, something that defines who you are. This gives you special, personal reasons to join in solidarity with others who share your passion and commitment. This is not to deny, of course, that everyone has *impersonal* reasons

---

30 Although what I will say will apply to both cases, it is worth recalling here the distinction between the reasons one takes oneself to have ['operative' reasons], and the reasons one really does have ['genuine' reasons] – the Mafia, for example, have reasons of the former but not the latter kind to act in solidarity with other members of the relevant family in advancing wicked ends.

to join the struggle; when they do – when they make the cause their own alongside others who have also made the cause their own – they then have further, personal reasons to continue the fight together.

Forst also suggests that solidarity cannot have non-instrumental value because its value is conditional, among other things, on meeting standards of justice. But doesn't this then make the value of solidarity *reducible* to that of justice (or to other values on which it depends)? What *independent* value would solidarity have? This objection elides the distinction between value that is *conditioned on something* and value that is *derived from it*. To illustrate: your desire to fight the occupation on the front lines might be *conditioned* on your mother not needing your care at home but it does not *derive from* your mother not needing your care. And so it is with solidarity: solidarity can have distinctive forms of non-instrumental value (such as the ones I discuss in the text), while this value is only realized when the solidarity in question does not promote or involve unjust ends.

Catherine Lu

Lu's illuminating response encourages us to consider failures of solidarity in conditions of structural injustice. My lead essay focuses mostly on instances when solidarity not only *succeeds* in bringing people together but is also *valuable*. Although I do mention cases of solidarity bent toward wicked ends, I don't discuss more nuanced cases where there is a mix of bad and good. And although I do discuss cases where people are alienated from groups for which they might otherwise act in solidarity, I only briefly discuss cases where there *should be* more solidarity than there is, and where such solidarity might itself be a demand of justice. In this response, I want to build on Lu's insightful remarks to see if we might make some further progress. I will focus on (a) the relation between justice and identification, (b) the variety of ways structural injustice can disrupt identification, and (c) problematic solidarities that are not wicked.

The reason I am reticent to say that solidarity can be a demand of justice turns on the place of identification in the overall account. While of course calls to joint action designed to overcome adversity can be demands of justice, and while of course the action required to realize such ends can, in appropriate circumstances, be subject to coercion, it is less clear whether *identification* as such can be mandated or coerced. But without identification, joint action that meets all of our other conditions is not a core case of solidarity; it may be a borderline case, but it is not paradigmatic. To illustrate: suppose that someone participates in joint action designed to overcome adversity, is willing to aid others in its pursuit, relies on others to do their part, but does it only because they are at the point of a gun. The person is not acting in solidarity, though they are acting *as if* they were in solidarity. Because there is no identification with the others involved, no trust, and no willingness – on the basis of one's identification – to set aside self-interest in overcoming adversity, this is not a case of solidarity. The same thing applies for someone who acts together in all the same ways as the person at the point of a gun, but who does so only because they are trying to impress their girlfriend, or because they have been paid a handsome sum to do so.

This has implications for how we ought to think of the relation between solidarity and justice. If justice commands the sphere of what Kant called 'external' actions, it does not touch on one's reasons or motivations or (broader) intentions in acting. On this view, justice commands us to do certain things – like pay our taxes or refrain from killing – but doesn't care why we do so. Similarly, if justice bounds the sphere of enforceable duties, then it mandates actions that can be coerced by an authorized enforcer (such as the state). Because solidarity reaches deeper than the sphere of the enforceable or the external, only the external *part* of solidarity can be enforced. Identification is, on this view, outside of the reach of justice. With respect to the coercive aspect of justice-based duties, this is as it should be: coercion cannot apply to identification without excessive incursion on our liberty. For similar reasons, I am hesitant – given the private, emotional, and intimate character of identification – to speak of *obligations* to identify with others. In part, this is why, in section 3, I wondered whether there could be moral obligations to act in solidarity with others, and focused on cases where people *already* identify but fail to act (when required) to aid the group in overcoming adversity. (I concluded that the normative force of the demand comes mainly, in such cases, from considerations of fairness.)

In such cases, there is no question of being obligated to *identify*, only of being obligated to *act*.[31]

Lu usefully reminds us that structural injustice can disrupt identification in myriad ways, and so stymie the possibility of solidarity where it is most needed. For the sake of this discussion, let us take structural injustice to mean injustice that is persistent, patterned (usually by unequal distributions of power possessed by different social groups), and highly resistant to change (even with the best of intentions). Typical examples include the persistent patterns of exclusion, vulnerability, marginalization, and exploitation to which subordinated groups are subject. As Lu points out, structural injustice can affect (and disrupt) the relations between members of oppressed ingroups just as it can disrupt the possibility of meaningful identification (and hence solidarity) between members of privileged outgroups and oppressed ingroups. Lu mentions several mechanisms, and we can distinguish several others. Most commonly, the mechanisms for such disruption are *material*, *epistemic*, *moral*, and *psychological*. Materially, structural injustice will reduce the access of subordinated groups to resources that could facilitate joint resistance to oppression while also enabling privileged groups to protect their privilege. Epistemically, structural injustice sows distrust, especially where it creates large cultural, economic, and social distances between and within groups.[32] It can also blind the privileged to the nature of their privilege, and so dampen the perceived urgency of political response. Distrust, in turn, makes identification either less effective or less likely, or both. Morally, structural injustice is reflected in broken relations between groups, and the mutual resentment that past strife and conflict creates between them. This gives a moral dimension to distrust, where distrust is a product not merely of being unable to rely on what others will do (given their track record) but also of diffidence and justified resentment. Psychologically, structural injustice can affect how ingroups perceive the likelihood

---

31 Of course, if we take a broader view of justice, where justice describes both constraints on external action as well as a virtue, then there is more scope for including solidarity within the domain of justice. But it strikes me as more clear to keep justice for the sphere of the external, institutional, or coercive.

32 See, e.g., Shelby forthcoming.

of success in collective action. The persistence of injustice can, that is, lead to desperation and resignation, which makes identification and joint action even less likely than it would otherwise have been. Privileged outgroups, finally, will often seek to justify and reinforce their privilege, not merely because of narrow self-interest, but because of the dissonance involved in recognizing their role in perpetuating the very same injustices they might otherwise have wanted to eradicate.[33] Lu is right to note the tragic paradox that sometimes solidarity is most needed where it is least likely to flourish.

Lu also raises the possibility of cases – like the Canadian Catholic Church – where solidarity can sometimes have effects that are mixed: good in some ways, but bad in others. In such cases, can solidarity have non-instrumental value? The Canadian Catholic Church, Lu suggests, has a high degree of internal solidarity. Catholics within the Church identify with one another, are prepared to struggle against adversity together, and are disposed to come to each other's aid. But their solidarity seems to give out when they are asked to promote healing and reconciliation efforts with the Canadian First Nations. While they recognize their past participation in forcibly assimilating aboriginal people (in an effort to destroy their customs and traditions), they are not as willing to repair for past wrongs as they are to fund a large and expensive church renovation. Lu suggests that this nullifies any non-instrumental value their solidarity would otherwise have. I'm not so sure. Remember that, in Lu's example, the Catholic Church raised $3.7 million for peace and reconciliation; even though this is thirty times less than what they raised for the church renovation, and far short of the amount they had initially pledged, it is still something. And yet Lu is surely right that, against a background of structural and past injustice, this failure to raise as much as had been hoped sends a message to the First Nations: 'you matter, but not all that much'. To come to a view about the value of Catholic solidarity in Canada, I think we need to distinguish three different cases. In the first, most favorable case, we can imagine that, *had there not been any internal solidarity within the Canadian Catholic Church*, Catholics in Canada would have given *even less* than $3.7 million. In this case, I believe we should say that, although Catholics within the Church are still blameworthy, their internal solidarity *is*

---

33 See, e.g., DiAngelo 2018.

both non-instrumentally and instrumentally valuable. It promotes, after all, not only important collective efforts involving Catholics but also efforts involving other groups, like the First Nations. Because non-instrumental value is conditional on instrumental value, it is enhanced (or at the very least preserved) rather than diminished in this case. While it would have been *even more* valuable had the full amount of their pledge been realized, it still retains value.[34] In the second case, the internal solidarity neither encourages nor discourages the peace and reconciliation effort. Catholics would have given the same, and in the same way, with or without a high degree of internal solidarity. They are still blameworthy, but their internal solidarity remains both instrumentally and non-instrumentally valuable. This is because their internal solidarity, we are assuming, promotes valuable ends generally (and does not undermine, or enhance, their peace and reconciliation efforts).

The final case is the most interesting one. Here we imagine that Catholic internal solidarity makes Catholics *less likely* to promote peace and reconciliation with the First Nations; Catholics would have given more, had they *not* had internal solidarity. This could be either because Canadian Catholics invest all their time and effort in improving the condition of those with whom they identify, which takes resources away from other pursuits, or it could be because their internal solidarity increases their prejudice, contempt, or animus toward the First Nations. In either case, both the instrumental and the non-instrumental value of their internal solidarity diminishes. There is no point in trying to say by exactly how much. Different people will come to different judgments depending on their overall assessment of the blameworthiness of their lack of concern, and the impact of Catholics' solidary beliefs and internal practices on that blameworthiness.[35] The important point is that the instrumental and non-instrumental value of Catholic solidarity, just as Lu suggests, decreases in this case.

---

34 Things would be different if one believes that no action on behalf of the First Nations would have been better than the paltry effort displayed by the Church.
35 This is a common critique of solidarity: solidarity within any one group can diminish solidarity with other groups. I try to address the general critique in Sangiovanni forthcoming.

References

Alfred, T. (2005), *Wasase: Indigenous Pathways of Action and Freedom* (Toronto: University of Toronto Press).

Anderson, E. (1995), 'Feminist Epistemology: An Interpretation and Defense', *Hypatia* 10: 50–84.

Asch, M., J. Borrows, and J. Tully, eds. (2018), *Resurgence and Reconciliation: Indigenous-Settler Relations and Earth Teachings* (Toronto: University of Toronto Press).

Bakunin, M. (1873), *Solidarity in Liberty: A Workers' Path to Freedom*. Available at: https://www.marxists.org/reference/archive/bakunin/works/writings/ch04.htm (accessed May 15, 2023).

Bettcher, T. M. (2009), 'Trans-Identities and First-Person Authority', in *'You've Changed': Sex Reassignment and Personal Identity*, ed. Laurie Shrage (Oxford: Oxford University Press), pp. 98–121.

Bratman, M. (1987), *Intention, Plans, and Practical Reason* (Stanford: Stanford University Press).

Conklin, A. L. (1997), *A Mission to Civilize: The Republican Idea of Empire in France and West Africa, 1895–1930* (Stanford: Stanford University Press).

Coulthard, G. (2014), *Red Skin, White Masks: Rejecting the Colonial Politics of Recognition* (Minneapolis: University of Minnesota Press).

DiAngelo, R. (2018), *White Fragility: Why It's so Hard for White People to Talk about Racism* (Boston, MA: Beacon Press).

Dickson-Gilmore, E. J. (1999), 'Iati-Onkwehonwe: Blood Quantum, Membership and the Politics of Exclusion in Kahnawake', *Citizenship Studies* 3: 27–43.

Durkheim, E. (1953 [1924]), *Sociology and Philosophy*, trans. D. F. Pocock (London: Taylor & Francis).

Durkheim, E. (1982 [1895]), *The Rules of Sociological Method*, trans. W. D. Halls (London: Macmillan Press).

Durkheim, E. (1984 [1893]), *The Division of Labor in Society*, ed. Steven Lukes (London: Palgrave Macmillan).

Durkheim, E. (1986), 'The Concept of the State', in *Durkheim on Politics and the State*, ed. Anthony Giddens (Stanford: Stanford University Press), pp. 32–72.

Durkheim, E. (1995 [1912]), *The Elementary Forms of Religious Life*, trans. K. Fields (New York: Free Press).

Fields, K. (2005), 'What Difference Does Translation Make? Les Formes Élémentaires de la Vie Religieuse in French and English', in *The Cambridge Companion to Durkheim*, eds. Jeffrey C. Alexander and Philip Smith (Cambridge: Cambridge University Press), pp. 160–80.

Fournier, M. (2005), *Marcel Mauss: A Biography*, trans. J. M. Todd (Princeton: Princeton University Press).

Hansen, P. and S. Jonsson (2014), *Eurafrica: The Untold History of European Integration and Colonialism* (London: Bloomsbury Publishing).

Harman, G. (1976), 'Practical Reasoning', *The Review of Metaphysics* 29: 431–63.

James, C. L. R. (2013 [1963]), *Beyond a Boundary* (Durham, NC: Duke University Press).

Kolers, A. (2016), *A Moral Theory of Solidarity* (Oxford: Oxford University Press).

Koskenniemi, M. (2002), *The Gentle Civilizer of Nations: The Rise and Fall of International Law, 1870–1960* (Cambridge: Cambridge University Press).

Kurasawa, F. (2013), 'The Durkheimian School and Colonialism: Exploring the Constitutive Paradox', in *Sociology and Empire: The Imperial Entanglements of a Discipline*, ed. George Steinmetz (Durham, NC: Duke University Press), pp. 188–209.

Sangiovanni, A. (forthcoming), 'Challenges to Solidarity', in *Solidarity*, eds. Andrea Sangiovanni and Juri Viehoff (Oxford: Oxford University Press).

Shelby, T., ed. (forthcoming), *A Tale of Two Tenths: Race, Class, and Solidarity* (Oxford: Oxford University Press).

Wagner, F. (2022), *Colonial Internationalism and the Governmentality of Empire, 1893–1982* (Cambridge: Cambridge University Press).

Zhao, M. (2019), 'Solidarity, Fate-Sharing, and Community', *Philosopher's Imprint* 19: 1–13.

Index

adversity
  Christian tradition 53
  Durkheim 41
  forms 78
  ground for identification 81–90, 91
  history of solidarity 34, 39
  joint action 23–4, 30, 34
  nationalism 48
  solidarity condition 23–4, 30, 34, 39, 41, 122
  critique 144–5, 209
Albania 4
Alcoff, L. M. 83n176
Alfred, G. R. 167, 169, 172
Alfred, Taiaike 169, 172, 174n39
Algeria 4
alienation 85, 92–9, 107, 122, 199, 200
Alpha Kappa Alpha (AKA) 80
altruism 4, 48, 67, 121, 223, 225
Amazon 100
Angola 4
anomie 43, 107, 251
anti-colonialism *see* colonialism
Arendt, Hannah 62n132, 211
Aristotelianism 217–19
Asians 4 Black Lives 92n190, 246
associational ethics 4, 117–18, 152, 202, 219, 224–5, 231
associative solidarity 193
asylum seekers *see* refugees

Australia, BLM *see* Black Lives Matter (BLM)
autonomy 55, 152, 176, 186, 205, 262

Bakunin, Mikhail 243
Balkan Crisis (1913) 161–2
Bangladesh 4
Bartky, Sandra 192
Bauböck, Rainer 90
Bayertz, Kurt 101n200
Beauvoir, Simone de 82n175
Bezos, Jeff 100
Bhutan 4
bioethics 3, 231
black community *see* Black Lives Matter (BLM); racism
Black Lives Matter (BLM)
  asymmetry 149–51
  Australia
  Bezos and 100
  deference to 244, 246
  diversity and 194
  joint action 20–5, 208
  logic of slogan 228–9
  origins 21
  solidarity and 3–4, 148
Black Lives Matter Global Network (BLMGN) 21n35, 22–3
Black nationalism 54–5, 175–6
Blais, Marie-Claude 40
BLM10 22

Blum, Lawrence 69
Bommarito, N. 106n208, 118n234
borderline cases 63–4, 119–20, 122, 259–61
Bouglé, Célestin 35n66
Bourgeois, Léon 35–9, 42, 51, 77, 154, 158–64, 211, 213
Bratman, M. 17n28, 23–4, 25n46
Brexit 113
Brown, Michael 21

Cameroon 4
Canada
  Catholic Church 233–4, 267–8
  First Nations 164–6, 174, 233–4, 254–6, 267–8
  settler colonialism 176, 233–4
cancer survivors 12, 14, 15, 16, 28, 85, 89, 93–4, 98–9, 119
caregivers 81
Catholic Church
  Canada 233–4, 267–8
  charity 60–1
  human diversity and 191, 193
  identification scenario 93, 95–6, 100–1
  social teaching 5, 49–53, 148, 189–90, 192n5
Chaplin, Ralph 45, 47, 73
charity
  Christianity 60–2, 65, 159, 213, 262–3
  joint action and 210, 211
  solidarity and 61–2, 64–5, 67, 121, 160, 213, 223, 225
Chile 4
Christian Democrats 45n86, 50, 51n102
Christianity
  brotherhood of man 56
  charity 60–2, 65, 159, 213, 262–3
  civil rights movement and 55–6
  equality and 60–1
  history of solidarity 49–53, 213, 226

  solidarity and 3
  see also Catholic Church
citizenship
  civic solidarity 5, 76–9, 163–4, 170, 198
  disagreements 78, 79, 170
  ground for identification 76–9
  patriotism and 79
civil rights movements 3, 53–6, 175–6, 189n3, 258
  see also specific movements
class conflict 35, 39, 43, 45–7, 214, 247, 250
climate change 12, 95, 182, 184, 191, 193, 199–200, 263–4
clubs 80, 138–42, 145
Coastal GasLink 164
Cohen, G. A. 106, 114n226, 145–6
Colombia 4
colonialism
  anticolonial solidarity 68n146, 164–77
  concepts 154–5
  Durkheim and 157–8, 248, 251–4
  exclusions 163–4
  French history 154, 156–62, 227–8, 247, 251–4
  history 155–64
  neglect of subject 154
  racism 21, 138–42, 145, 152, 163–4, 172, 227–8, 241–3, 248–9
  Rawls and 164
  self-determination 165, 168–9
  settler colonialism 171, 174, 176, 229, 233–4, 254–6
  Trinidad 137–42, 145, 152, 241–3
  violence 174
commitment
  condition of solidarity 23–8, 33, 207, 261
  Kolers critique 143–4

lovers 26–7
shared fate 24–8
Comte, Auguste 5, 35
concepts of solidarity
　concepts and conceptions 31–2, 205–20
　conceptual overlaps 211–12
　diversity 4–5
　empirical v normative uses 29–33, 225
　Forst 205–20, 258–64
　history *see* history of solidarity
　overview 9–33
　quasi-contract 37–8, 158, 162, 164
　solidarity as modern concept 34
　unifying 5–9, 206, 225
　see also nature of solidarity; specific concepts
conceptual engineering 7n12
condition
　ground for identification 11–16, 81–90, 93–4, 173, 175–6
　intersectionality 86–8
　sisterhood 81–6
Congo (DRC) 196
constitutionalism 4, 254
Cooper, Anna Julia 227
cooperation
　19th century French solidarity 38
　charity and 62, 65
　concept 211, 257
　cooperative activity 23
　Durkheim 41, 43
　joint action and 23–4
　Rawls 217. 219
　reciprocity 106
　solidarity and 243, 246, 260, 262
　value 107–8, 110, 111, 120, 123, 170n31, 213, 232
coordination 18–19, 20, 36, 41, 64, 122, 208, 210, 211, 213
corporatism 50
cosmopolitanism 115–16
Coulthard, Glen 174

Covid-19 pandemic 4, 52, 182, 187, 188, 195–6, 222, 223

Dakota Access Pipeline 256n25
Debs, Eugene 139
deference 28, 57–60, 91n189, 149–50, 244–7
Deloria, Vine 167–8, 172
Demolins, Edmond 160–1
Denmark 21–2
Derpmann, S. 4n5
Deveaux, M. 81n171
disability 53, 175
disagreements
　civic solidarity and 78, 79, 170
　identifying 32
　indigenous people 170–5, 254–6
　solidarity and 22, 170
　structures 30–1
　tolerating 95
　values 103
distributive justice 158
diversity 191–4
division of labor 36–7, 39–45, 51, 80–1, 156, 157, 158, 163, 226, 250
doctors *see* healthcare
Doran, K. 191
Du Bois, W. E. B. 172, 173
Durante, Jimmy 242
Durkheim, Émile
　anomie 43, 251
　collective consciousness 40–1
　colonialism and 157–8, 248, 251–4
　corporations and 214
　critique 211, 213
　history of solidarity 35, 39–45, 51
　mechanical solidarity 40–1, 157, 248, 254
　negative solidarity 41–2
　new morality 250–1
　organic solidarity 39–45, 157, 248

professional grouping 44–5
race and 248–9
on religions 249
social solidarity 5
Dworkin, Ronald 112n219

Ebola 196
empathy 13, 89, 185n2
empowerment 189–90
environmentalism 93, 95, 96–7, 165, 199–200, 209, 263–4
equality
  charity and 158
  Christianity 60–1
  colonialism and 162, 254
  Forst critique 210–11, 213
  French 19th century 160, 162
  history of solidarity and 56–60, 158, 214, 226–8
  intersectionality and 28
  joint action and 211
  racism and 228
  solidarity and 27–8, 34, 149–50
  structural injustice 222–36
  symmetrical relations 210–11, 246–7
European Union 4, 90, 113, 207
eurozone crisis 90
exclusion 115–16, 163–4, 172, 174–7, 191–2, 266
experience
  ground for identification 81–90
  intersectionality 86–8
  sisterhood 81–6
external actions 265–6
Extinction Rebellion 27, 28

fair play 71n151, 72n153, 97, 98–9
Feinberg, J. 101n200
fellow-feeling 4, 5, 10, 33, 66, 121, 224–5, 263
feminism
  2nd wave 58n122
  debates 209

history of solidarity 53–4
intersectionality and 86–8
sisterhood 53–4, 80, 81–6, 88, 115
solidarity and 3, 175, 262
feudalism 44, 157, 161
Forst, Rainer 205–20, 259–64
Foster, Krys 245n4
Fouillée, Alfred 39n73, 159
Fourier, Charles 35, 45
France
  2nd Republic 10
  3rd Republic 35, 156–7, 162
  19th century concept of solidarity 34–45, 156–63, 213–14
  Civil Code 156
  colonialism 154, 156–62, 227–8, 247, 251–4
  ethnology 253
  fraternity 35, 227
  long depression (1873–92) 43, 158
  Paris Commune (1871) 43
  Revolution (1789) 35, 227–8
  slavery 228
  Solidarité Républicaine 10
Francis, Pope 52, 191, 193, 233
Fraser, N. 117n233
fraternities 80
fraternity 35, 37n70, 57n118, 159, 219, 227
free-riding 24n41, 71, 72n153, 76, 79, 89, 90, 191
Freire, Paulo 52–3

Gardner, John 17–18
Garner, Eric 21
Garveyism 55, 175
Garza, Alicia 194
Germany
  Christian democracy 51n102
  Erfurt program (1891) 46
  eurozone crisis 90
  fall of Berlin Wall 118, 208, 259–61

Index 275

nationalism 214–15
solidarity with West Germany 91
Goebbels, Joseph 215
Gould, Carol 13n22, 231
Greece, eurozone crisis 90
grounds for identification
 adversity 81–90, 91
 alienation from 92–9, 122
 causes 90–2
 Christian tradition 51–2, 53
 conditions and experiences 81–90
 Forst critique 215–17, 263–4
 nationalism 48–9
 normative issues 67
 overview 66–103
 personal v impersonal 263–4
 roles 72–81
 roles and conditions 11–16, 17, 27, 146–51, 167
 scenarios 92–9
 shared interests and values 101–3
 socialist tradition 47
 value and 6, 8
 ways of life 67–72
 see also specific grounds
Gutierrez, Gustavo 53, 210

Habermas, Jürgen 114n225, 209n2
Haiti 227–8
Haslanger, S. 85n179
healthcare 74–6, 92–3, 98–9, 231, 245n4
Hegel, Georg 107
history of solidarity
 Christianity 49–53
 civil rights movements 53–6
 colonialism and 155–64
 concepts 33–4, 226
 equality condition 56–60, 226–8
 Forst on 213–15

French 19th century 34–45, 213–14, 247–54
 importance 32–3, 155–6
 nationalism 47–9
 overview 33–66
 reciprocity 57
 socialism 45–7
 solidarism 35–9
 uses 8, 33–4, 121
Hitler, Adolf 215
Holley, Jared 68n146, 154–77, 247–56
Honneth, A. 117n233
hooks, bell 53–4, 82
hope
 Black Trinidadians 242–3
 Erfurt Program (1891) 46
 mustering 200–1
 transformative value 182–203
human rights 3, 118
human solidarity, meaning 5
humanitarianism 34, 63, 65, 67, 209, 211, 212–13, 262–3
Hume, David 108, 110, 123

identification
 19th century French concept of solidarity 39, 41
 antecedent identification 140–1
 Black nationalist movement 54, 55
 charity and 62
 Christianity 50, 53
 core condition 10, 11–16, 33, 99–101, 207
  critique 137, 144–5, 263–4
  Lu on 225, 228–9, 266–7
 de re and *de dicto* 12–13, 15–16, 26–7, 121
 Durkheim 41
 form 11–12
 grounds *see* grounds for identification
 justice and 264–6
  structural injustice 266–7
 meaning 11

nationalism 47–8
normative conception 32
overlapping consensus 81, 146–8, 183, 199, 258
transformative value 229, 257
value 122
who are we? 145–51
imagined communities 47, 65, 227
immigration *see* migrants
inclusiveness 191–4
indigenous people
  anti-colonialism 168–9, 171, 174, 229, 254–6
  Canada 164–6, 174, 233–4, 254–6, 267–8
  Dakota Access Pipeline 256n25
  disagreements 170–5, 254–6
  nationalisms 167–8
  political movements 168
  resurgence 165, 167, 170, 174–5, 176, 254–5
  self-determination 165, 168–9
  Tanzania 168–9
  ways of life 68–71, 167, 255–6
individualism 35, 39, 147, 161, 186, 194, 199–200, 249–50
institutionalism 164
intentions *see* shared intentions
International Convention of Arbitration (1907) 161
intersectionality 28, 86–8
Iran 24
Israel 4
Italy, Covid-19 pandemic 222, 223

James, C. L. R. 138–42, 145, 152, 241–3
Japan 21, 162
Jim Crow 54
John Paul II, Pope 49, 51, 52n104, 60–1
joint action
  adversity condition *see* adversity
  Christianity 61
  commitment and 23–7, 33

  cooperative activity 23–4
  coordination and 18–19, 20
  equality and 211
  Forst critique 208–10, 213, 259–62
  justice and 117
  Kolers critique 137–52
    response 241–7
  nationalism 48–9
  shared goals 17–20
  shared intentions 211
  silent solidarity 119
  social movements 20–5
  socialist tradition 47
  solidarity as 10–11, 16–28, 65–6, 121, 224, 225
  transformative value *see* transformative value
  trust and 25–6
  value 108
justice
  Durkheim, colonialism and 251–2
  identification and 264–6
  negative duties 116, 123
  solidarity and 112–18, 123, 212, 218–19, 224, 225, 230–1, 264
  structural injustice 222–36, 264–8
    identification and 266–7
    instrumental value of solidarity and 224–30
    non-instrumental value of solidarity and 230–4

Kant, Immanuel 97n197, 112, 114, 117, 265
Kautsky, Karl 46
King, Martin Luther 55–6, 175–6
Kolers, Avery 57–9, 67n142, 91n189, 137–52, 241–7

Laplanche, J. 12n20
latent solidarity 63–4, 210–11, 262

law, nature 7–8
League of Nations 158, 161, 162, 252n14
Leo XIII, Pope 51
Leroux, Pierre 35, 62n132
Leroy-Beaulieu, Paul 160, 161, 162
Levy, N. 79
LGBTQ movement 53, 58, 60, 175
liberalism
   19th century France 156
   Rawls 164
   solidarity and 112n219
liberation theology 52–3, 209, 210
Locke, John 144
love
   Christianity 49, 60, 62n132
   solidarity and 26–7, 223, 225
loyalty 47, 69, 70, 91n189, 218
Lu, Catherine 222–36, 264–8
Lyshaug, B. 193

Maasai people 168–9
McEwan, Ian 18
Madagascar 159
Mafia 29, 111, 117, 123, 213, 217–18, 232, 263n30
Malcolm X 19n33, 55, 175, 257–8
Malinowski, Bronislaw 254n20
Malone, Dudley Field 63n133
market society 107
Martin, Trayon 21
Marx, Karl 46
Marxism 46, 209
Mason, A. 170n31
Mauss, Marcel 253
Mazzini, Giuseppe 47–8, 213
medicine *see* healthcare
mercy 61
metalinguistic negotiation 30n58
MeToo 4
migrants 21, 87, 182, 184, 198, 229
   see also refugees

Miller, David 103n204, 167
Millikan, R. G. 29n56
Mills, Aaron 174, 176
Mills, Charles 164
Mohawks 165, 169, 255, 256n23
Moore, G. E. 103n205, 109n214
moral solidarity 36, 37, 38
Morocco 4
mutualism
   Christianity 50, 55–6
   history of solidarity 34
   mutual aid societies 35
   solidarity and 65–6, 78, 143–4, 262–3
   value 110–11

National Farm Workers Association 188n3
nationalism
   anti-colonial 68n146, 167–77
   Black nationalism 54–5, 175–6
   civic solidarity 76–7, 79n167
   history of solidarity 47–9, 213–14
   identification 29–30, 227
   identity and 170
   indigenous people 167–8
   methodological nationalism 247
   nationhood 167–8
   self-determination 165, 168–9, 172, 253, 255
   solidarity and 3, 215
   territoriality 167
   vaccine nationalism 223
   way of life paradigm 67–8
NATO 91
natural solidarity 36, 38
nature of solidarity
   adversity *see* adversity
   autonomy 152
   commitment *see* commitment
   concepts 9–33
   conditions 66–7
   consequentialism 151
   empirical v normative uses 29–33

Forst on 205–20, 259–64
identification *see* identification
joint action *see* joint action
Kolers definition 142–5, 151–2
manifest collective action 151
non comparative approach 9
not an institution 9–10
overview 120–4
New International Economic Order 168–9
Nozick, R. 109n214, 111n217
Nyerere, Julius 168–9

Occupy 4, 20
O'Neill, Onora 65n139
organic solidarity 39–45, 157, 248
organic unity 109, 111n217, 112
outgroups 58–60, 69, 91–2, 103, 152, 244–6, 266, 267
overlapping solidarities 199

Pan-Africanism 68n146, 167, 168
parenthood 80–1
Paris Peace Conference (1918–19) 162
passive solidarity 118–20
Pasteur, Louis 40n74
patriarchy 54, 82–3, 176
patriotism 48–9, 79, 207
Paul, Alice 63n133
Paul, L. A. 187, 198
Paul VI, Pope 50–1
Pesch, Heinrich 50–1
Pius XI, Pope 51n102
Plunkett, D. 30n57, 30n58
Poland 49, 74n155, 261
poltical solidarity, meaning 5
Pontalis, J.-B. 12n20
poverty 47, 78, 223, 229
premodern societies 40, 43, 248, 249, 250
prisoners 62–4, 122, 262
prisoners of war (POWs) 118, 119, 120, 122
private society 107–8

projects 12, 39, 49, 74–6, 80, 98–9, 113–114, 196–7, 216, 263
Protestantism 49

quasi-contract 37–8, 158, 162, 164
quasi-solidarity 148–9

racism
  Black nationalism 54–5, 175–6
  civil rights movements 55–6
  colonial Trinidad 138–42, 145, 152, 241–3
  colonialism 163–4, 172, 227–8, 248–9
  deference and 244–6
  diversity and 194
  Durkheim and 248–9
  intersectionality and 86–8
  joint action 209–10, 257–8
  nationalism and 227
  race alienation 93, 94–5, 96–7
  reasons for identification 93
  shared goals 19–20
  social structures 21–2
  sororities and fraternities 80
  White supremacy 172, 227, 229
  see also Black Lives Matter; indigenous people
Rawls, John 37n70, 57n118, 107–8, 112n219, 115n227, 158, 163–4, 217–18, 219
reciprocity
  19th century French solidarity 36, 39
  expressive value 106–7
  free-riding and 71
  history of solidarity 57
  outgroups 92n191
  threshold 247
  value 110–11
Red Power movement 68n146, 167

refugees 21–2, 32, 64, 113, 114, 207, 262
relational ethics 189–90, 202, 219–20
relationships
  Bourgeois 37–8
  Christianity 50, 51
  collective power 195
  deference 150–1, 245
  Durkheim 41, 44
  identification and 122
  relationship-based roles 80–1
  social relationships 4
  solidarity and 66, 70n149, 117–18, 176, 182–3, 224
  transformative value 185–6, 196, 202–3, 256–7
Renan, Ernest 47, 213, 227
Renaud, Claude 35
Rippe, Klaus 112n219
roles
  activities 80
  citizenship 76–9
  condition distinct from 73–4
  ground for identification 11–16, 17, 27, 72–81, 146–51, 167
  non-project roles 80–1
  relationship-based roles 80–1
  sectoral roles 74–6
Roma 263
Roman law 24n43, 34, 156
Romania 4

St. Hill, Wilton 139–41, 241–3
Saint-Simon, Henri de 35, 45
Scanlon, T. 112
Scheffler, S. 69n149
Scholz, Sally 29n54, 182–203, 256–8
Schwenken, H. 193
Schwiertz, H. 193
self-determination 165, 168–9, 172, 253, 255
self-sacrifice 118n234, 120
servility 28, 57, 144, 244

shared fate
  betrayal 151
  Brexit and 113
  Christian tradition 53
  civic solidarity and 79
  commitment 24–8, 39, 146, 247
  condition of solidarity 17, 151, 207, 246–7
  critique 145–6
  Durkheim 41, 45
  European Union 113
  ground for identification 31, 90, 92
  indigenous people 256
  interest groups and 102
  joint action and 17, 121, 142, 145
  nationalism 49
  obligations 47, 50
  prisoners 63
  silent solidarity and 118–19
  transformative value 257
  variable 29, 145
shared intentions 17–18, 23n41, 25, 79, 121, 142–3, 152, 208, 211, 261
shared interests 44, 50, 101–3, 216–17, 229
shared values 101–3, 216–17, 229
Shelby, Thomas 23n39, 70n150, 81n171, 192–3
Shklar, Judith 230
Shut Down Canada 165
silent solidarity 118–20, 243
Simmons 69n148, 72n153
Simpson, A. 174
Simpson, Lianne 175, 176
Sioux 68–71, 167, 169–70
sisterhood 53–4, 80, 81–6, 88, 115
slave trade 21
slavery 23n41, 54, 55, 149, 176, 227–8, 244
Sobrino, Jon 52

social contract 37
social debt 24, 37, 39, 158, 159–60
social democracy 46, 158, 214
social movements
  associational ethics 118
  civil rights 54–6
  joint action 20–5
  justice concept 231
  new social movements 20–5
  outgroups 58–60
  solidarity and 3–4, 113, 175, 226
social union 107–8, 110
socialism 3, 30, 35, 45–7, 158, 213–14, 226
solidarism
  Christianity 50–1, 61
  French tradition 35–40, 51, 156, 158, 160–1, 247
  history 214, 226
sororities 80
South Korea 196
Soviet Union 91
Spain 4, 245n6
Spencer, Herbert 35, 249
Straehle, Christine 193
Strawson, P. F. 25, 151
strikes 32, 35, 75–6, 145, 188n3
subsidiarity 51–2
substance template 29n56
Sundell, T. 30n57, 30n58
sustaining solidarity 197–8

Tanzania 168–9
Taylor, Charles 48
Tedros, Adhamon Ghebreysus 195–6
terrorism 29, 111, 123, 232
Tiny House Warrior Project 165
Tischner, Jósef 49–50, 60
trade unions 73–4, 145, 147, 158, 245n5
transformative value
  beyond solidarity 199–201
  collective power 194–6, 258

diversity and inclusiveness 191–4
empowerment 189–90
fluid connections 198–9
identification and 229, 257
living in solidarity 183–203, 256–8
meaningful personal decisions 188, 198
mustering hope 200–1
personal transformation 184–90
Scholz 183–203, 256–8
selves in the social 184–8
solidarity goals and 196–9
solidarity group value 190–6
sustaining solidarity 197–8
transformative mobilization 65, 202, 226
Trask, Huanani-Kay 168, 172
Trinidad 138–42, 145, 152, 241–3
trust
  requirements 25–6
  solidarity and 25–6, 78, 144, 247
  structual injustice and 266–7
Tully, James 172n33
Tuomela, R. 19n32, 208

Unist'ot'en Nation 165
United Kingdom
  BLM 21
  Brexit 113
  junior doctor strikes (2016) 75
  London marathon 24–5
  miners strikes 246n6
United States
  2020 presidential election 80
  Black nationalist movement 54–6, 175–6
  BLM see Black Lives Matter (BLM)
  civil rights movements 55–6
  farm workers' strike 188n3
  feminist movements 63n133
  Native Americans 68–71, 168, 170, 255–6
universalism 55, 175, 253

value of solidarity
  conditional value 111–12
  egalitarianism and 62
  expressive value 105–6, 120
  Forst critique 216, 217–20
  grounds and 6, 8
  impersonal value 103–4
  instrumental value 103, 122
    structural injustice and 224–30
  justice v solidarity 112–18, 123
  non-instrumental 103–12, 122–3
    Forst 217–19, 264
    structural injustice and 230–4
  organic unity 109
  overview 103–20
  silent/passive solidarity 118–20
  social union 107–8, 110
  transformation *see* transformative value
  valuable goals 264
values *see* shared values
Van Parijs, P. 6n11, 65n138, 65n140
victimhood 230
Viehoff, Juri 99n199, 112n218, 117n231
Volta Congress (1938) 254n20

ways of life
  ground for identification 67–72, 170n31, 175–6
  indigenous people 68–71, 170, 255–6
we-perspective 13n23, 18, 145–51, 208, 210
welfare state 5, 6, 9, 31, 34, 76n158, 144, 148, 206
Wet'suwet'en Nation 164–5, 174
White Coats for Black Lives 244, 245
White supremacy 172, 227, 229
Wiggins, D. 116n230
Wilson, Woodrow 63n133
Wolheim, Richard 12
World Council of Indigenous Peoples (WCIP) 169, 171, 172, 173
World Health Organization 195–6

Young, Iris Marion 83–6, 87, 88, 229, 231–2

Zhao, Michael 56n116, 106n208, 118
Zimmerman, George 21

EU authorised representative for GPSR:
Easy Access System Europe, Mustamäe tee 50,
10621 Tallinn, Estonia
gpsr.requests@easproject.com

www.ingramcontent.com/pod-product-compliance
Ingram Content Group UK Ltd.
Pitfield, Milton Keynes, MK11 3LW, UK
UKHW021824140426
5217IPUK00004B/77